MAKE IT OURS

Also by Robin Givhan

Everyday Beauty

The Battle of Versailles:
The Night American Fashion Stumbled
into the Spotlight and Made History

Michelle: Her First Year as First Lady

MAKE
IT

Crashing the Gates
of Culture with
Virgil Abloh

OURS

Robin Givhan

CROWN

NEW YORK

CROWN
An imprint of the Crown Publishing Group
A division of Penguin Random House LLC
1745 Broadway
New York, NY 10019
crownpublishing.com
penguinrandomhouse.com

Library of Congress Cataloging-in-Publication Data has been applied for.

Hardcover ISBN 978-0-593-44412-2
Ebook ISBN 978-0-593-44413-9

Editor: Kevin Doughten
Editorial assistant: Jessica Jean Scott
Production editor: Terry Deal
Text designer: Aubrey Khan
Production manager: Jessica Heim
Copy editor: Elisabeth Magnus
Proofreaders: Ruth Anne Phillips and Tracy Rothschild Lynch
Publicists: Mary Moates and Josie McRoberts
Marketer: Chantelle Walker

Manufactured in the United States of America

9 8 7 6 5 4 3 2 1

First Edition

The authorized representative in the EU for product safety and compliance is Penguin Random House Ireland, Morrison Chambers, 32 Nassau Street, Dublin D02 YH68, Ireland, https://eu-contact.penguin.ie.

To my parents,
whose love makes everything possible

CONTENTS

CONTENTS

5
The Art Project and
Something for Himself

6
Sneakers

7
A Win for the Culture?

8
A Once-in-a-Century Storm

PROLOGUE

CHICAGO. On Sunday, November 28, 2021, just a few days after Thanksgiving, the country was enjoying an interlude of calm after nearly two years of tumult brought on by a pandemic, an insurrection, and the beginnings of a racial reckoning.

And then news broke: Virgil Abloh had died. He was just forty-one years old, and he'd made history as the first Black artistic director at Louis Vuitton—the fashion world's largest luxury brand.

More than 3.5 million people died in the United States in 2021. An estimated 460,000 of those deaths were related to Covid-19. Among the dead were baseball player Hank Aaron, who battled racism while setting a home run record, actor Cicely Tyson, who shattered cultural stereotypes about Black women, and Vernon Jordan, who was the rare Black man who took control of Washington's levers of political power. Abloh was lauded in their ranks.

He has been described as a fashion designer, but that description isn't quite right. Fashion made him widely known. His role at Louis Vuitton menswear made him a hero to some, but he had no formal training in patternmaking, tailoring, or draping. He didn't fit into any established school of fashion, meaning his work could not be categorized as avant-garde, minimalist, or deconstructed. He was an American working in Paris, but unlike earlier generations of his compatriots he hadn't come to the birthplace of haute couture seeking validation. Frankly, he wasn't that insecure. Nor was he a creative misfit—someone too unorthodox for the stubbornly pragmatic sensibilities of New York's Seventh Avenue—who sought sanctuary among Europe's fashion adventurers.

Instead, Abloh was part of an egalitarian community of creative souls, young men interested in sneakers, music, art, and personal identity. He may not have been the most inventive of that group. He certainly was not the most outspoken. But he had charisma and curiosity, confidence and calm. He was smart. He was genial. He was talented.

His existence complicated the binary tensions that were central to the work of writer Lawrence Otis Graham, who also died in 2021. Graham had made a career chronicling the dynamics of race, class, and achievement among a certain category of successful Black men and women—those who were raised in relative comfort, rather than poverty or deprivation, and whose ambitions had them striving to preside over the establishment, not dismantle it.

"That's the problem with being raised in the Black upper middle class," Graham said. "You are living in a White world but you have to hold on to Black culture. You have to please two groups. One group says you have sold out and the other never quite accepts you."

Like Graham, Abloh had a foot in both worlds. But in Abloh's case, both worlds hailed him as a conqueror. One commanded his allegiance. The other swooned over his affability. Upon his death, Abloh was mourned like the people's prince.

Two weeks after his passing from a rare cancer, his grief-stricken family, friends, and collaborators came together at noon on December 6 at the Museum of Contemporary Art Chicago, where Abloh's work had once been celebrated in a sweeping exhibition. The museum sits between the city's Magnificent Mile and the shores of Lake Michigan. It's a stone's throw from the Ralph Lauren flagship, Nike Chicago, and the well-heeled neighborhoods of the North Side where Abloh had a home. The museum, which opened in 1967, consists of two aluminum-clad symmetrical wings connected by a soaring glass atrium and has hosted exhibitions exploring the work of Andy Warhol, Lorna Simpson, Jeff Koons, and other giants of the visual arts. But on that cold winter day, it was a secular church where hundreds sat shoulder to shoulder in the museum's central corridor—its nave.

A translucent lectern—a pulpit of sorts—was placed on a makeshift stage in front of a melancholy chorus of roses in shades of pink, brown, and white. Rich Wilkerson Jr., the charismatic pastor of the nondenominational VOUS church in Miami with whom Abloh had formed a bond, prayed. Representatives from high culture and popular culture remembered Abloh: artist Arthur Jafa; rapper Tyler, The Creator; singers Dev Hynes and Lauryn Hill; fashion entrepreneur Michèle Lamy; Louis Vuitton president Michael Burke; and Kanye West. Jafa offered a poem in which he compared Abloh to "god in the flesh." The mourners wept and they sang, and they considered all that Abloh had accomplished.

"He did what he *knew* he could do," Tyler said, "and did not care what anyone thought he *couldn't* do."

And yet. What exactly did Abloh do? He hadn't invented a new fashion vocabulary. His design output, though prolific, was uneven. His own company, Off-White, was young and its future not assured. Abloh's rise and acclaim were the result of colliding circumstances. He was a beneficiary of the changing times and someone who was well prepared to make his own good fortune.

Abloh's presence altered fashion; his success was made possible because of the ways in which fashion had already evolved.

He prospered on ground tilled by social upheaval. He climbed atop a foundation poured by his predecessors. He stood tall on a stage built by cultural transformation. Abloh was the right man for the times. He crafted a career for the ages.

His story is fashion's next chapter.

Introduction

BY ANY MEASURE, Virgil Abloh's career trajectory was re-markable. In the span of a decade, he launched Off-White c/o Virgil Abloh, captured the imagination of fickle consumers and demanding sneaker aficionados, and was catapulted into the upper ranks of a luxury fashion industry that was in flux and, in some ways, lost. Few designers make such professional strides in their entire career. Even fewer capture the imagination of consumers in such a way that they are hailed as groundbreaking.

Abloh's death was announced to the public by LVMH Moët Hennessy Louis Vuitton, the French luxury conglomerate that runs such pillars of status and extravagance as Dom Pérignon, Bulgari, Dior, Givenchy, and, of course, Louis Vuitton. Abloh was part of that elite tribe. In 2018, LVMH executives thrust Abloh, a young Black man without a design degree but with a keen understanding of the power of community and popular culture, into rarefied air when they appointed him artistic director of Louis Vuitton menswear. Abloh's elevation made him the first Black person to serve as lead designer for the brand, whose origins date to 1854.

But more important, more fitting to the story of Abloh himself, the news of his death was also relayed on his personal Instagram account with its millions of loyal followers. It was there that young Black acolytes and dreamers gathered for a virtual wake to celebrate his historic career and to mourn the brevity of it.

For three years, Abloh sat atop a fashion world that had long defined luxury and desirability from the point of view of White men and women. It was a world that exalted those with a monied pedigree, Eurocentric good taste, and a résumé filled with traditional fashion data points: the right design school, an impressive apprenticeship, a long-suffering fealty to the way things had always been done.

Abloh ascended despite not having any of that—maybe even *because* he lacked those familiar bona fides. The culture, after all, had evolved. Abloh rose during a time of existential angst for a fashion industry trying to make sense of its responsibilities to an increasingly diverse audience, its power to shape identity, and the challenges of selling status to a generation of consumers who fetishized sneakers, prioritized comfort, and had little use for rhapsodic nostalgia. If the twentieth century saw fashion shift from haute couture to ready-to-wear, the twenty-first century saw fashion evolve from ready-to-wear to streetwear. Or as designer Kim Jones preferred, clothes without boundaries. "The term *streetwear* doesn't really mean anything to me," Jones said.

ABLOH WAS A striking figure among fashion's creative types. He stood six feet, three inches tall. He had a neat beard and a nearly bald pate. He was a lean, dark-skinned Black man with soft features and a voice that sounded like he was perpetually battling a head cold. His default mood was calm. He maintained an old-fashioned reserve. He was dignified. People *liked* him. This was no small thing. Abloh succeeded in a time when even the most committed optimist would seek out reasons to *dislike* people or at least distrust them. Abloh had a demeanor that was equally appealing to decision-makers in corporate boardrooms, high-minded aesthetes who would entertain his murky theories about creativity, and the swarms of fervent consumers who swooned to his siren song of sneakers.

Abloh was a fashion outlier in other ways. His common cause was with those who hovered around the business's edges—the neighborhood street vendors looking to launch a fashion line one day, the shoppers who bought designer key chains hoping to some-day afford a handbag, accomplished men and women who felt un-welcome in designer boutiques because of their skin color, their class, or their youth. Abloh inspired them because he made them feel as if one of their own had broken through. For his admirers, he was the Black man who had breached fashion's glittering wall and left an opening through which others might shimmy. He exuded ease with that identity and with that burden.

Abloh's professional path provides a road map to a better un-derstanding of the power of race, diversity, gender, and celebrity, themes that have been driving an evolution in fashion and that are at work in the larger world. Abloh wasn't the first Black designer to reach fashion's lauded inner circle. He wasn't the second; he wasn't the third. But those who preceded him didn't have social media's megaphone. They didn't have the digital tools to rally thousands of discrete voices of support into a boisterous, powerful chorus cheer-ing them on. When Abloh stepped into his role at Louis Vuitton, it didn't matter that he wasn't a designer—at least not in the way that fashion had long demanded. He was an aficionado of hip-hop and skateboarding who had an eye for luxury. He was seemingly inde-fatigable and dizzyingly collaborative. From the very beginning, he envisioned himself as an example of what was possible. He pro-jected humility as well as sure-footedness. He saw himself as a leader even as he was still finding his own way. He claimed as a men-tor anyone he admired or who inspired him, even if they'd never offered him a single word of advice. For him, a mentor was simply an example, a template for others. And by that definition, Abloh in turn had countless mentees.

ABLOH BROKE INTO the popular consciousness in a way that other Black designers before him did not. He was helped along by the maturation of sneaker culture into a lucrative collectibles business and by the rising influence of menswear in general. Abloh came to the fore when menswear, after generations of incremental shifts, was the driver of the most significant changes in the way both men *and women* dressed.

Abloh was a new kind of designer who took lessons from his love of music and deejaying—work that taught him how to set the mood of a party, draw folks to the dance floor, commune with them, make them believe they were invincible, and keep them spinning and yearning for more. Deejays didn't write songs; their skill was in knowing which refrains, beats, and chords to stitch together to create something irresistible. Abloh was a child of that kind of cut-and-paste improvisation. He was generation Tumblr, Instagram, and Pinterest.

He had a degree in architecture that allowed him to see ideas in three dimensions. He was practiced at standing in front of skeptics, critics, and judges and explaining his ideas. Architecture was both artful and practical. It wasn't fashion, but it was a form of personal style. It was a way of seeing and understanding one's environment.

Abloh absorbed a version of youth culture and reflected it back from fashion's runways as well as the stages of this country's storied institutions, using the vernacular of art and architecture intellectuals, social media influencers, hucksters, and hype-masters. He reached deep into cultural expectations and turned them inside out, making people reconsider their long-held assumptions. Over time, he worked out a personal design language that explained, clarified, and sometimes justified his manipulation of preexisting products or the technical lapses in his designs. He spoke in detail about his belief in a 3-percent doctrine, an often-repeated oversimplification of copyright laws in the United States: alter an object by some modest percentage—3, 5, 10—and it can be considered transformed into something entirely new. When critics suggested this philosophy was simply a convenient way of redefining plagiarism as a high-minded intellectual exercise, he liked to respond that "Duchamp is my lawyer," a reference to the twentieth-century artist Marcel Duchamp, who championed the idea of ready-made art and whose 1917 *Fountain* sculpture, a prefabricated porcelain urinal signed "R. Mutt," disrupted the art-world orthodoxy. The truth was that Abloh had numerous lawyers at Epstein Drangel, among others, protecting his interests. He filed to trademark a series of diagonal lines; he claimed ownership of banal phrases; he petitioned to protect a red zip tie. He did this even as he made liberal use of other companies' brand names, insignias, and aesthetic gestures. He sued to protect his own intellectual property; he was sued for making use of others'.

If there was any aesthetic through line for Abloh's work, it was irony. Quotation marks were his most favored design element, his calling card. A little black dress bore the words "little black dress"—quotation marks included. A pair of boots read "for walking." The quotation marks added a layer of meaning and gave a commodity a high-minded reason to exist. The black dress wasn't merely another basic good; it was a commentary on commerce, a snubbing of the rules of propriety and appropriateness. The quotation marks meant that *his* fashion—and by extension, *his* customer—was in on the absurd traditions of fashion, an industry that often took itself too seriously, even as it regularly failed to accept its broader responsibilities within the culture. The dress became a wry comedy, a bit of performance art, a marketing gimmick, a branding exercise. Abloh

5

reflected the tensions that had long existed within fashion but that were being pushed to the surface thanks to influencers, exasperated customers, and a new generation of designers who were trying to make their way in a system that seemed both outdated and impenetrable.

Abloh had a catholic approach to popular culture that grew out of the 1990s, a time when city kids and suburban youth united in their love for hip-hop, grunge, and skateboarding. He came of age when individuals with niche interests could form a global community linked by blogs, chat groups, and social media. Abloh slipped into the comments to chat up strangers. He direct-messaged people about whom he was curious. "He wouldn't network. He liked organic meetings," said his friend Kim Jones. "He would reach out to people he admired and say, 'I really admire your work.'" His sincerity opened doors.

Fashion can be a closed industry. This often comes as a surprise to those who see vendors selling graphic T-shirts or handmade jewelry at a flea market. The business looks simple enough, with a low cost of entry: a few bolts of fabric, a bag of colorful beads. But the fashion industry thrives on exclusivity and aspiration. Its allure is rooted in its perpetual inaccessibility, in its never-ending promise of something just a little bit better, a little more magical, a little more privileged than what one already has or that already exists. No matter what frocks hang in a person's closet, there is always another more satisfying prize to win. There is always another trinket just a little bit more inaccessible and thus, better.

Abloh didn't dismantle the fashion system's reliance on exclusivity and status. He recognized how the system was changing and exploited those changes for his own purposes.

Traditional fashion houses had long used a single product to propel them into the financial black and cement their identity in the public consciousness. Louis Vuitton's flat-top, modern trunks could be stacked one atop the other; Christian Dior's New Look, with its generous use of fabric, heralded the return of haute couture following World War II and years of rationing. The products defined the brands.

Abloh began with a T-shirt, but he wasn't attempting to perfect a particular silhouette or drape. It was not a performance T-shirt. He was creating an identity, a name. If a T-shirt could be an expression of tribalism for music lovers and sports fans, then it could be that for fashion devotees as well. And a T-shirt—a big, unisex garment that required no tailoring and was easy and inexpensive to mass-produce—was the perfect blank slate on which to write the beginnings of his fashion story.

Abloh formalized his T-shirt making with Pyrex Vision in 2012. He called it an art project, but he introduced it in the context of fashion. He followed that with Off-White in 2013. He expanded Off-White from menswear to women's attire, and he presented those collections in Paris, where fashion is revered as a national treasure and where men and women come from across the globe to see if they're good enough to compete on the industry's most acclaimed stage. In asking that Off-White be judged against fashion's prevailing standards of excellence, he forced the question: Whose standards are these? His answer was "ours: yours, mine, your next-door neighbor's, the kid's down the street." Creativity did not have to be exalted by White men in suits or White women in haute couture for it to be excellent.

In March 2018, just before he joined Louis Vuitton, Abloh put his Off-White fall women's collection on the runway in Paris. It was the last collection before his name started to be trailed by superlatives like "king" and "g.o.a.t." The evening's setting was an elegant event space on a narrow block just off rue Cambon on the city's Right Bank—a stone's throw from the world of Chanel, the Hotel Ritz, and the Louvre. But the streetside entry had been transformed into a heaving mosh pit of overexuberant, pushing, screaming fans made up of mostly young men of various races and ethnicities. They hadn't come for the clothes; they'd come because of the sneakers and because Abloh, who shared so much about his work on social media, had posted the address—something he'd done in the past in the name of inclusivity, and something practically no other designer in Paris would ever consider doing. It was an open-door policy that perturbed the organizers of Paris's fashion week. Skittish after recent terror attacks, they worried that a mob of unvetted fans could pose a security risk. But Abloh had begun collaborating with Nike, and he'd tapped into the voracious appetites of sneaker collectors—a global community dominated by men whose identity was wrapped up in the canvas, leather, and rubber on their feet.

The excitement stemmed from Abloh's point of view, the way in which he was defining fashion and in particular luxury. Abloh was doing his part to further eradicate the dividing line between high and low style. He was part of a generation of designers who didn't look at luxury fashion as something unattainable but rather as something that was just as much theirs as anyone else's. They might have felt that the fashion industry was foreign territory, but they didn't believe that it was off-limits. They weren't trespassing. They were blazing a new trail. They saw no reason why the rich and the older generations should define luxury. They didn't see access to luxury goods as an inherited birthright. Luxury was simply an object of desire—a pair of limited-edition sneakers was as much of a treasure as a pair of custom-made brogues. Abloh's cohort knew what they valued. They had no interest in gatekeepers, either metaphorical or literal.

RACE WAS INEXTRICABLY linked to Abloh's passions. Streetwear's forebearer was hip-hop fashion. And it had been sidelined by many retailers despite its influence. Department stores referred to it as "urban" even if its consumers were suburban, and retailers separated it from other sportswear on the sales floor. Hoodies were an emblem of antiestablishment bravado when worn by a White technology mogul like Mark Zuckerberg; and they were a sign of danger and violence when worn by Trayvon Martin, a seventeen-year-old Black teenager, who was stalked and killed in 2012 by a neighborhood vigilante who saw Martin as a threat rather than just a kid in sportswear.

Abloh was part of a generation of designers for whom community was not only a marketing notion but also a way of defining and protecting themselves. There was strength in numbers. Groups of consumers using social media had the ability to judge a brand guilty of discrimination or insensitivity or racism in the court of public opinion and force incremental change—or at least a public mea culpa.

Weeks after the chaos at Abloh's Paris show, Louis Vuitton announced him as the new artistic director of its menswear division, the successor to Kim Jones, who had moved to Dior Homme. Abloh entered that space with confidence but without hubris. He had the kind of focused determination that is often the hallmark of children of immigrants—in his case, of Ghanaian immigrants—who didn't have the internalized burden of America's legacy of enslavement. He was a child of Rockford, Illinois, a modest manufacturing town where residents were surrounded by midwestern farmland rather than steel and glass skyscrapers. Abloh arrived at Louis Vuitton secure in the knowledge that while what he had to offer was not design-school approved it was dynamic and relevant—and most of all, desirable, nearly riot-causing. In hiring Abloh, it was clear that Louis Vuitton was not just interested in reinventing its menswear; it was ready to reimagine its customer, something that was long overdue.

Abloh's time at Louis Vuitton coincided with a season of global tumult. The world shut down during the pandemic and reopened with the arrival of lifesaving vaccines and a new approach to work and play. The country lived through a summer of racial unrest after Derek Chauvin, a Minneapolis police officer, pressed his knee into George Floyd's neck for nine minutes and twenty-nine seconds as the Black man begged for his life, called out to his mother, and took his last breath.

Abloh was at the top of an extremely White fashion industry as the United States—and cities around the globe—were galvanized by marches for racial justice, hashtags about Black solidarity, and symbolic gestures of inclusivity. Against that backdrop, a community of fans and casual observers thrilled at his success because a member of the Black diasporic family had achieved some measure of greatness.

VIRGIL ABLOH DIED after being diagnosed in 2019 with cardiac angiosarcoma. The rare cancer is situated within the heart's blood vessels. Diagnosis can be difficult because the symptoms can be subtle. It is also fast-growing. For those faced with it, the prognosis is grim. Some die within months of diagnosis; longevity is typically twelve to thirty months. Abloh survived more than two years. During that time, he lived his professional life with urgency, at a breakneck pace—just as he always had.

He engaged in an endless list of creative pursuits. He explored his artistic interests. He designed stage sets and album covers for Kanye West, water bottles for Evian, furniture for IKEA, cars for

Mercedes-Benz—and most importantly, sneakers for Nike. While some designers are loath to discuss their aesthetic philosophy or their creative methodology, preferring to attribute it to alchemy or instinct, Abloh was a voluble conversationalist. He lectured at the Harvard Graduate School of Design, the Rhode Island School of Design, the High Museum in Atlanta, and Columbia University's Graduate School of Architecture, Planning and Preservation. He sat for interviews, participated in panel discussions, and brainstormed with countless students. He could be both profound and glib in his discourse. He contradicted himself—sometimes during the same lecture, sometimes within the same sentence.

Abloh's contradictions—his attempts to explain his creative gestures, his desire to wrap intellectual gravitas around his work and place it within a continuum of artistic thought, his natural gift for gab—emerged at a pivotal time in the fashion industry. The business was wrestling with the definition of luxury. How do you impart status and meaning to track pants and sneakers in order to make them desirable to luxury shoppers? How does a historically homogeneous industry speak to an increasingly diverse consumer base in a way that feels authentic and confident? How does an industry in love with its own history connect to the future?

Fashion—high fashion—was essentially questioning the reason for its own existence. Abloh offered a balm for fashion's worries. For generations, luxury conglomerates had talked of their brand's DNA: the traditions, the specific silhouettes, the craftsmanship. All of this was in service to the brand. Abloh reverse-engineered fashion. He created a brand and the products followed. He didn't allow himself to get bogged down striving for perfection. In the evolving fashion environment, there were more important things than that.

Abloh maintained an intimate relationship with his customers. He wrapped a narrative around his work that was far more considered and audacious than the typical designer's. His predecessors and contemporaries wove tales about an exiled princess or about a starving artist as a way to explain a collection filled with ball gowns or overcoats made with bits of upcycled fabric. Abloh aimed higher. His professional outbursts amounted to a treatise on fashion, which he suggested was simultaneously steeped in meaning and also meaningless. He made his work feel important and thus made his customers feel important too.

In the wake of Abloh's brief but spectacular career, we are left to wonder: What is fashion selling to the rising generation of aspirational consumers that he nurtured? What is considered valuable in the twenty-first century? And who among us gets to decide?

This book uses Abloh's extraordinary career trajectory to explore those questions. To consider the ways in which he changed fashion but also the ways in which fashion transformed so that this Black man, this outsider, had room to flourish.

A Seventeen-Year-Old in Rockford

"**E**VERYTHING I DO** is for the seventeen-year-old version of myself." Abloh would repeat this sentence like a mantra. He measured his accomplishments against the dreams and passions of a teenager teetering on the cusp of adulthood. He tailored his creativity and messaging to the wonder and skepticism of adolescence.

Many designers have used childhood memories as a source of inspiration. The tale of having been infatuated watching their mother or aunt or older sister or best friend prepare for an outing is practically a cliché. It is a stock element in the origin story of almost every male designer—the way they came to understand fashion as a transformative endeavor. But rarely has a designer spoken of his own teenage self as the inspiration for his adult work.

"When I was starting, I was very much to the left. Formality was at the root of what high fashion was, and I said, to make a name for myself, I'm not going to wave a magic wand and speak from that perspective. I'm going to speak from the perspective of what I was as a seventeen-year-old kid and what I saw from these brands that I could relate to," Abloh stated. "Instead of making my career about myself or the industry, it's permanently focused on the seventeen-year-old that will be in my seat next."

For much of his professional life, Abloh engaged in a conversation with his younger self and with the youth around him. This was a sign of his enduring optimism. It was also his savvy understanding of the power of a rising consumer.

It was a sentiment that made sense for a man whose career success relied on an intimate understanding of the desires and anxieties of young men. It was a way of acknowledging his constant engagement with youth culture. And it was a way of exempting himself from the industry's traditional expectations of luxury. He was talking to the teenagers, not the suits. Indeed, he often said he still *felt* like an adolescent even as he was moving into his forties.

Abloh, a tall, lanky teenager, grew up in Rockford, Illinois, at a time when it was undergoing racial upheaval, demographic shift, and political tumult. A tenacious soccer player, he was surrounded by mostly White and Latino teammates. He was someone with a sense of community and an attitude of generosity. He was a style-conscious teenager at a time when it was almost impossible not to be. Fashion's creativity—Ralph Lauren, Stüssy, Tommy Hilfiger, Nautica, FUBU—was colliding with youth culture and social responsibility in a way that it had not since the 1960s. He was a kid from nowhere America learning about the wider world of style from glossy magazines published in Europe and Japan—precious analog commodities ordered from the local Barnes and Noble bookstore. Rockford was not a hotbed of experimental art and fashion.

Instead, for a time, Rockford had the ignoble title of Screw City. From the first World War through the Cold War, the modest Rust Belt town led the way in the country's production of screws and bolts. This gave Rockford bragging rights of a sort, along with a sturdy economy built on manufacturing. Rockford proudly made things—until making things was no longer valued.

The city's modern-day population is about 146,120, a number that has fluctuated by only a few thousand over recent decades.

Outsiders sometimes referred to Rockford as a suburb of Chicago. But that only served to rile up locals who saw a unique identity in their city that others could not. Geographically and temperamentally, Rockford is closer to Dubuque, Iowa, and Beloit, Wisconsin, than it is to Chicago, which is about ninety miles southeast. Rockford is part of a swing county of centrist voters. Chicago has practically defined Democratic machine politics. Chicago sits on the sparkling shores of Lake Michigan; Rockford is bisected by the meandering Rock River as it flows from Wisconsin into the muddy Mississippi. Abloh grew up on the thriving, prosperous side of the river that delineated the town's demographics.

Rockford was settled in 1834, by a group of White New Englanders. Over the years, the city's population grew thanks to a steady stream of Swedish immigrants, who were skilled woodworkers and furniture makers, as well as new arrivals from Ireland and Italy. These immigrants, most notably the Swedish, dominated the population and culture of Rockford and helped to transform it into an industrial center.

The first wave of Black residents arrived during the years surrounding World War I. Their increased numbers sparked tensions and violence from the many Italian and Irish residents whose animosity toward Blacks grew out of their own striving toward Whiteness and the privileges that accompanied a higher rung on the country's racial hierarchy. Still, the number of Blacks remained relatively modest, and thus unthreatening, until the Great Migration in the middle of the twentieth century, when scores of African Americans streamed in from southern states in search of more personal freedom and the greater financial opportunities afforded by industrialization. Ultimately, these Black Americans came north to claim their place in the civic life of their country. By 1949, *Life* magazine described Rockford as "nearly as typical of the U.S. as any city could be."

Rockford thrived economically for decades, thanks to the manufacture of cars and paint, the light industry, and all those screws and bolts. But eventually its fortunes turned, and it was plagued by many of the same economic and social ills—unemployment, gang violence, and drug addiction—that hollowed out so many cities and tormented so much of the Black population. In 1991, Rockford even had its own *Do the Right Thing*–style protest and scuffle between an Italian American business owner and his mostly Black customers. Joe's Dariette, a walk-up ice-cream parlor in the southwest part of the city, was housed in a small cinder block building. It had been in the neighborhood since the 1940s, when Italian immigrants dominated the area. As the surrounding modest homes changed hands and the neighborhood filled with African Americans and Hispanics, these new residents put more pressure on the family-owned ice-cream shop to hire Black workers and contribute to local charities. The flap was eventually settled—and without a trash can being hurled through a window. But the protests at Joe's Dariette would be memorialized in the historical record and the community's psyche as emblematic of the city's embedded racial tensions. Eventually, Black residents would grow to 21.8 percent of Rockford's population—the largest minority group in a city that is 55.5 percent White and with a significant Hispanic community. Abloh was a Black kid growing up in a predominantly White city with an undercurrent of racial animus.

In appearance, Rockford could be almost any medium-size city in the Midwest that saw the energy drain out of its central business district and flow into outlying neighborhoods, where much of the White population fled. Rockford's cityscape was dominated by brick commercial buildings and warehouses from the first half of the twentieth century, along with the earnest rehabbing and unimaginative landscaping efforts that epitomized the tail end of it. The downtown bore the marks of a shrinking industrial city, one trying desperately to reclaim its lost stature in a country whose manufacturing economy had shifted to an information one. From a bird's-eye perch, the city's core appeared to fade into a horizon of . . . nothing. It was as though Rockford proper simply dropped off a ledge along with the setting sun.

Over the years, the Rock River separated the city not only geographically but also economically and racially. It served as the dividing line between the more prosperous east and the struggling west. There were so many lessons within Rockford's geography about disparities of opportunity. Rockford was both urban and rural. It was struggling and expanding. It was Black and White. It was multiethnic. It was tilted toward a future of exurbs and big-box stores; it was mired in the past of segregation.

Most Black residents lived on the west side of the river. The houses there were modest; neighborhoods quickly evaporated into open fields; and the lack of commercial vitality was striking. Most of the city's public housing was also built on the west side of the river; the impacts of crack cocaine and gang culture were felt most acutely in that part of town. "The west side was not considered a safe place," said Deryk Hayes, who grew up in Rockford during the 1980s and '90s, the same time as Abloh.

Hayes graduated from Auburn High School, a large public high school founded in 1960 on the west side of town. At Auburn, student achievement was often overshadowed by the surrounding community, with its boarded-up houses, overgrown lots, psychic struggles, and day-to-day perils. But for every educator who viewed teaching there as professional purgatory, there were others who aimed to instill pride and possibility in their students. Auburn housed programs for the performing arts and gifted students. Among its graduates, it lays claim to Michelle Williams, who found success as part of Destiny's Child, and more recently basketball player Fred VanVleet.

On the west side of town, Hayes was surrounded by working-class Black Americans, many of whose roots reached back to the South and enslavement. His own family hailed from Mississippi. He was also surrounded by Sicilians and Hispanics. For all these folks, there was a shared history of hardship and hope, as well as pride.

East of the river, wide boulevards were crowded with the chain stores and restaurants that defined middle-class America. These sprawling shopping areas were part of the suburban dream: spacious houses with a yard, good schools, and well-scrubbed teenagers hanging out at the mall.

The east side was mostly White. The few Black families in this part of town tended to be more recent arrivals to Rockford, or to the country itself. They made their way to these neighborhoods of new residential developments and commercial zones in the 1970s and '80s.

That's where Abloh grew up—in a well-cared-for tan brick ranch-style house on just under a half acre of land. His parents had chosen this lot when it was just a patch of empty ground, when the house—one of six in a quiet cul-de-sac—was just a notion. They built it in 1978. Its front was modest; its garage held two cars; its footprint was restrained. But its broad back deck just off the kitchen looked out over the pristine grounds of a golf course.

Abloh was born September 30, 1980. He came of age in a city struggling against all the ills that were affecting so many urban, and some suburban, environments: drug infestations, faltering industry, rising crime, attacks on the social safety net. But he was the son of Eunice and Nee Abloh. He was the younger brother of Edwina. He was a middle-class kid. His youth was not impoverished. He didn't suffer the callousness and indifference from local institutions. He had watchful parents who believed nothing came before his education. School was his full-time job.

Eunice Abloh was a tall, brown-skinned woman with curly hair. Her manner was reserved, but she moved with the brisk efficiency of a businesswoman. Eunice was an accomplished seamstress and remains one of the best known in town. She received clients on the house's lower level. Customers brought in trousers and jackets for alterations. They came seeking her expert eye. Eunice taught her son to sew not by holding his hand and guiding him but by her example. Virgil asked her to tweak garments, to alter them to better suit his taste. He would watch her, and he'd go on to do things she never could imagine.

Nee Abloh was also tall with a medium build. He had high round cheeks and the same deep ebony complexion as his son. He spoke quietly and deliberately—sometimes gazing into the middle distance as he searched for the right words to convey his thoughts. He was precise. He moved through his home with a straight-backed, dignified gait.

The Ablohs immigrated to the United States from Ghana. Eunice had grown up in Accra and Nee had grown up in Tema, a coastal city about fifteen miles away. Like so many immigrants from this West African country, they were chasing education and opportunity. Nee, who had spent time working on the docks in the capital city, came to the United States in 1971. Eunice followed a few years later. Nee finished his master's degree and then took a job at the Glidden paint company in Chicago. Later, after being hired by Valspar in Rockford, where it was once headquartered, he made the leap westward. Nee preferred Rockford: the quiet, the lower cost of living, the easy quotidian rhythms. He was close enough to Chicago to drive in upon occasion, but he didn't have to contend with the hassles of traffic and parking day after day. His home's bucolic setting, in a nice, quiet neighborhood, with a view of the links, practically defined the American dream. No matter that he didn't golf, even in retirement. The setting was a victory.

The home was cozy; the public rooms neat but not spare. The living room celebrated family. Over the years, pictures of the Abloh children in a glass curio cabinet were joined by photos of Virgil's wife Shannon and their daughter Lowe and son Grey.

Nee called a room tucked away in a corner on the home's lower level his "junk room," but objectively it was a combination storage space and man cave. Affixed to the wall was a notice from June 1994. It marked the year Virgil was one of the top one hundred middle school students in Rockford Public School District 205. For the Ablohs, there was value in education that meant more than fame, hype, or fashion.

Education was the key that unlocked almost everything. It was the pathway to stability and success. And while it couldn't fend off all harms or insults, it could be a potent defense. For generations of Americans, education had been viewed as a stepping-stone to a better financial future. For African Americans, it was a pathway to a good job, a talisman for success, a path up the social ladder, a bartering chip in a bid for respect. Education was the realization of their ancestors' most dangerous dreams.

But for many African immigrants in particular, education meant even more. It was a way around racism, a way of *defying* it. Education was akin to a shield, with each degree, certification, or academic award serving as an additional protective layer. When Nee considered how he navigated race in America and how he taught his children to negotiate it, he said: "We came from a long way . . ." The subtext to his declaration was that he had come to the United States by choice, in search of something. He had had the *wherewithal* to come. And for all these reasons, he simply did not understand those who chose to cease their education after high school, who didn't continue to devour knowledge to fortify themselves, who offered excuses for their failures, or who simply gave up. He and Eunice made the decision to have two children because "we could only afford to educate two," he said. And, he pointed out, both of those children would eventually finish master's degrees.

"A lot of the Africans that came in the 1960s and '70s were very practical," said Shawn Agyeman, who grew up in Chicago and whose parents are also Ghanaian. "Education was going to save you. There's Jesus and your master's degree. My parents saw [education] as the greatest insulation against a poor social or economic outcome. . . . They believed you could use education to insulate against joblessness, against anti-immigrant sentiment, against racism."

Agyeman met Virgil Abloh in 2008. Agyeman was an admirer of his work, and he interviewed Abloh about his creative drive and aspirations. But the two spent much of that time discussing their family background and what it meant to be a child of Ghanaian parents.

"Being an African in Africa is the equivalent of being a White man in America," Agyeman explained. "If you keep that attitude, and add to that with hard work, that undergirds your ability to win. [My parents] wouldn't say, 'You have to be twice as good to succeed.' You already know you're that good."

Nee and Eunice took pride in the way their son navigated race and racism. He acknowledged hurdles but demonstrated the capacity to think his way over, around, or through them. Abloh was a Black man in America, but one who moved through the world as if he were in Africa.

THE ABLOH HOUSE sat just blocks away from Guilford High School, the best that the city's public school system had to offer. It was Abloh's neighborhood high school. Its students were predominantly White, and the school offered a strong college preparatory curriculum. It's where his sister went to high school. But Abloh asked to go to Boylan Catholic High School. It wasn't a matter of religion. Abloh had been raised in the Episcopalian church. But he thought he'd get a better education at Boylan, his father said. The parochial school was situated closer to the center of the city and had a long history. It was an institution that was respected for both its scholarship and its sports teams—and Abloh loved soccer. But Boylan also allowed Abloh to disengage from the most contentious issue facing Rockford students and parents: race. It freed him from a public school system steeped in the bigotry of low expectations.

By the time Abloh entered high school, Rockford public schools had been accused of systemic racism in a federal lawsuit that was filed in May 1989 and whose consequences dragged on for a decade, at a cost of more than $166 million. The lawsuit pulled the city into a long, tense argument about race, money, and this country's unresolved history of inequality.

"I remember it being a big issue from the time I started school," Hayes said. "I remember getting bussed out to various schools on the east side. It was a huge discrimination case. By high school it was over on paper, but the racism was systemic."

White residents were taken aback by the lawsuit; many saw it as unnecessary agitation. Black parents were resigned to it; for them, it was inevitable. It was the only option left to force change.

Joe Kirby, a young reporter who had grown up in the Bronx and who worked at the *Chicago Tribune,* found Rockford conservative, segregated, and disconcerting. The *Tribune* was the state's largest newspaper, and Kirby, who was assigned to its Schaumburg bureau, was tasked with reporting on areas northwest of Chicago. Rockford rarely merited much coverage by the big city paper. The one glaring exception was its school system, the lawsuit, and the way the city treated Black students.

"I was amazed something like this could happen so close to Chicago," Kirby recalled. "I was amazed it could happen in a sizable city in the North."

De facto segregation had been a part of Rockford's school system for generations. In a 1970 lawsuit, civil rights organizations confronted Rockford officials for their failure to make much progress in the aftermath of the Supreme Court's 1954 decision in *Brown v. Board of Education,* which ruled segregated schools unconstitutional. The district responded to the 1970 lawsuit with lackadaisical busing efforts and nonchalant attempts at magnet schools. By 1981, even those modest efforts had faded away.

So a group of parents started the fight all over again a few years later. The legal battle, led by a local activist named Ed Wells, began in 1989, after the school board announced a plan to close ten schools—a half dozen of them on the city's mostly Black west side. The board also wanted to create several mega schools. These schools would have been part of a massive educational community of nearly two thousand students—most of them Black and Hispanic. The plan would essentially have created an educational ghetto.

When a federal judge finally issued a report resulting from the lawsuit over Rockford's schools in the fall of 1993, the 537-page assessment was a blistering rebuke of decades of neglect, hostility, disastrous busing, and sweeping failures. The report described students being placed onto educational tracks from which they could rarely escape, with Black and Hispanic students regularly trapped in lower-level classes regardless of their abilities or desires. It detailed practices that harkened to the Jim Crow era, with Black and White students kept in separate classrooms and expected to use separate bathrooms. These separate facilities were not equal. Minority students typically received poorer-quality buildings, classrooms, and opportunities compared to their White counterparts.

By 1994, as Abloh was preparing to enter high school, Rockford officials had begun working with the federal courts to desegregate its schools at a cost of hundreds of millions of dollars. The uproar, which consumed the entire community, spoke to the ways in which institutions undervalue and underestimate young Black people. It was American racism with all its familiar contours.

It was a controversy that Abloh didn't confront. As a high school freshman in 1994, with his parents' blessing, he simply avoided it by choosing Boylan. Or at least, he made a worthy effort to do so. It was an early example of his seemingly instinctive refusal to get mired in a tug-of-war over race. His parents had come from a long way. He didn't have to work to be twice as good as his White classmates to succeed. He was already great. Guilford, his neighborhood public high school, despite being one of the best in the city, was still part of a district that had never shaken off the racism of Jim Crow America. Even worse, the district hadn't really tried.

Abloh's parents paid the yearly tuition of $3,275 at Boylan Catholic High School. For them, education was all-important, no matter the financial sacrifice. Their son joined the class of 1998 and committed himself to making good use of his parents' hard-earned, middle-class largesse. He studied engineering. This was the sort of serious scholarship his parents expected, and Abloh felt a duty to make his parents proud.

"Virgil was an African American in Hispanic circles and predominantly White circles," Hayes said. "Those circles would have shaped him."

Boylan preached scholarship, sports, and old-fashioned propriety. The young men were expected to wear dress shirts and ties, and the school took pride in impressing on its students the importance of the soft skills of adulthood: being punctual, offering a firm handshake, engaging in social pleasantries.

The building occupied significant acreage north of downtown and just west of the Rock River. It resembled a suburban rambler that just kept expanding in a disorderly and not especially pleasing manner. As one approached the main building, Boylan's athletic field—home of the Titans—sat off to the left. A parking lot constituted a front lawn.

The school was founded in 1960, when the Catholic Church built a host of institutions to cater to the young baby boomers who were entering adolescence. It was constructed before the city's population shifted east in earnest. For years, Boylan was the only Catholic high school in the Rockford region, a diocesan institution, not a Jesuit one—and at its height of popularity, the school enrolled some 1,200 students, both Catholic and non-Catholic, with some even traveling from Wisconsin. When Abloh arrived in 1994, the student population was closer to 1,000.

Rows of beige lockers lined the hallways, as did examples of student artwork—a counterbalance to the celebration of sports. "We never have a problem getting on the front page of the newspaper because of our football team or our basketball team," said Boylan president Amy Ott. "But you have to turn the page to find the arts."

A drop ceiling gave the school, with its winding hallways, a dated appearance, as if its last do-it-yourself renovation was sometime around 1975. Each month, the school's gym, which had remained virtually unchanged since the 1960s, was transformed into a makeshift chapel for mandatory mass. The green-striped wooden bleachers were pulled out over the lacquered floor. The basketball nets faded into the background. And students were instructed in theology and the teachings of the Catholic Church. Abloh might not have been Catholic or a committed churchgoer later in life, but the fundamental tenets of Christianity stayed with him.

In the 1990s, Boylan's student body was some 85 percent White. Hispanics made up the bulk of the school's minority population. Abloh was a minority within a minority. His dark skin distinguished him in his yearbook photographs—as part of the junior varsity soccer team in their green and white uniforms, as one of the junior valets at prom all dressed up in their white shirts and black bow ties, as a varsity athlete declaring his teammates "determined" and assessing their commitment in the face of loss like a seasoned professional: "We still managed to pick ourselves up and play at our full potential." The school's trophy cases burst with state and division championship trophies in football, basketball, and soccer.

Abloh was a soccer player on the school's junior varsity and varsity teams. He wasn't a star when his varsity team reached the state championships in 1997. But he was a solid Titan who in his senior year snagged jersey number 23—the same as revered basketball player Michael Jordan, who won six NBA championships with the Chicago Bulls between 1991 and 1998. Abloh wasn't a star on the Dorian club team on which he played either. Dorian was a small club. Its logo was a helmet; its colors were red, white, and navy. Team members wore Adidas gear and candy cane–striped socks. "He was a part of the whole process. He wouldn't expect anything," said Eric Eiss, who coached him at both Boylan and Dorian. "You would never hear Virgil complain. He was just trying to do the work. He knew he would get limited minutes because out of a roster of twenty, he was a sixteen, seventeen, eighteen, nineteen, kind of guy. And he understood that. He also knew that him putting forth his best effort and training every day was also making the team good." Eiss had no idea of Abloh's fashion ambitions, but he also wasn't terribly surprised when he learned about his ultimate success. Abloh was calm—perhaps preternaturally so. "He just floated," Eiss recalled. "It's not like he was going to take things by storm; he wasn't pushing things on you. A lot of doors opened, and he stepped through those open doors."

Abloh was an introvert, which is not to say that he was shy, because he was a talker. He spoke in long paragraphs, explaining himself and musing about his ideas. He was thoughtful; he approached problems and possibilities in a considered manner. He was watchful and dutiful.

IN 1997, ABLOH TURNED SEVENTEEN. That's a pivotal age. A young man has completed a few years of high school. He's had time to get his bearings and to grow from an insecure underclassman into a confident upperclassman. It's the time before senior year when things turn serious, when college applications must be filed and futures considered. It's a moment in a young man's life when childhood lies in the distance and adulthood still feels like a place of possibility and freedom, rather than responsibilities and challenges.

As a seventeen-year-old, Abloh was part of a youth culture in which music was a distinctly uniting force. Abloh didn't study art in high school; he wasn't one of the theater kids. In his free time, he was a skateboarder and a deejay with a love for techno, which was the brand of house music that originated in Detroit and found acclaim in Europe. Techno, the dance music that merged the urban grittiness and steady rhythms of house with an overlay of synthesized strings and melodic vocals, was a percolating subculture that linked Black and White kids in the Midwest with those across the Atlantic in London, Berlin, and Belgium.

Techno had a stake in fashion too. It was distinguished by its fascination with futuristic attire: wraparound sunglasses, patent leather, black clothing, and most anything that suggested a digitized, sleek cool. Techno wasn't pessimistic about the future. Tomorrow was one step closer to utopia.

Abloh also loved hip-hop, which was ascendant and moving from urban settings into suburban ones. It was becoming the dominant cultural language, and it was speaking to the complexities and dangers of modern life.

An earlier generation had faced its mortality through the lens of the Vietnam War. Abloh's cohorts had the tenuous nature of their mortality made plain right here at home. In 1994, President Bill

Clinton signed the Violent Crime Control and Law Enforcement Act. It would become known as the 1994 Crime Bill. It included a ban on assault weapons and offered protections for women in violent relationships. It also designated billions of dollars to the construction of prisons and instituted a mandatory life sentence without the possibility of parole for those convicted of a third violent felony or drug-trafficking crime. The bill brought more police officers to Rockford and focused attention on gang violence there and in other smaller communities throughout Illinois. The bill would widely be described as a catalyst for the mass incarceration of young Black men. It would be blamed for the creation of an entire generation of disenfranchised, unemployable, disillusioned ex-felons.

The thriving hip-hop scene reflected much of the trauma unfolding on city streets. Tupac Shakur was murdered in 1996; then, in 1997, the Notorious B.I.G. died. The music was also documenting the violence and the political discourse surrounding it. In his 1997 book *Fight the Power*, Public Enemy's Chuck D wrote about the unifying effect of the music: "Rap is now a worldwide phenomenon. Rap is the CNN for young people all over the world because now you can hear from rappers in Croatia and find out what they talk about and how they're feeling. Rappers from Italy, rappers from Africa. Rap has become an unofficial network of the young mentality."

Hip-hop also represented hope, creativity, and entrepreneurship. That enormous cultural shift was happening before Abloh's eyes and during his most formative years.

Hip-hop lovers were starting to use fashion to communicate their financial aspirations as well as their cultural identity. The term *metrosexual* was buzzing around in marketing circles and in mainstream media as a way of describing young, straight—typically White—men with an affinity for fashion and expensive grooming. But long before trend forecasters thrust the word into popular culture, Black men had embraced style as a form of self-definition, a statement about belonging, and a pleasant way to peacock and pose.

"Black male elegance is an essential element of our complex humanity," said social critic and activist Cornel West. "In a society so deeply shaped by White supremacy that it regards Black bodies with disgust and degradation, Black style acts as a type of aesthetic resistance to the various racist myths."

Hip-hop zeroed in on brands such as Tommy Hilfiger and Ralph Lauren that signified Americana and a country club version of success and appropriated them for their own messaging. A breakdancer might choose an oversize fit—or stitch together multiple garments to make a single enormous silhouette—to make movement easier. But as a political statement, the baggy shapes allowed the wearer to take up more space, to be seen more vividly, and to command greater attention. Those enormous rugby and polo shirts were both an acknowledgment of the social hierarchy and a usurping of it.

Hilfiger responded to the attention by playing along. The logos on his clothes got bigger, and so did the silhouettes. In February 1996, rappers Sean "Puffy" Combs—as he was known back then—and Coolio walked the runway for a Hilfiger menswear show decked out in basic black tailoring. Anthony Shawn Criss, better known as Treach from Naughty by Nature, modeled a custom black leather Tommy Hilfiger suit after having signed with Bethann Management, the same agency that represented model Tyson Beckford. Beckford broke barriers in 1993 when he won an exclusive contract with Polo Ralph Lauren. It wasn't the first time a Black man had represented the classic tailoring and American mythology of Polo; Rashid Silvera, with his patrician, slender elegance, preceded Beckford. But Beckford made a different kind of statement. He had a deep brown complexion, full lips, and a muscular physique. He brought no less dignity to his advertising campaigns than Silvera, but it came with an evocative strut.

"Everyone likes the pretty boys, but they're also starting to like someone with a hard edge," Treach said. "Like a 'Tyson' and like me."

At the time, casting Treach and other rappers seemed like little more than a publicity stunt, a way for Hilfiger to acknowledge the role that young Black consumers were having on the company's bottom line and to encourage them to spend even more money. In hindsight, though, a seed was planted. Hilfiger advised a generation of hip-hop's entrepreneurs—Russell Simmons, Sean Combs—as they entered the fashion industry. Instead of viewing them as competitors or distancing himself from them as some designers had, Hilfiger shared his knowledge about the pitfalls and machinations of an unforgiving Seventh Avenue.

Lauren didn't change his design sensibility to garner more attention from the hip-hop community, nor did he become a consigliere to its aspiring entrepreneurs. He stayed true to his formal tailoring, his New England preppiness, his romanticized vision of a Jazz Age New York. But he invited hip-hop into his world. And that community adopted Lauren's dress code.

Hip-hop also took note of Lauren's ethos. He was playing the long game. He wasn't trafficking in trends. He was constructing a world. "I'm not fashion," Lauren said. "I don't want to be this year's look. I want to be exciting, but I want a certain taste level. I never felt I was in the fashion business."

Lauren's company went public in 1997. It was bringing in wholesale revenue of nearly $3 billion, and it was selling its vision of wealth, power, and Americana in the suburbs and in the cities, to corporate titans and rappers. The Ralph Lauren Corporation became emblematic of the kind of empire that designers like Abloh ultimately yearned to create for themselves. It was a company with such a strong brand identity that anything bearing its mark *became* Ralph Lauren. The brand stood for a sensibility, a way of life, not a fad.

And to some degree, Lauren himself served as a template for how an outsider could become a pillar of the establishment. He was a Jewish kid who never went to design school; instead, he studied business at Baruch College, which is part of the City University of New York education system, but enlisted in the U.S. Army before he graduated. He was an outsider who became a self-made man. "I knew what it was like to have nothing," Lauren said. "I grew up in the Bronx. I played basketball in the streets. I went to public high school.

"I earned the money."

When Ralph Lauren went public, it was a big deal in high fashion, on Wall Street, and within popular culture because the brand had such an enormous footprint. It was a mall brand, after all. And Abloh was a mall kid.

But Ralph Lauren was also the rare American brand that was part of fashion's aspirational economy, alongside Louis Vuitton, Gucci, and Fendi. At the tail end of the twentieth century, when Abloh was a dreamy-eyed seventeen-year-old, these brands were beginning to represent something deeper. Acquiring them was not just a reflection of one's bank account; they were being equated with identity. They were becoming tribal.

When Abloh was seventeen, fashion was in the midst of one of its most pivotal moments. It was bloated with a new generation of designers who would become cultural disruptors. They would become the fascination of filmmakers; their businesses would usher in an era of tremendous financial growth for luxury conglomerates; their work would break out of the fashion bubble and into the popular consciousness.

The industry churned out a host of debut collections whose cumulative effect was to draw a dividing line between the old and the new. Fashion was experiencing its second "youthquake." The first had been in the 1960s, when the baby boom generation stepped into

33

the spotlight and their interests and needs as both creators and consumers were prioritized. Three decades later, fashion was turning its attention to Gen X and beyond. The year was so significant that the Musée de la Mode de la Ville de Paris dedicated an entire exhibition to it: "1997 Fashion Big Bang."

That was the year that a tiny handbag changed the fortunes of a family-owned Italian fashion label, helped cement Hollywood as an extension of the fashion industry, and instigated a reconsideration of the importance of accessories in the fashion ecosystem. The Fendi Baguette hit the market. The small handbag with the truncated shoulder strap fit under the arm like a loaf of bread being carried home from the neighborhood bakery. Designed by Silvia Venturini Fendi, the bag came in a kaleidoscope of iterations—beaded, sequined, embroidered. It morphed into a pop cultural phenomenon when it became a plot point on *Sex and the City*. In the two years after its introduction, Fendi sold three hundred thousand of the bags, which had a starter price of about $1,000. The Baguette begat an entire generation of "it" bags—purses that became such objects of desire that they could keep whole companies afloat from one season to the next.

Legacy houses were in transition. A host of American designers, with an expertise in youthful, sophisticated sportswear, stepped into the spotlight, lured to Paris by LVMH. Marc Jacobs was appointed to Louis Vuitton, where he was tasked with creating the first ready-to-wear collections for the company, which was then mostly known for its luggage. Michael Kors was brought in to energize Céline. Narciso Rodriguez was hired at Loewe. There was change elsewhere too. Stella McCartney presented her first collection at Chloé, and although she had a formal fashion degree from the highly respected Central Saint Martins in London, it was her celebrity pedigree as the daughter of Paul McCartney that captured headlines. This was also the year that Nicolas Ghesquière was named creative director of Balenciaga. After having worked as a freelancer for the brand, he was tasked with brushing off the dust and making the stately house relevant again. He made his mark by bringing his interest in futurism and science fiction into his work. In doing so, he welcomed another one of the subcultures of the popular imagination into luxury fashion.

In the United States, grunge had hit the catwalks. A short-lived fashion trend, it was born out of the scruffy rock music from the Pacific Northwest. Grunge was the sound and look of bands such as Pearl Jam and Nirvana, which were part of Abloh's eclectic musical taste. The style was characterized by dishevelment and waif-like models. It was the antidote to the Amazonian supermodels and hyperglamour of the 1980s. Heroin chic added a layer of desperation, austerity, and rawness.

"One aspect of fashion, initially more underground, focused on the waif-like models, whose slim silhouettes seemed more natural to us. There was less fuss over hair and make-up, and they wore unconstructed clothes. To us they seemed to convey authenticity, much more than overly manufactured glamour and perfection ever did," wrote Long Nguyen in *My Beutyfull Lyfe,* a book celebrating the photography of Davide Sorrenti. Nguyen, a style director for *Detour* magazine during the 1990s, was simultaneously credited with and blamed for the rise of heroin chic.

The style was popularized by fashion's gatekeepers, but it was inspired by underage kids hanging out in dingy clubs, quirky teens who were considered outcasts by the old standards of popularity. As Abloh stood on the cusp of adulthood, reading his style magazines and swooning over the latest skater brands, he also saw a fashion industry consumed by the desires, anxieties, and frailties of adolescence.

In large measure, 1997 marked the implosion of heroin chic with the death of twenty-year-old Sorrenti, whose work had placed him in the center of a fashion aesthetic that was unpolished and accessible but also glorified a drugged-out, emaciated hollowness, as well as addiction. The story of Sorrenti's death, along with the fashion industry's belated recognition of the devastating power in the images of decimated youth, appeared on the front page of *The New York Times*.

Even the White House had something to say about the way in which fashion was engaging with Abloh and his peers. President Clinton pointedly admonished Seventh Avenue during a meeting at the White House with thirty-five mayors who'd assembled to discuss drug trafficking and substance abuse. "American fashion has been an enormous source of creativity and beauty and art and, frankly, economic prosperity for the United States," Clinton said, "and we should all value and respect that.

"But the glorification of heroin is not creative, it's destructive," he added. "It's not beautiful; it's ugly. And this is not about art; it's about life and death. And glorifying death is not good for any society."

Fashion's creative experimentation—an attempt to strip away artifice and embrace individual identity—had trickled into the broader culture. But once fashion was loosed from the atelier, once it was out there in the wild, its practitioners received a harsh lesson. Freedom came with certain responsibilities. In the aftermath of the president's rebuke, the fashion industry's sensibility shifted. It wasn't so much that editors, photographers, and stylists were shamed by D.C. or the sorrows they'd exacerbated. It was that the glamorization of pain had run its course. It was time for fashion to move in a new direction.

Few designers had a more profound impact on the way that Abloh's generation of young men thought about fashion than Raf Simons. He also offered a way forward from grunge that still felt youthful and authentic, but not nihilistic.

"What drew me to his work was his intellectualized view of current culture. His approach is so reality-based. His early work is social commentary on being young, and that approach to fashion resonates with me the most," said Abloh, who discovered Simons's work in the pages of Japanese style publications. "The 2003 collection is burned in my mind."

The Belgian-born Simons, who founded his menswear label in 1995, presented his first runway show in Paris in 1997. Much of the inspiration came from the attire of American college students and English prep schools. The show audience was seated no more than a foot away from the models as they made their way around the crowded room on a dead-end street in the eleventh arrondissement of Paris, not far from Père Lachaise cemetery. There was painfully little racial diversity on Simons's runway; the cast was overwhelmingly White. In that way, his models were hardly revolutionary. But they stood out in at least one way: they were not all finely chiseled models for hire. Mostly they were thin and gangly. They had the build of boys rather than men.

The show foreshadowed the ways in which Simons would alter the definition of menswear, which is to say that it wasn't really a reflection of the obsessions of men but of adolescents—or of men perpetually in conversation with their seventeen-year-old selves. Simons rejected the "masters of the universe" grandiosity of the 1980s; he eschewed the self-conscious elegance of Giorgio Armani's soft tailoring; he refused to indulge in the macho glamour of rock and rollers. Instead, he was moved by skateboarders and club kids. He brought subcultures onto the runway in a manner that imbued them with respect and importance.

Fall 2003 was one of Simons's most revered collections and not just by Abloh. Simons collaborated with one of the world's best-known graphic designers Peter Saville, who'd created the album covers of the new-wave band Joy Division and its reconstituted iteration,

New Order. Saville had used the painting *A Basket of Roses,* by the nineteenth-century French artist Henri Fantin-Latour, for the cover of New Order's 1983 album *Power, Corruption & Lies.* The result was a jarring aesthetic tension. A classical still life served as the marketing symbol of an album of electronic music—music that was deeply reliant on modern technology. The groundbreaking cover was even memorialized on a stamp. Simons referenced that famous cover in his 2003 collections' prints.

From the very beginning of his career, Simons staked a claim on the moody romanticism that was one of the obsessions of young men coming of age as the world transitioned from analog to digital, when the internet still seemed like a place where organic connections could be made, before online life became so isolating and radicalizing. Simons helped move youth culture from the cynicism of grunge and the morbidness of heroin chic to something more optimistic—or at least something not so destructive.

Another alternative to heroin chic that would have appealed to Abloh was the dynamic, sexy monied style that emerged during this time, much of it led by Tom Ford at Gucci. It was fueled and embraced by Black entertainers and athletes—notably basketball players whose lean, muscular physiques made them prime models for more daring menswear and whose league rules prohibited them from wearing shorts and tank tops while on team business. And once these Black tastemakers knew what it felt like to be in fashion's spotlight, once they saw just how lucrative fashion could be in terms of cultural currency, as well as marketing potential, they were eager to move to center stage and do the work to remain there.

Ford's glamorous aesthetic was deeply connected to hip-hop. During runway show season in Milan, Ford would regularly check in with Emil Wilbekin, editor in chief of *Vibe* magazine, which chronicled the music and style of a rising culture. "Gucci, especially under Tom Ford, really embraced hip-hop and hip-hop culture. When I'd go to Milan for men's [fashion shows] I'd have a one-on-one with Tom Ford. He wanted to know what was happening on the street, to understand how the community was reacting to his work and what they were wearing," Wilbekin said. "The Black community and the Latinx community would embrace what he was doing and remix it."

The year 1997 was fashion's great year, a time of creative urgency and an era of adventure. The industry was in the midst of a racial reckoning—one of many that it would have over the decades. At the start of the 1990s, Black models essentially disappeared. It was a period when White models so dominated the runways and magazines that the effect was akin to "white washing." The homogeneity was so stark that activists raised their voices in protest. In 1997, the pendulum began to swing back toward diversity—or more specifically, it started to be *pushed* toward diversity, as fashion media could not ignore what had become so painfully and dreadfully obvious.

That year, Jean Paul Gaultier, who'd created Madonna's famous conical bra, presented a collection in Paris inspired by the African diaspora. Mounted in the Salle Wagram, a historic auditorium in Paris's seventeenth arrondissement, the collection was a blend of Harlem, the African continent, jazz, and hip-hop. It steered clear of easy stereotypes and focused on the dignity and majesty and variety in Black culture. It demonstrated what was possible when a designer looked beyond the old tropes. Gaultier's collection was still deeply rooted in the fashion tradition, but he'd cracked open the door and embraced contemporary Black culture along with Black people—if only for a season. It had not been difficult; Gaultier only had to look around him. It "was an homage to different Black women that I admire, like Miriam Makeba, Josephine Baker, Angela Davis . . . and also to the elegance that Black women have," Gaultier said. "The inspiration was also coming from different kinds of typical Black music like jazz, rap, and funk. I had the image of the wife of an ambassador of an African country living in a city like New York or Paris. . . . That woman is dressed in an Occidental way but she keeps her African roots with some accessories like a turban and big jewelry."

Designers had become personalities: Gaultier and Rei Kawakubo, along with Alexander McQueen, who debuted at Givenchy in 1997, and John Galliano, who showed his first collection at Dior the same year. Givenchy and Dior were both affiliated with the LVMH corporate family. They were controlled by Bernard Arnault, a billionaire who viewed himself as a patron of fashion's creative spirit and who saw himself as an instigator in the broader popular culture. There was a limit to the number of handbags and pairs of shoes Arnault could sell. But there was no limit to the dreams and aspirations he could exploit and monetize.

"The mid-1990s were a period of incredible creativity with few boundaries, when fashion designers broke barriers and fashion embraced identity and freedom in a way that is unrecognizable today," Nguyen wrote. "Wearing particular designers wasn't about portraying a luxury lifestyle, the clothes lent the wearers a sense of belonging and shared values."

One of the cultural moments that defined 1997 was the death of Princess Diana, who was killed in a car crash in Paris only weeks after designer Gianni Versace was murdered in Miami Beach. Diana's death prompted global mourning, and for those who had an emotional investment in her wedding and marriage to Prince Charles, it was also the end of a fairytale, a death blow to idealized love—or at the very least, the loss of a glamorous icon who had excelled at revenge fashion.

It's hard to imagine seventeen-year-old Abloh—soccer player, engineering student, skateboarder—as someone interested in British fairy tales and princesses, but Diana's death was a cultural moment: an estimated 2.5 billion television viewers watched her funeral. One didn't have to be actively paying attention. The news surrounding her death was a media event so all-consuming that simply existing meant absorbing the emotional impact. Ghana, Abloh's parents' country of origin, had been a British colony referred to as the Gold Coast until 1957 and is today a member of the British Commonwealth. Diana was one of the few members of the royal family not fully tainted by its colonial past. Years later, as the designer of his own label, Abloh would create a womenswear collection inspired by Diana, one that would nod to her voluminous wedding gown as well as her woman-about-town bike shorts and oversize sweatshirts.

In other corners of the culture, Black men and women were beginning to dominate. Music was fertile ground for Black aspirations. Black musicians brought such valuable cultural currency that fashion couldn't turn away.

In sports, Michael Jordan was in his glory; the Chicago Bulls were supreme. And Abloh was among the many basketball fans who idolized him. The hoops star's Air Jordan sneakers were setting a new standard for how an athletic shoe could look, how lucrative a cultural collaboration could be, and how hungry young men were for a way to communicate both style and affiliation through what they wore. Black athletes grabbed hold of their admiring young fans—of all races—and directed their gaze toward their sneakers, their clothes, and then fashion itself.

The menswear that would eventually emerge was, in many ways, the result of the union between the two worlds in which young Black men saw a lucrative path forward: music and sports. The cliché of teenagers dreaming of becoming a rap star or a basketball star expanded to include becoming a designer—a dream that could begin with a T-shirt. Fashion allowed for personal storytelling in a way that was more accessible than other forms of creative expression. The barrier to entry seemed low and inexpensive. And the power of brands was expansive and alluring.

No one is shaped by only a single year in their lifetime, but the year to which Abloh so often referred was a time when his own sense of style was constrained. He had to wear a de facto uniform to school. He wore a uniform to play soccer. Skateboarding and listening to hip-hop were as much expressions of his personal style as anything else. At the mall, he admired brands like Nautica, Ralph Lauren, Tommy Hilfiger, and Timberland. He loved Stüssy. He held Supreme in the same high regard as Hermès and Louis Vuitton. If his sense of aesthetics had distinct gestures, it was in combining the formal traditions of his daily schoolwear with the informality and creativity of streetwear brands that were still in their infancy.

The year of Abloh's obsession was pivotal in ways that were both extraordinarily intimate and far-reaching. When he was a high school student, his small city—well past its manufacturing glory days—was in turmoil, stressed by its stubborn refusal to move beyond racial divides that reached back generations. Rockford was a city whose geography made inequality plain; it drew a line between the predominantly White neighborhoods worthy of economic investment and the mostly Black ones that were afterthoughts. The river that had attracted White settlers seeking opportunity also told a story about how access to opportunity still was not equal.

Abloh had grown up in an immigrant household, and this fundamental fact shaped the way in which he thought about race and dealt with racism. It would make a difference in the way he was perceived in the fashion industry, where he was typically referred to as the child of Ghanaian immigrants rather than simply African American. The former implies choice. It's tinged with the radiance of the American Dream. The latter bears the stain of the country's original sin.

To come of age in the late nineties meant hearing fashion begin a conversation about race and authenticity that would continue into the next millennium. The dialogue would sometimes reach a crescendo before falling silent, only to be resuscitated. Logos would continue to identify aspirational brands, but they would begin to signify community, not simply wealth. Some of the most desirable brands had little to do with how much money a person had and everything to do with how deeply enmeshed in a particular subculture that person was. Street style would change the hierarchy of value. And eventually that would mean that a Black son of immigrants without any formal fashion training would sit atop the menswear division of Louis Vuitton, the world's largest luxury fashion brand with annual revenue of more than 20 billion euros.

Tilling the Soil

IT'S IMPOSSIBLE TO understand Virgil Abloh's success within the fashion industry without looking back to those Black designers who came before him. No one breaks barriers on their own. They're aided by folks who put cracks in glass ceilings, who mitigate senseless fears, who prove stereotypes wrong. The ways Abloh's predecessors dealt with race, wrestled with it, make it clear how much the industry changed for the better over the years. The skills they had that lifted them to the top of the fashion industry provide a contrast to the ones that ultimately helped Abloh rise. Their stories are inextricable from Abloh's.

"When you're a first, sometimes it's quite difficult," said Edward Enninful, who was the first male and first Black editor of *British Vogue*. "When you're the token or the only one, you can exist in solitude, or you can say, I'm going to bring in people with me.

"For the first, you open the way for the next generation," Enninful continued. "The brilliance of Virgil came along because the world was opened."

BEFORE THERE WAS Virgil Abloh, there was Edward Buchanan. And it was lonely being Buchanan: a Black designer at one of Europe's legacy brands.

In 1995, Buchanan was the design director at Bottega Veneta, where he was tasked with establishing a ready-to-wear collection for the Italian company. Bottega Veneta was founded in 1966 in Vicenza, an elegant city in northern Italy between Verona and Venice. The company began as a leather goods house, one focused on craftsmanship and subtlety. It spurned logos and the look-at-me flashiness of the 1980s, so it was not a brand name that had made its way into popular culture. It was dignified and it was family owned.

Buchanan was an unlikely choice to build a luxury ready-to-wear collection from the ground up. Like Abloh, he was a child of the Midwest. He grew up in Cleveland, Ohio, and in 1995 graduated from Parsons School of Design, where Gordon Henderson had been his mentor. Henderson was part of a new wave of young designers that fashion editors saw as writing the next chapter in the story of American sportswear. That Henderson, who was Black, was part of that group was notable because it was uncommon.

By the mid-1990s there had been successful Black designers, but the list of Black designers who'd built their own multi-million-dollar businesses and broken into the broader public consciousness was short: Willi Smith and Patrick Kelly. They had done so through extraordinary means.

Smith always said that he didn't aspire to dress the queen but rather to dress the folks who lined the streets and waved as she passed by. He was a populist who wanted to bring thoughtful design to the everyday shopper. Smith was inspired by the cotton fabric he sourced from India, the men and women he saw on the street, and his own ideas about comfort and cool. He called his brand Willi-Wear, and it was, in some ways, one of the earliest precursors to streetwear.

But it was political royalty that pushed Smith into the popular imagination. He designed the navy linen suit that Ed Schlossberg wore when he married Caroline Kennedy in July 1986. The suit itself was not particularly audacious. But it stood out for its easy silhouette, closer to an Ivy League sack suit than a Savile Row suit of armor. It had a modern, jaunty flair; it exuded youthfulness. And, of course, Smith himself signified change. But the designer died the following April from AIDS at thirty-nine, and much of his legacy died with him.

Mississippi-born Patrick Kelly was more of a couturier. He was six years younger than Smith and a joyful provocateur. Kelly learned to sew in high school and perfected his craft by remaking thrift-shop garments. He adorned his frocks with buttons and bows and appropriated racist caricatures like Golliwogs and pickaninnies into his work, turning them into a commentary on Black history and cultural resiliency. Kelly found success as an expatriate in Paris and in 1988 became the first American admitted to the Chambre Syndicale du Prêt-à-Porter des Couturiers et des Créateurs de Mode, France's prestigious organization of ready-to-wear designers.

His fashion shows were effervescent and cast with models of different races. They smiled and twirled and expressed their personality with a wink or a particularly dramatic sashay. He gave his audience party favors, tiny little brooches in the shape of Black baby dolls. The little plastic infants with their articulating arms and legs had swirling black curls and bright red lips. They weren't caricatures of Black babies; they were homages to them.

Kelly died in 1990 at thirty-five from AIDS-related complications. His company died with him.

Kelly's work could not have been more distinct from Smith's. But something as simple as leaning into one's individuality was a powerful lesson for designers who are too often described as "Black" before anything else.

The award-winning Henderson was hailed by the industry press as a fresh face, the next big thing, a designer on the verge of greatness. He grew up in California, assisted Calvin Klein, and graduated from

Parsons. And far from being the sort of designer who indulged in Hollywood theatrics, he was a pragmatist. He celebrated the traditions of great American sportswear but loved oversize silhouettes. He was a designer for the people. "I could have really taken you to Cuba or Mexico, had the donkeys coming down the runway," he told *The New York Times* after a show in 1989. "But this is about clothes. When you start becoming theatrical apart from what your clothes stand for, there's no reality."

Henderson was a realist; he focused on clothes that were understandable, desirable, and wearable. And that was the kind of designer that Buchanan would grow to be.

"Gordon was amazing for me. He was super, super talented and super handsome, and he was just, for me, the prototype of what it was to be a designer. And then, to see a reflection of myself on the other side, he was essentially doing what I wanted to do in that time," Buchanan recalled. "He's the one who actually placed me in front of Donna Karan; he placed me in front of Calvin Klein; he placed me in front of Ralph Lauren. None of which hired me, but he placed me in front of them at the time when I was in New York."

To help finance his education, Buchanan worked as a window dresser—this in an era when brick-and-mortar stores were dominant and their street-facing vitrines were a powerful marketing tool. Another window dresser alerted him to an enticing job prospect: Bottega Veneta was looking for a designer. The optimism and fearlessness of youth led Buchanan to apply despite having little experience. He visited the brand's New York boutique; he perused the handbags; and he assembled a presentation that he presented to Laura Moltedo, whose family owned Bottega Veneta.

"Laura created, in the seventies, the Bottega Veneta that we know today. The first boutique was on Madison Avenue in New York City, so that's where I met her," Buchanan said. "I think back at that time, for me, being this Black American presenting myself to a luxury house, I didn't understand what the power of that was. But I was impressed when I think back to how open and accepting she was of me as a creative, not based on who I was or what I looked like. I just presented this project. And not even a month later, I was hired."

Buchanan didn't speak Italian. He didn't know what he was undertaking. But he was thrilled because he had a job in fashion—a massive one for a kid fresh out of Parsons. He was Bottega Veneta's new design director.

When he was growing up in Cleveland that was what he'd been eager to do. He wanted to create clothes for regular folks—the hardworking ones, the aspiring dreamers, the accomplished professionals. He wasn't interested in dressing celebrities for the red carpet. He wasn't lusting after fame. He was a designer's designer, someone who was fascinated with fabrics and silhouettes. Over time, he became a knitwear expert, someone who could look at a little squiggle of yarn from a mill and know exactly how it would look knitted into a sweater.

As Buchanan prepared to begin his fashion career in Italy, he was still in his twenties; going out on the town was like a part-time job. He knew nothing about building a design team and communicating production orders to factories. Bottega Veneta had taken a leap of faith; and so had Buchanan.

When he arrived in Italy in 1995, he landed at Venice's small, regional airport. Italy was used to welcoming visitors on the grand tour and college students taking a study year abroad, but it was also a bluntly homogeneous society struggling to accommodate increasing numbers of poor immigrants, especially those flowing in from Africa. Young Italian men had physically attacked Black immigrants in Florence, and North Africans had been firebombed out of their makeshift shelter in a middle-class Florentine neighborhood. Racist literature was sprouting around the country. Racist comments were common. Populism was on the rise, particularly in the north. And many frustrated police officers, aggrieved shopkeepers, and fearful everyday folks blamed rising crime on the Black newcomers.

When Buchanan tumbled off his long, overnight flight from New York, he walked into an Italy that was especially wary and suspicious of Black faces. Buchanan had long dreadlocks and was wearing jeans and a hooded sweatshirt. He walked over to the baggage area to claim his luggage. Five police officers approached him and asked him to step into a private room.

"They start checking my bags. And they say, 'Listen, if you have drugs, just give them to us, or tell us about them.' And I was like, 'I don't have drugs. I don't do that. I don't even smoke cigarettes.' It was two hours that they held me. And they stripped me down and did a cavity search. This is my very first trip to Italy.

"It wasn't the first time that I was dealing with microaggressions or passive racism, because I dealt with that in New York City or even in Ohio, for that matter. But it was just so shocking to me that here I am being hired as a designer for a luxury house and I'm arriving in the country, and I'm somehow treated like I've done something wrong. That really stuck with me.

"It didn't create fear. It created information or tools for me for the future, to be very aware of the spaces that I was going in and how people actually viewed me in those spaces. It was informative for me."

Buchanan was sad that his youthful, gap-toothed self, someone with a ready smile, full of excitement and nervousness, was treated with suspicion and disdain. And the insulting coda? After the violating search revealed nothing illegal, there was no apology. No admission of wrongdoing. No one attempted to excuse the inexcusable.

"There was no formal 'Okay, we're done. We thought you were someone else.' I've heard that stuff before where they're like, 'Oh, we're looking for a Black man with a parka on.' And I just fit the bill. But there they were just, 'You look like you have drugs. We're going to check you for drugs. We're actually going to strip you down naked and search between your cheeks. And now that we see that you don't have drugs, just go on your way.'

"I didn't have the knowledge and the guts at that time to say, 'What the fuck is going on here?' I just had to pull myself together because I was there to start doing something that would actually change the trajectory of my career, my life."

Buchanan was breaking ground. He was there turning the soil for the next generation. But he had little recourse. He had nowhere to vent his frustration. His treatment at the airport became his personal cautionary tale—that shattering moment when he realized that his success would be forged through the infuriating and stubborn heartache of stereotypes, prejudices, and racism. The incident embedded itself into his coming-of-age story. It became scar tissue.

Buchanan walked away from the police. In that moment, surviving the encounter was a victory. Shaken, he called his colleagues at Bottega Veneta. And they came to retrieve their new design director.

After several modest seasons of quiet showroom presentations, Buchanan's first formal runway show for Bottega Veneta was in October 1998 at Palazzo Serbelloni, an ornate eighteenth-century palace in the heart of Milan. The debut was duly recorded by the fashion press. *Essence* magazine, which celebrated Black women and Black achievement, chronicled Buchanan's work with pride. *The New York Times* gave his first show two sentences of shoulder-shrugging criticism. The *Toronto Star* offered kinder words, but they were packed into a single sentence.

Buchanan had been given a clean slate upon which to write a ready-to-wear story in his own vernacular. That degree of freedom in fashion was rare and remains so. In his work, he focused on details and on craftsmanship. As a result, he won over the owners of Italian fabric mills, the expert knitters, and the veteran seamstresses.

He rose above the prejudices. Buchanan didn't deliver blockbuster collections, but he eventually found his rhythm and helped set Bottega Veneta up for future success. His clothes were unfussy and relaxed, but with an air of grace. They were the epitome of quiet luxury.

Still, Buchanan's tenure at Bottega Veneta wasn't discussed beyond fashion's borders. His rise was not celebrated as a historic victory in the United States. Fashion had not yet burst out of its small, clubby world. People didn't see this as any sort of cultural victory. Buchanan came to Bottega Veneta as an unknown. He lacked a larger-than-life personality to draw lights and cameras his way. "The majority of the Italian press didn't even take note. They were talking about other things at that time. They were talking about Tom Ford [at Gucci]. They were talking about Alexander McQueen. They were talking about [John] Galliano. They were talking about Nicolas Ghesquière. But they were not talking about Edward because his appointment didn't matter. It did not matter in the mix," Buchanan said. "I took the bows after the collections. The pictures were there on Style.com at the time, but there was not much conversation."

Buchanan spent six years at Bottega Veneta. He built a foundation of expertise and know-how so that he could have a long-lasting career in fashion. He transformed from an idealistic young man into a clear-eyed adult. He was still sometimes stopped on the street and asked to present identification. And when he pulled out his shiny blue American passport, he would swiftly be sent on his way. He often wondered how quickly he'd be dispatched if he produced a passport from Nigeria or Ghana or any country filled with Black people that didn't have the global economic, cultural, and military might of the United States. These moments were too disconcerting to be characterized as microaggressions. They were more than minor violations or inconveniences. They were the kind of cuts that don't draw blood but nonetheless leave a body aching. But Buchanan kept moving forward—for himself and for others—because retreating simply was not in him.

During his time at Bottega Veneta, only a handful of other Black designers were working inside fashion's European luxury goods companies, men such as Eric Wright at Fendi and Warren Davis at Jil Sander. But Buchanan was even more unusual because he was the lead for ready-to-wear. He didn't have the creative director title; Laura Moltedo claimed it. But he was setting the vision, and the two took their bows together.

"To see someone like me in a position like that was very rare. Very, very rare," Buchanan said. "So rare, in fact, that I often thought to myself, 'How did I get here?'"

BUCHANAN SHOWED THE INDUSTRY that a young kid from the Midwest could step into a legacy fashion house and create something from scratch. He demonstrated that despite being an outsider he could speak in the vernacular of the fabric mills and the seamstresses. Over the years, Buchanan learned Italian, but he also proved that fashion was a universal language.

After Buchanan came Ozwald Boateng. He emerged as Abloh, having graduated high school, was working to wrap himself in thicker and thicker protective layers of education, first a bachelor's degree and then a master's. Abloh had yet to commit to his personal creative impulses in fashion. His artistic outlet outside the classroom was behind a turntable as a deejay or designing T-shirts.

Then in December 2003, LVMH sent out a press release announcing that the luxury group had hired Boateng as creative director for Givenchy Homme. While Buchanan had been at a small family-owned house in Italy, Givenchy was in Paris. It was part of a luxury conglomerate. It was an entirely different level of prestige and responsibility. Boateng would paint a monumental picture of what was possible for a Black man in fashion.

He was tasked with creating the first cohesive menswear vernacular for the respected fashion house. Givenchy already produced menswear, but the clothes didn't have a designer's point of view. They were garments by committee. As beautifully manufactured as they were, there was nothing singular about them.

Boateng represented a momentous choice not simply because of what he was hired to do at Givenchy but because of who he was. He was the company's first Black creative director, preceding Abloh into one of LVMH's corner offices by fifteen years.

Boateng and Abloh had a great deal in common. Although Abloh was a son of the American Midwest and Boateng was born in North London, they were both children of Ghanaian immigrants. Boateng's parents came from Ghana to the United Kingdom in the 1950s—his father, a teacher, and his mother, a freelance seamstress. Both Abloh and Boateng came to fashion sideways. They tapped into popular culture as a route to success. They were entrepreneurs. They both had a beguiling manner: Boateng was full of charismatic bluster and easily served as the best model for his clothes; Abloh was admired for his warmth and good humor.

Boateng stood well over six feet tall. He had a slim, athletic physique and he moved with both grace and confidence. He was compelling in a sculptural way, a beautiful composition of lines and angles, light and shadow. He had a handsome bearing, but that wasn't unusual in an industry that focused on appearance and attracted people who were willing to work diligently to look their best. Besides, handsome—like pretty—quickly becomes dull. Boateng had something much more intriguing, a convincing suaveness. And that was a potent ingredient in his success. He was not especially humble, but to be clear, that does not mean he was cocky or arrogant, an assessment most often used to remind Black men that they shouldn't think so highly of their skills or desires. Boateng had always been aware of what made him great and believed wholeheartedly in his abilities.

After a career that took him from Savile Row to Paris, Los Angeles, and New York and back again, his accent drifted from posh to hipster slang to a slushy mixture of working-class ennui and bemusement.

Unlike Abloh, Boateng was a skilled tailor at a time when expertise mattered more than anything else. That's what ultimately fueled Boateng's success. His sharp, refined cuts, with his distinctly lean, athletic silhouette, were in conversation with the work of Tom Ford as well as Hedi Slimane. He also had a sophisticated color sense, able to inject shades of fuchsia and tangerine into a sleek business suit without ever overwhelming its unique elegance.

While Louis Vuitton was the most lucrative of the LVMH fashion properties, Givenchy was one of its most esteemed. It rivaled Dior in the cultural imagination. Founded in 1952 by Hubert de Givenchy, it had nobility in its core. The tall, elegant Hubert was born a count and studied under designers Lucien Lelong, Elsa Schiaparelli, and Cristóbal Balenciaga, who was considered the eminence grise of haute couture.

Hubert's work was valued for its attention to line and proportion rather than a reliance on embellishments. He was a minimalist. And the works he crafted in collaboration with actress Audrey Hepburn for the films *Breakfast at Tiffany's* and *Sabrina* were perfect examples of his sensibility. He understood the sensuality in an austere neckline, the grace in exposing the curves of a woman's back, and the perfect balance between extravagance and refinement. In the brand's heyday, which was from the 1950s through the '70s, Givenchy was favored by women who dominated the international fashion circuit and the society pages, back when such things not only existed but also were revered. He dressed Princess Grace of

Monaco, Bunny Mellon, the Duchess of Windsor, Jacqueline Kennedy Onassis, Babe Paley, Marie-Hélène de Rothschild, São Schlumberger, and Deeda Blair, among others. In short, Hubert dressed the influencers of his day, women whose photos appeared in newspaper columns rather than Instagram grids.

At that time, fashion trickled down from the couture houses of Paris to the ready-to-wear companies on Seventh Avenue and into the closets of everyday women. That meant that Givenchy was among those design houses that dressed the world.

In 1988, Hubert sold his brand to LVMH, but he stayed on to lead its creative team until he retired in 1995. By the time the founder stepped away from the atelier, the brand was catering to an older, tradition-bound clientele. It had lost its cultural urgency. And by the time Boateng was hired to craft a menswear vocabulary, its womenswear division had become a revolving door through which talented designers cycled. John Galliano directly succeeded the brand's namesake, but after only a year at the helm he moved on to Dior. He was replaced by Alexander McQueen, who stayed until 2001, when he left to focus on his own label. Julien Macdonald was designing the women's collection when Boateng's appointment was announced but was receiving terrible reviews from both the press and retailers. He would be out by 2004.

Boateng's appointment to Givenchy was startling. It came at a time when fashion had powerful gatekeepers and there were no easy ways to get around them. Young designers could not simply broadcast their talent on social media. They couldn't crowdsource financing. Corporate headhunters scoured top fashion schools looking for talent or worked to hire star designers away from other houses. Boateng didn't have a battalion of social media warriors to help him push open the doors. An aspiring designer typically had to convince someone to let them into the room.

Boateng did that by establishing himself within the London

community of Savile Row, which since 1843 has been the geographic center and mythical heart of the most formal and prescribed men's tailoring. After he got his bearings, this was the area where Boateng set up shop, in a small space on Vigo Street where the carpeting was marigold yellow, the walls were cherry red, and the window panels were turquoise. On any given day, James Brown shouted his exhortations from the sound system. Boateng was the youngest tailor to open his own studio there and the only Black one. And while he was assuredly a disrupter whose mere presence drew press attention, upon his arrival he made it plain that he had not come to dismantle tradition but to preserve it by making bespoke tailoring relevant to younger generations. He injected color into this dusty gray world where street numbers were gauche and the words "By Appointment to Her Majesty the Queen" were all the advertising a tailor needed.

Boateng always described himself as self-taught. That was part of the fable he crafted about himself. It's more accurate to say that his beginnings in fashion were untraditional. He didn't follow a straight path from fashion school to internship to design assistant and finally designer. The story that he told most often began in the 1980s when he was a student at Southgate College, which is now Barnet and Southgate College. Southgate was a technical school founded in 1962, and Boateng was there to study the unglamorous but promising subject of computer programming. He was heading down the road his parents sanctioned. His father, the academic, saw a future for his son in the legal profession, perhaps even in politics. While in college, Boateng met a girl—his first girlfriend. And he was dizzy from the magic of their dewy relationship. The girl was an artist, a creative dreamer who painted and sculpted and dabbled in fashion. When she was preparing for a show, she asked Boateng for help. She sat him down at a sewing machine and he stitched away at her direction. She was impressed by how quickly he caught on. Over time, he made himself a few frocks—trousers, a jacket—from bolts of African fabrics his mother had in storage. And when he wore these garments, people asked if they could buy them. Vanity and capitalism were powerful elixirs. He began to see fashion as an entrepreneurial opportunity.

The truth behind his I-did-it-for-love story is that he already knew how to sew.

"My mother used to make clothes at home, and the thing is, I used to look at her doing that and say, 'I will *never* do that job. You will *never* see me at that machine,'" Boateng said. But one summer, when he'd just entered his teen years, his mother told him he needed to find a job. To hear Boateng tell it, he was practically punching a clock from the time he was tall enough to see over a rail. "That's what happened back then, in the seventies. It was a different world. At seven years old I was delivering newspapers," he said. "And so, my mom was like, 'Listen, it's the summer, you've got to work.' And I'm like thirteen and I go find a summer job.

"I ended up going down in the East End of London and I basically got offered work in a factory sewing linings and jackets; I'm thirteen years old. I lied about my age and said I'm sixteen," he said. "In those days the checks and balances were a bit loose.

"They taught me how to sew. You go eight hours a day sewing in a straight line, suddenly you can do that blindfolded," he said. "I did it maybe two summers and I said, 'I'll never do this type of work ever again.' Because it's so tedious.

"The only time I stopped fighting was when they said to me, 'Oh, I want to buy this.'"

Boateng switched his studies from computer programming to fashion. He made his own clothing and was his own best model—both a blessing and a curse that followed him into his professional life. Observers would see Boateng in the sleek silhouette and he looked so fantastic that they'd fret that only tall, slim young men with staggering self-possession could pull off the sharp suits with their brightly colored lining. A friend who was a researcher on a television music show invited Boateng to sit in the studio audience—to essentially wear his clothes in a place where cameras would be. Perhaps the cameras would pan the audience and someone with money or clout would catch a glimpse of him. Perhaps he'd meet one of the show's musical guests and make a fruitful connection.

Boateng built relationships one by one. He was introduced to Savile Row's rigor through the work of Tommy Nutter, who was famous for sending a jolt of high fashion and youthful energy into traditional tailoring in the 1960s. Nutter made clothing for Mick Jagger, David Hockney, and Diana Ross, but his most visible work may well be on the cover of the Beatles 1969 *Abbey Road* album, on which three of the four band members photographed mid-stride in a crosswalk are wearing Tommy Nutter bespoke suits. In Nutter's edgy, of-the-moment work, Boateng saw possibilities for himself.

Boateng didn't apprentice in a design house. But he was perceptive and analytical and, of course, charming. He wove excitement into his garments with boasts and assurances. He learned by trial and error. "There is something about being self-taught. You make a lot of mistakes. And so, as a consequence, you don't fear making mistakes," he said. "The learning is different. I was constantly challenging the rules, you know? Because I didn't have the formal training—and I'm still living off that today—it creates a curiosity."

Boateng liked traditional British tailoring with its high armholes and compressed waists and slim lapels. He brought a youthful vibrancy to his severe cuts with his unflinching embrace of color. Instead of banker gray and navy, he chose violet and pumpkin. And when he *did* opt for a more subdued flannel or wool, he paired it with vivid linings that quietly reminded the wearer that he wasn't like all those other sops stuck in the grind of expectations.

Boateng moved forward in his work propelled by idealism.

Because things had been falling into place, his certainty about his point of view grew. But in the mid-1980s, when he asked for and was granted a meeting at London's Browns, one of the most influential retailers in the world, he was asked a question about his collection that he couldn't answer: What's the concept?

He realized that he was being asked *why* he made clothing. What was the point of it all? He didn't know. So he took some time to consider an answer until he finally realized what was driving his passion.

"I love the tradition of being British," Boateng said. He loved everything about it with the kind of determined glee of someone who knows what it's like to be both an insider and an outsider and has made a decision to be inside.

What Boateng didn't say at the start of his career was that he injected traditional British tailoring with the flair, soul, and vibrancy of his Blackness. The most obvious distinction is his color palette, alive with the bright hues of the African textiles his mother stocked. But there's more. The clothes have a look-at-me sensibility that balances flamboyance with dignity. It's a difficult skill that calls to mind the ways in which Black men have for generations improvised their own fashion in order to define themselves, make their presence known, and command respect—or at least recognition. There's a lot of "the dandy" in Boateng's work. And that has been an archetype long embraced by Black men as they negotiated their identity within the broader culture.

Boateng declared his version of bespoke tailoring staunchly British. In doing so, the long-held belief of what Britishness is became more alive and relevant and complex because of what Boateng was pouring into it. His tailoring argued in favor of diversity and inclusivity. It was a win for the culture—even if the culture didn't fully acknowledge it and even if Boateng was uncomfortable talking about it.

In these early years, Boateng didn't discuss race. He didn't run away from it; that was an impossibility. But race wasn't part of the narrative that he told the world about himself even though Black culture was expressed in his use of color, in the mood of his shop, and in the electrifying tension he created by tugging on aristocratic themes. Indeed, in the early days of his business, when he was starting to draw the attention of style magazines such as *i-D* and *The Face*, he was a garrulous and compelling interview, but he dodged being photographed.

"I didn't want anyone to know what I looked like because I didn't want to cloud what I was saying by the way I looked. I didn't want to have that conversation of, oh, he's Black and he looks a certain way and how that affected the kit. Because of the language I was communicating with, you know, people thought I was, in effect, some White guy," he said. "My name couldn't be more distinctively African, but they would associate it with someone, something completely different. So I basically liked the fact that no one knew."

Boateng wanted the work to speak first: that's what he wanted to be judged on, and he didn't think he would be if people saw him. He was an anomaly, and he knew his story was irresistible. What journalist didn't want to tell the story of a rare creature? But he didn't want the clothes to be lost in a story about identity. He didn't want his Blackness to be the reason people cheered for him.

As a designer, Boateng steered clear of identity politics with vigor and determination. He didn't see himself representing niche communities or subcultures or outsiders. He didn't work that way. He simply wanted to make a credible case for his craft. That was the more urgent task.

But finally he relented. He was photographed for a story in a British newspaper. It raised his profile, but it also heightened his internal conflict. Much of the article, he said, focused on his appearance. Anyone who dressed with the aplomb of Boateng, who wore suits in shades of violet, sapphire, and persimmon, harbored a desire to draw attention. But he was uncomfortable with his identity being the message rather than the clothes. He struggled to untangle the two. His race made him a unique presence in fashion. But it didn't make his fashion. Or did it? Would his slim cherry-red suits have the same tantalizing sizzle if they were designed by a White guy? Would his clothes be looked at differently if his identity was the focus and not just the subtext?

"It's a different world now because you're more in charge. Back then, there were gatekeepers. The gatekeepers determined if you're in or out," he said. "Now you don't have that. People judge you on the work."

Or at least, that's how it should be. But fashion continues to be a form of identity. That has become its fundamental purpose. Who do you claim to be? With whom do you align?

By 1994, Boateng had begun to insinuate himself within the Paris fashion system. He traveled there to mount his first runway show. Paris show invitations were wildly creative. In addition to simple paper invitations, designers sent embossed leather wallets and carnival trinkets, as well as invitations floating in strange gelatinous substances or embroidered on bits of actual garments. Instead of just sending an invitation on nice card stock with the guest's name in calligraphy, Boateng sent one that came with a video missive on VHS tape. A short film starred Boateng himself as he carried an enormous trunk of clothes from London to Paris—by train, by car, by foot. The designer who had once refused to be photographed was now a video star.

He held the show in a converted gallery space on rue de Paradis. Remnants of the building's original owner—a ceramics manufacturer—distinguished it from its surroundings. A ceramic mosaic decorated an inner courtyard, and an oversize urn on the facade welcomed guests. The collection was everything that Boateng had long preached: the formal cuts, the bold colors, the dashing, lean men, the staunch Britishness.

For the massive undertaking, Boateng mortgaged his home. The time and energy he devoted to it strained his marriage. But in the end, Boateng had alerted Paris to his presence. And the next year, he opened his London Vigo Street shop.

Like all designers of the modern era, Boateng cultivated a celebrity clientele: Jamie Foxx, Laurence Fishburne, Will Smith, Forest Whitaker, Gabriel Byrne, Spike Lee, Mick Jagger, David Bowie, Paul Bettany, and a host of other actors and musicians who were regularly in the spotlight. When they were promoting their latest creative projects, Boateng dressed them for interviews; he dressed them for the Oscars and other red-carpet events; he created costumes for their film roles. He was enmeshed in popular culture. He even had a film crew trailing him for more than a decade, capturing the successes and failures in both his professional life and his personal one. He starred in the resulting documentary, as well as *House of Boateng*, a reality show that chronicled his efforts to bring his collection to the United States. As his reputation within fashion grew, so did his wider visibility.

Like so many independent fashion designers, Boateng also struggled. For a time, he was unable to deliver merchandise to retailers because he ran out of money. But he had an aristocrat's confidence in the face of his punishing debt. He was impeccably dressed; his upper lip was stiff; and he pressed onward.

And then LVMH came calling. In 2002, Boateng moved into a new shop directly on Savile Row, and to mark this step up he shut down the street for a fashion show. It was a brash display with nearly fifty models, one thousand guests, the mayor of London, and plenty of sniping from the street's old guard, who couldn't stomach so much flash in their gray-haired, tweed-suited midst.

Unbeknownst to Boateng, on the night of his Savile Row show,

Louis Vuitton was hosting a party at its new London store, and a parade of guests abruptly left that party to attend Boateng's shindig. The irresistible lure of a Boateng extravaganza had not gone unnoticed by LVMH bosses. Yves Carcelle, who had been the president of Louis Vuitton but had recently taken on the task of running the entire LVMH fashion division, was intrigued.

Shortly after he interrupted their party, Boateng was invited to a dinner hosted by Louis Vuitton in London. It was one of those grand events regularly hosted by luxury houses as a display of prestige and cultural might. Boateng was seated at a premium table with Carcelle and his wife Rebecca. Over the course of the evening, Rebecca Carcelle invited Boateng to Paris to make a suit for her husband, an invitation that Boateng found odd because while he was happy for the commission, he didn't ordinarily travel to the client for fittings. The client usually came into his workroom.

"So then I go back to my studio, and a close friend of mine was working late. He says, 'Look, it's not about the suit. Just get on the plane or the train and if he takes you out on the balcony, you know, they're going to offer you something.'"

Carcelle's office was the stuff of fashion folklore. The suite was the size of an immodest apartment. And Carcelle, an energetic and ebullient man, used a stroll onto the balcony as a way of breaking away from the formality and stiffness of a meeting across a table. The balcony signified intimacy and, perhaps, a meeting of minds.

Boateng traveled to Paris and indeed Carcelle invited him onto the balcony. They talked about Kenzo and the possibility of his taking over the brand's entire range of products from ready-to-wear to housewares. The scope was overwhelming and would certainly have required Boateng to give up his own business, which he was unwilling to do. The talk then turned to Givenchy, which intrigued Boateng.

Carcelle, who died in 2014, asked James Greenfield to meet with Boateng. Greenfield, who'd just joined Givenchy as the director of the men's division, went to Boateng's London shop and was impressed by the tailor's color sense, his silhouettes, and, as the French like to say, his *savoir faire*—an embedded understanding of creativity and craftsmanship.

The idea of working on menswear for Givenchy, a narrowly focused position, seemed to Boateng like something that could be balanced with his own brand. He was excited by the possibility, the resources, and the enormous stage, and he didn't want to make the same mistake he'd made years earlier when his name had been floated for the Dior Homme position that eventually went to Hedi Slimane.

After a year of courtship, Boateng signed a one-year contract for about a half million euros—to start. He consulted with Hubert de Givenchy himself, telling the retired couturier that he wanted to create a template for the modern French gentleman, one that men around the world would want to emulate. The two men, both with a tall and elegant posture, shared a preference for spare tailoring. And the executives at Givenchy were excited to see how Boateng would use his Savile Row expertise to inform the company's menswear.

The division needed to be reorganized, but mostly it needed attention. "There was a lot of change just prior to his arrival," Greenfield said. "We were preparing for the day that we could have someone sit in that role, to enter and to do amazing things."

When Boateng arrived at Givenchy on Avenue George V, he was trailed by his documentary camera crew—a fact that left much of the staff flummoxed. This wasn't exactly the predigital era, but it still predated people reflexively filming life's every moment lest it didn't actually occur. Dressed in a camel overcoat and red turtleneck, Boateng climbed out of his car and strode to the entrance. He was escorted to the atelier to meet the modest design team. Boateng glanced through an existing advertising campaign and proceeded to confuse a male model for a woman. He expressed admiration for the preexisting efforts that essentially served as a placeholder. He declared that Givenchy menswear needed "a message," and Greenfield formally presented Boateng with his company identification badge.

For his first show, in July 2004, the company took over the Musée d'Art Moderne on Avenue du Président Wilson. For the collection, Boateng drew upon the style of the founder. He rooted the color palette in navy, gray, and white. The cut wasn't as slim as in Boateng's signature line. But the lines were neat. *The Daily Telegraph*'s fashion critic Hilary Alexander wrote, "His models crunched down a catwalk strewn with one-and-a-half tons of anthracite chips. The collection was sharp and sophisticated, merging French chic with Boateng's slick, hip urban signature. In joining Givenchy, part of the vast Moët Hennessy Louis Vuitton empire, Boateng, 37, has acquired membership of the fashion world's most exclusive 'club.'"

Other reviews weren't as enthusiastic. "Boateng's collection displayed more self-belief than actual talent, with baggy, poorly cut trousers repeated ad infinitum," pronounced *The Guardian*.

While LVMH doesn't disclose the financial results of each fashion house, its 2004 annual report told shareholders that "Givenchy benefited from the enthusiastic reception for Ozwald Boateng's first men's ready-to-wear collection."

Boateng's time at Givenchy was both an accomplishment and a frustration. He created a vocabulary for menswear there and drew even more attention to his skills as a tailor. He brought celebrities to the brand, men like Lenny Kravitz who would spontaneously turn up at the offices for a casual fireside chat with Boateng. The designer's charisma and connections jolted the house with electricity.

"We really embraced it. We thought it was exciting," Greenfield said. Boateng had an "amazing personality. His work was amazing. We thought it fit in so well. There were only positives there."

But as the documentary *A Man's Story* revealed, the demanding travel schedule took a toll on Boateng's personal life. The designer was not mentioned by name in subsequent annual reports as Givenchy struggled to get its financial bearings. Boateng continued to focus on making the menswear sing.

His designs were elegant, but they never had the élan of his personal brand. Boateng's menswear at Givenchy was also overshadowed by the more provocative sensibility of Hedi Slimane, who created a splash at Dior Homme with a silhouette that one-upped the narrow proportions for which Boateng was known. Slimane cut his jackets, jeans, and trousers for such a skinny body type that they were most easily worn by adolescents rather than adults. They were not clothes for muscular men or even men who regularly consumed three square meals a day.

Slimane mined youth culture. Boateng was intent on teaching young men how to dress like smart gentlemen. Slimane was helping grown-ups put on the guise of rock and roll–obsessed boys. Slimane's clothes demanded a physique that exuded youthful disconsolateness—a palpable irritation at one's own privilege. He preferred his models with an expression of disregard, a look only partially visible on the runway, as he also liked models with hair that hung across their face like a curtain. And mostly, he preferred that they be White. Diversity was not a key element in Slimane's runway casting.

Slimane's taste in models received criticism from industry observers. But there was little apparatus in place to push against it or hold him to account. Still Slimane's design aesthetic, just as Raf Simons's did, opened the door to luxury menswear labels looking to youth culture for inspiration. The kids out there in the clubs, skateboard parks, and online hangout spaces dictated what was cool. The seventeen-year-olds held sway. And Abloh would be obsessed with them and their interests.

In the meantime, Givenchy brought in a new boss: Marco Gobbetti. Just months after Boateng was hired, the Italian-born Gobbetti, who was educated in the United States, moved to Givenchy from Moschino, where he'd been chief executive. Almost immediately, Boateng felt friction.

He ascribed the tension he felt with Gobbetti to race. It was a situation that left Boateng baffled and exasperated. Race had always distinguished him in the fashion industry, but he hadn't leaned into it. Boateng wasn't pulling from his African roots to inform the work of Givenchy. Race was not part of the story he was trying to tell at the French house. He talked only about the clothes. And yet, the clothes seemed to be the precise things that were being ignored.

"I'd never experienced that type of conflict—directly in my face—to that level. It was proper like in your face, racially charged. It was purely racially charged because it didn't make any sense and I couldn't understand it," Boateng said. "I was used to dealing with racism. I've been dealing with it since I was a kid in this country. I never would have got here on the Row if I didn't know how to handle that. The only way you handle that is by delivering the goods. And so, for me, I didn't understand why [Gobbetti] was being this way and he hadn't even seen the work.

"When my first show was hugely successful, you know, he didn't acknowledge it," Boateng said. "He was quite literally trying to figure ways of getting me out."

Gobbetti was temperamentally the opposite of Boateng: an introvert. A reserved businessman, who has been described as open-minded, forward-thinking, and results oriented, Gobbetti had bigger concerns than the company's menswear. Givenchy had a womenswear problem. It needed a new designer.

Boateng was doing fine work. He was garnering attention in London, where editors paid special attention to their hometown guy. But much of Paris, which was the only place that really mattered to this couture house, was at best cautious and at worst dismissive. When the subject turned to Givenchy, all eyes were trained on the women's collection in a kind of breathless, exasperated anticipation of an announcement of a new designer.

For Gobbetti, the problem boiled down to resources. "The thing that we needed to do was to create an identity and to streamline and develop the business," he said.

A big LVMH brand like Dior could afford to have separate creative directors running the men's collection and the women's. But it didn't make sense for Givenchy to follow that model. It was too small. Givenchy's revenue was a pittance compared to that behemoth's, and the menswear finances were mediocre, Gobbetti added.

"The last possible thought about it was a question of race," he said. "I have to say Ozwald has a great personality and he's a great personality, but the results were not excellent and the brand could not afford to have two designers. The brand could only afford to have one designer. And so this is how we came to part ways with Ozwald."

Gobbetti finally hired Riccardo Tisci, a young Italian who was only six years out of design school. He described Tisci as a "perfect fit for us."

"A lot of people say, 'He is very young,' but I think he's ready for it."

And indeed, while Tisci's first presentation, which was for fall couture, was described as poorly organized, it also revealed his talent. "Of twenty-nine outfits there were three or four that suggested Mr. Tisci has a modernist vision, and three or four is enough," wrote Cathy Horyn in *The New York Times*. "He has a natural feeling for drapery, an eye for modern proportions, and he may be more Givenchy than any of his better-known predecessors."

Boateng stayed at Givenchy until 2007.

Despite his struggles, he demonstrated what was possible in a part of the fashion world where the faces were mostly ivory and the traditions of a house were considered so immutable that they were referred to as DNA. He made the idea of a Black man—with skin the color of night, a gleaming shaved head, and full lips—running a stately atelier a reality. A place that once had seemed impenetrable to all except the privileged few became accessible to someone for whom privilege was a hurdle to be overcome, not something to be enjoyed.

Boateng made a dream real in a way that Buchanan did not. Buchanan had been an unknown entrusted with outsize responsibility at a small fashion house. Boateng was a fully formed designer with a reputation that preceded him. Buchanan's contribution to Bottega Veneta has nearly been erased. But Boateng's time at Givenchy became part of the Givenchy story and ultimately part of the larger fashion one.

And yet. There was little public acknowledgment of the history Boateng made. Instead, there was number-crunching curiosity about Givenchy's desire to expand its menswear business, which made up about 35 percent of the company's revenue. Writers mused about how Boateng's aesthetic might modernize and energize the company's menswear, which could best be described as staid. And Boateng took personal blows. His confidence was perceived as distracting arrogance. As a writer for the *Times* said, "He has more charm than Hogwarts and a near demonical, charismatic self-confidence that often seems to sit at odds with his august and discreet neighbours on the Row." Boateng was a peacock.

Even though he summited one of fashion's highest mountains, his success didn't reverberate into the broader culture. Boateng was a successful designer but he wasn't a folk hero. Some might argue that the minimal focus on his skin color was laudable, that fashion wasn't looking at everything through the prism of race. But in its failure to see race, the industry failed to see Boateng clearly. The industry's attitude was akin to that of an individual who boasts about being color-blind in their hiring or in their friendships. They believe their self-declared blindness is a demonstration of openness, of their reliance on a pure meritocracy. But it also suggests a failure to recognize the degree to which history shapes the way in which a person moves through the world. It ignores hurdles unique to that person's professional path. It dismisses the exceptional gifts that they alone possess. It downplays what an individual success might mean to a community of similarly situated others.

There's no public record of LVMH making a formal announcement when Boateng left Givenchy. After his departure, Tisci took on the role of menswear designer in addition to his duties with womenswear. One of Tisci's most memorable and influential contributions to the menswear conversation would come in 2011. It wouldn't be a suit. It would be a Givenchy T-shirt printed with the face of a rottweiler.

After leaving Givenchy, Boateng retreated to London to focus on his signature line. And fashion moved on.

Chicago, Crown Hall, and Building a Community

LIKE SO MANY YOUNG PEOPLE from the Midwest who had big dreams, like so many American fashion designers before him, Abloh looked east to find his future. He cast his gaze toward Chicago, the city of house music and hip-hop, the Magnificent Mile and the South Side, Jesse Jackson and Barack Obama, midcentury and modernist buildings.

Abloh went to Chicago to study architecture—a field that influenced the way he engaged with his own creativity and the imaginings of others. The city introduced Abloh to the buildings of Ludwig Mies van der Rohe, whose work would be an enduring inspiration.

The architecture school at the Illinois Institute of Technology, where Abloh studied, was one of the most famous in the world, not just because of the quality of the education students received there, which was top-notch, but because of the main building that housed it. S. R. Crown Hall, designed by the widely admired van der Rohe, was built in 1956. It stood as a masterpiece of modernism and has been described as "the architectural father of open-space buildings." It was the structure that sent generations of homebuyers and HGTV fanatics on the hunt for open-concept dwellings and turned everyone into an expert on "flow." In 1982 the U.S. Postal Service issued a twenty-cent stamp featuring Crown Hall, and in

2001 Interior Secretary Gale Norton declared it a national historic landmark.

The low-slung, rectangular building, measuring nearly twice the size of a football field, was set back on a grassy esplanade and was framed by rows of mature, stately trees. Crown Hall's exterior walls were glass, the lower third of which were etched, providing privacy for the students working inside while shielding them from outside distractions. Ten travertine marble stairs led to the main entrance and the building's terrazzo-tiled ground floor.

There were no interior walls. Crown Hall was a wide-open space that managed to feel airy without being overwhelming. This sort of freewheeling interior was startling because it was constructed in an era defined by pre–World War II buildings with decorative molding and closed-off rooms—each one with a specific, formal purpose. Van der Rohe's design provided significant flexibility for those working inside Crown Hall but also connected them with the surrounding elements. The beauty of the building was in its elegant simplicity, the way that its appearance was quietly distinctive—its architecture refraining from overpowering its environment. At night, when the building was lit from within and surrounded by darkness, it appeared to magically levitate just above the ground.

This impressive building was named after Sol Crown, who died in 1921 at age twenty-seven. He, along with his siblings Henry and Irving, founded the perfectly blandly named Material Service Corporation, which bought and sold building supplies such as sand and gravel. Eventually that company merged with General Dynamics and the family's holdings grew exponentially. At one time they even included the Empire State Building. But the architecture school was renowned for the man who designed it, not for the family whose name was written on it.

The German-born van der Rohe came to the United States in 1937. He'd been the last director of the Bauhaus school in Germany before it was shut down by the Nazis in 1933. The Bauhaus design ethos merged simplicity, rationality, and practicality. It connected the various arts and taught a version of modernism tinged with warmth and humanity. Van der Rohe brought these ideas with him to IIT along with a welcoming belief in technology.

Van der Rohe himself helmed the College of Architecture from 1938 to 1958 and oversaw the development of the campus. IIT bore van der Rohe's imprimatur in its buildings and in the architecture school's curriculum, which emphasized understanding materials, constructing three-dimensional models, and following the philosophy that "less is more" and "God is in the details." When Virgil Abloh stepped through the doors of Crown Hall for the first time as a graduate student in 2003, he was mesmerized by the building's design and its clarity of purpose. He didn't know *why* he was so captivated; he knew next to nothing about van der Rohe, who'd died in Chicago in 1969. But he knew the building was special, and he was intrigued and energized by its spirit.

Abloh was fresh from his undergraduate graduation at the University of Wisconsin, where he'd earned a degree in civil engineering. Neither of those data points—his alma mater or his major—had been something about which he was passionate. His parents encouraged him, *told him*, to study engineering. Like so many children of African immigrants, he was expected to enter one of three fields: law, medicine, or engineering. They were careers that immediately commanded respect. To practice law was to be presumed a success. A doctor was heroic. Engineers built things. There was nothing fuzzy or scattershot about these professions.

The decision to become a University of Wisconsin badger was a matter of geography and timing. The school was just over an hour's drive north from Rockford, and since Abloh had missed the deadline to apply to the engineering school at the University of Illinois, he turned to Wisconsin, which had a later deadline. While in

Wisconsin, Abloh divided his time between deejaying—something that had captured his imagination in high school and had given his mother Eunice heartburn—and schoolwork. His mother literally cried when she realized something so whimsical was getting a significant share of his attention. She worried even more when he installed a turntable in his dorm room. But he was a good student, suffering through advanced mathematics and all, so she couldn't really complain. Music and skateboarding were his creative outlets.

Then, just before graduating, he discovered a new one. He took his first art history class. It focused on the Renaissance, a period in European painting stretching from the fourteenth to the sixteenth centuries and including artists such as Raphael, Michelangelo, and Leonardo da Vinci—an early multihyphenate. He also discovered Caravaggio and his manipulation of light and shadow known as chiaroscuro. He was excited to learn that the artist, who had begun working at the end of the Renaissance period, had helped to usher in a completely new style of painting. An artist changed the way people thought.

Abloh made his way to architecture because it was both a creative pursuit and a practical one. It was a method of problem-solving within an aesthetic context, and it was a natural extension of his undergraduate education. "Architecture would be my bridge between the rational world of engineering and these emotive forms I was always drawn to," Abloh said.

He moved to Chicago, a city of architectural wonders and an urban mecca for a host of young people from smaller cities and towns all around the Midwest.

It was a city of distinct ethnic neighborhoods, as well as a place with a legacy of deep racial divides. Chicago had a history of racial violence that erupted during the Great Migration, when Black southerners made their way north in search of greater opportunities.

The story of the suburb of Cicero illustrated how dangerous that simple human urge could be. In 1951, residents in this all-White community were so incensed by the arrival of a single Black family that they rioted. They destroyed the Black family's apartment and their possessions. Then they destroyed the entire building. If the White residents couldn't have Cicero all to themselves, no one could have it.

Chicago remained a divided city and one with stark class differences. It also had hipsters and artists, old-timers and new arrivals. It was the birthplace of house music and an incubator of rappers with a streak of social consciousness, such as Common and Kanye West. Chicago had an edge, but it wasn't as cutting as New York's could be. It was the Midwest after all. That's not a criticism. It was a point of pride.

Chicago was a city whose history was filled with blue-collar grit, where the fashion sensibility had been defined by dignity and social ambition rather than personal creativity. "Women from this city, when they traveled internationally, met with negative ideas of what the city was," fashion historian Timothy Long said. "They used fashion to convey a visual message: We are not blue-collar, unsophisticated. We are not hog butcherers."

To prove their style intelligence, "women who could buy Balenciaga would buy the signature item," Long said. They would buy the most distinctive garments from a collection to broadcast their fashion credibility. "Chicago was the second largest city for so long. If you're third, fourth, or fifth, you're not going to fight as much. But if you're in a race just behind the winner, you're going to try harder."

Chicago was not a city striving to mimic New York. It was its own epicenter; it had its distinct problems and possibilities. When Abloh arrived, the city was governed by Mayor Richard M. Daley, who'd just been elected to his fifth consecutive term with nearly 79 percent of the vote. Daley was part of a political dynasty that had been running Chicago for more than thirty years except for a brief interlude when, in 1983, the city elected Harold Washington, its first Black mayor. Washington died a few months into his second term in 1987.

Chicago struggled with deadly violence. In 2003, it had more homicides than any other city in America, ending the year with a tally of 598 killings. But by 2005, the city was feeling the effects of a national trend of falling crime. Barack Obama was serving in the Illinois state senate and representing a diverse district that included Hyde Park, with its multiracial population of college-educated residents. Hyde Park residents had a median income that was some 50 percent higher than that of Obama's constituents living in South Shore, a predominantly Black neighborhood where most residents do not have a college degree. The breadth of Black ambition and politics, frustrations and possibilities was told in this small quadrant of the city.

The Illinois Institute of Technology sat nearby in a community known as Bronzeville. As a student there, Abloh stood on inspiring but complicated ground. The story of Bronzeville and Crown Hall was rooted in race, ambition, and self-invention, all things that would influence Abloh's rise.

Bronzeville was a neighborhood with a notable history of Black creativity. Some have compared the cultural heft of Bronzeville, which was called Chicago's "Black metropolis," with that of New York's Harlem. Its greatness was a by-product of discrimination. As Black southerners moved north in the early part of the twentieth century, segregationist housing laws and traditions limited where they could live. Bronzeville, an area south of the downtown business district and north of Hyde Park, became a community of industrious Black entrepreneurs, professionals, and artists. It was home to Black-owned financial and real estate institutions, newspapers, and performing arts centers. Those who once called Bronzeville home include Louis Armstrong, Sam Cooke, Mahalia Jackson, Katherine Dunham, Richard Wright, Ida B. Wells, and Gwendolyn

Brooks, who even wrote a novella-length poem titled "In the Mecca," which was set in the neighborhood's grandest apartment complex.

The Mecca Flats was an architectural wonder. It was born out of the 1893 World's Fair, which commemorated the four-hundredth anniversary of Christopher Columbus invading these shores. After Chicago bested New York and Washington, D.C., as the host city, organizers decided to stage the fair in Jackson Park along the shores of Lake Michigan. The park had been designed by Frederick Law Olmsted and Calvert Vaux, who'd mapped out the contours of New York's Central Park. In 1881, after a public call for suggestions, Chicago's new green space was named after President Andrew Jackson, much to the dismay of residents of Hyde Park. The nation's seventh president was deeply committed to the institution of slavery, which was the source of much of his wealth. Two generations later, in Jackson Park, in celebration of Christopher Columbus, a group of the country's best architects designed a series of gleaming ivory beaux arts buildings for the fair that were referred to as "the White City."

In preparation for the influx of tourists attending the fair, developers also constructed the Mecca Flats in Bronzeville. The stately residence, designed around a central courtyard with ornate iron railings, was intended to serve as both a hotel and an apartment building. Its distance from Jackson Park, however, made it unpopular with the tourists attending the fair, so it was fully converted into an apartment complex. Initially, it housed only White residents, but as the demographics of the neighborhood shifted, Black households were accepted, and it eventually became home to members of the striving Black population that made up Bronzeville. With its expansive atrium and Romanesque arches, the Mecca was decidedly fancy; it was unabashedly elegant. At the time, it was one of the largest apartment buildings in the country, an architectural accomplishment, and a measure of civic pride. And it sat in the middle of a predominantly Black community.

In the years surrounding 1940, the Illinois Institute of Technology purchased the Mecca Flats with the intent of tearing it down and expanding the school's campus. The Black residents, dressed for battle in suits and ties, heels and hats, gathered to fight off that initial assault through protests and legal filings. They won a reprieve. Over time, however, through neglect by its owner that was anything but benign, the building lost its luster, and the Black tenants finally lost their war against urban renewal.

In 1952, the Mecca was torn down, and S. R. Crown Hall rose in its place. History has always been composed of a series of vantage points: from the top of the heap, from the troughs, from the flatlands. Buildings are not merely structures; they are politics, economics, and social contracts. And, as Abloh came to understand, design is not just a matter of aesthetics; it is about identity and power and desire. Part of the function of design is to create order—or disorder—to delineate importance. It has the ability to transform whose stories are valued and whose are erased. Whole communities rise and fall on the substance of a blueprint—or a sketch.

At the Illinois Institute of Technology, Abloh enrolled in a course of study designed for those who were coming to architecture as fully formed professionals working in a different field or as graduates who'd received their bachelor's degree in another subject. The rigorous three-year program was intended to give students the tools and education they needed to become a licensed architect, or to at least think like one.

"The interesting part about architecture training, in my opinion, is you learn to present. You learn to present the work for design reviews," said Frank Flury, an associate professor at the college of architecture who had Abloh as a student. "It doesn't make a big difference if you're a painter, an architect, or a salesman. The important part is that you learn to present. This is a very important part of our discipline and why some people study architecture.

"They learn to dress properly, go out to talk to people, to be self-confident—because if you need to sell your idea or your design project, you need to be convincing to people."

Flury was born in Germany and spoke with a distinct German accent, which gave his words a sharp precision. He was a tall slender man, balding and with a watchful gaze. When he walked through a studio dotted with students laboring on architectural models, he took in their work, assessed it in a glance, and offered guidance with the speed and facility of an educator who had seen, if not everything, a heck of a lot. Flury was direct but kind and unafraid to disagree with orthodoxy. He was not one to swoon because everyone else was doing so. In addition to being an architect, Flury was a master carpenter, and it was important to him that his students understood the ways in which materials interacted with the human body, aged, and transformed. He had worked with hundreds of students. Yet he remembered Abloh. In part, this was because Abloh was a visual curiosity. To an architecture professor who was a study in unremarkable neutrals, Abloh's clothes were offbeat concoctions, like a hoodie with fur stitched around its edges. Abloh, who'd become more attuned to fashion as a college student freed from the formality of Boylan High School, conjured his clothes from his imagination, and his mother realized them with her sewing expertise. But his building models also stood apart from those of his peers.

"I wouldn't say he was necessarily the top architect or designer, but he was always very, very much interested in graphic design. So his drawings were all always compositionally very, very interesting," Flury said. "The scale was different. . . . He designed and made things a little different than other students."

Abloh never intended to work as an architect, something he never explicitly confided to his parents. But he expressed a kinship with its method of problem-solving and its creativity. He enjoyed intellectualizing, theorizing, and hypothesizing. He could expound on anything. He had a compulsion to explain. He was fond of the word *practice,* as both a noun and a verb. He used it as a way of describing his work in fashion: he was applying ideas and theories to real-world situations. With fashion he took disconnected notions on a mood board or laptop and turned them into garments. "I liked the idea of taking a program, thinking of a solution and being able to defend it," he said. "I think I always had a sense of how to internalize that method and apply it somewhere else."

Unlike many of his peers in the fashion industry, Abloh was at peace with the fact that everything he produced was not in its perfect form. It was, after all, a practice. Everything was a work in progress.

"Virgil always was like, it's a prototype," said designer Matthew Williams, whose friendship with Abloh dates to the early 2000s. "He was never so precious about the output. It was always like, 'Put it out. Next idea, make it better.' At the beginning, when I was starting, I was so precious about every idea. I was like, 'This is the last jacket I may ever create! I need it to be perfect!' With every stitch and button placement and the thickness of the leather, I would obsess, obsess, obsess. He was much more like, 'Out into the world. Keep it moving.'"

This sentiment is practically heresy in fashion. Designers are known to fret over the details. Style revolutions have been premised on centimeter shifts in silhouettes. Fashion shows have run hours late just so a seamstress could finish a garment to a designer's exacting specifications. For the architecture student who never intended to construct buildings, everything was a proposition, an idea that could absorb criticism, a notion that could be improved upon in its next iteration.

"That inspired me to allow more of that way of working into my work," Williams said. "I think it's a good way to be because things take on a new life once they enter the world. It's also just less drain-ing. You're affected less by others' judgment or negativity if you're able to care about the work but put it out into the world and know you're okay with it—not be so precious about it that you have to go stay in your bedroom for a month if somebody says something neg-ative about it.

"Virgil dealt with a lot of—I dealt with lots of—negative feed-back in our careers, but, you know, especially him," Williams said. "There were times when people said really mean stuff, and he al-ways kept it moving, kept doing his thing and pushed through and didn't let it matter."

During Abloh's first year at IIT, the new student hub, McCor-mick Tribune Campus Center, had its ribbon cutting. Designed by deconstructivist architect Rem Koolhaas, the center opened in 2003. It represented a dramatic shift in the aesthetics of the campus that van der Rohe had designed. The $48 million campus center was ap-plauded by critics for its vivacity, its mischievousness, and its inten-tional disruption of a landscape whose well-balanced order had grown stale over time. The preexisting restrained architecture was "as apt to conjure notions of institutional conformity as of social harmony."

The interior of the new center was like an urban neighborhood with diagonal boulevards and excavated lounges. Digital murals, graphic icons, and a sixty-foot-long light box were the work of 2 x 4, a global design consultancy based in New York City. The interior introduced Abloh to the breadth and influence of graphic design.

One of the most distinctive features in Koolhaas's architecture was the metal, sound-deadening tube that wrapped around the city's elevated rail tracks that ran above the building and cut through the campus. The tube almost appeared to be squashing the building itself. The design quickly captured the imagination of students, who adopted the tube as a logo.

The campus center allowed Abloh to see up close and daily the point of view of a contemporary architect whose game-changing work absorbed van der Rohe's modernism and responded to it. Koolhaas made Abloh think of architecture as a kind of social manipulator. It didn't simply house people; it dictated the way in which those people moved through their lives. Architecture demanded things from society.

"You could think about deconstruction as taking something apart. But deconstruction was really about looking at the political context for work and seeing that as a factor that drives the way things are," said Michael Rock, a founding partner of 2 x 4 and a colleague of Koolhaas.

A building could actually *cause* different kinds of social conditions to exist. An architect could reflect the asymmetry and disharmony within society through a building's design. A building could do more than simply make a statement about corporate might. "So a lot of those buildings became really complex because it was about complexifying relationships between people," Rock said.

Koolhaas was a provocateur and a theorist. He hadn't honed a singular vision so much as fed new and jarring ideas into his work process. He shook up established conventions, something that offended those who believed in tradition, and delighted those who found traditions either suffocating or insufficient. Koolhaas was a free-range thinker. He worked for a time as a journalist and wrote *Delirious New York,* a book that found soulfulness in the New York of the 1970s, when the city was mired in financial disaster, crime, political dysfunction, and graffiti. He lent a high-minded intellectualism to fashion with his design for Prada's flagship store—or "epicenter," as the brand referred to it—which opened in 2001 in New York's SoHo neighborhood. The space included a performance stage as well as a massive, curved zebrawood wall that resembled a two-story skateboarding ramp.

Abloh held an abiding fascination with Koolhaas, something that was relatively common among his generation of architecture students. In the most simplistic terms, Koolhaas approached architecture less as a matter of structure and shelter than as a form of discourse.

"It's a way of analyzing something, a way of trying to see relationships and to channel those relationships into the made world in some way," said Rock, who often worked with Abloh. And so, for Abloh, when he turned his attention to fashion, "It's not about the structure of a dress, it's about the social relationships where the dress has happened." He wasn't interested in the way a dress functioned on a woman's body. He was concerned with what a "dress" meant to a luxury consumer.

Other designers have a background in architecture or have been deeply influenced by it. They include Narciso Rodriguez and Gianfranco Ferré. One can see architecture in their work, in the engineering of garments, in the lines and angles. Abloh's work didn't have precision. It wasn't classically architectural in the way fashion has always understood it, which typically means some form of minimalism.

"I think some of the criticism of [Abloh] as a dressmaker comes from the fact that he wasn't really that concerned about dressmaking. He was concerned about what [the dress] represented and what it stood for as a brand and as an object and what he was saying with it," Rock continued. "And that's almost the exact same criticism that's leveled at Koolhaas, which is that he was never thought of as a good architect in terms of his detailing. His buildings were almost like models, like full-scale models about ideas."

In Chicago, Abloh began building a foundation on which to hang his fashion. He heeded the discipline required to construct models, took note of the complexity of meaning that can be associated with an object, grasped the power of graphic design in telegraphing community and identity, and practiced the confidence and charisma necessary to sell an idea.

The tabletop model for his master's thesis depicted the Chicago skyline with its famous skyscrapers, all constructed from dull blue foam. The city was merely a backdrop, present but not central. The building he'd designed stood out—a tall, angular block of cherry-red acrylic. The structure reached skyward and tilted toward Lake Michigan "like a tree bending toward sunlight." In his work, Abloh hadn't designed the tallest building or even one with the largest footprint. Instead, the structure stood out because of his use of color and material. His most powerful choices were rooted in aesthetics rather than engineering.

He'd offered an idea of a building and shown its relationship to the city's natural environment, the one that had always existed rather than the one that had been formed by the city fathers and grandfathers. His building was part of the skyline but existed on its own terms.

Architecture demonstrated the power of branding, which is not merely the use of a symbol to identify a particular company but rather an organizing principle and a statement of tribalism. The fashion industry's approach to branding had always put the product first. The products told the story of the brand. Gucci was bamboo-handled purses. Hermès was the Birkin. Chanel was quilted handbags and bouclé jackets. For Abloh, branding came first. It was more like a language that could be used to talk about anything.

"He recognized that if you had a visual brand—something like the slash mark or the quotation mark—anything could be brought in under that umbrella. And then if you weave a story around that, a narrative around it, which he was really skilled at through social media, you can build something. You could build an idea around it," Rock said. "But you need that touchpoint, that visual brand, to make it come together."

WHILE ABLOH WAS in Chicago immersed in architecture and the heady conversations around it, other cultural shifts were happening in the background. Rap impresario Sean Combs launched his own fashion brand, Sean John, which was a celebration of Black masculinity that blended track pants and fur coats. He debuted the line in 1998 at a Las Vegas trade show, but by the 2000s he was organizing enormous runway productions in New York at a Cipriani event space and filling the front rows with celebrities such as singer Mary J. Blige. Combs was inspired by Ralph Lauren, mentored by Tommy Hilfiger, and embraced by Bloomingdale's late fashion director Kal Ruttenstein. Combs hadn't gone to design school, but he knew what he liked; he knew what the people who bought his music wanted to wear. He wasn't another celebrity looking to put his name on a product and cash a check. He wanted more. Combs intended to join the fashion industry.

The gatekeepers let him in, with a caveat. To accommodate his Sean John brand, as well as other fashion companies launched by those who'd grown up in hip-hop culture, the fashion industry came up with a new term: *urban*. Initially, the designation made sense. Hip-hop was a phenomenon born in cities, and its earliest fans and producers came from urban environments. It was a way of noting that these collections drew much of their inspiration from the streets. They weren't created in some hermetically sealed atelier from a designer's fantasies. The clothes, often based on athletic wear, were created by people who were active participants in the culture of hip-hop—most often, but not always, Black people.

In the beginning, "urban" brands had a distinct sensibility that set them apart from so-called traditional sportswear. They were younger, more informal, and, quite simply, cooler. But soon enough, *urban* became synonymous with *Black*. It was applied to casual styles that grew out of hip-hop culture; it was applied to sportswear created by Black-owned brands. It became sloppy and prejudiced verbiage.

Hip-hop had moved from cities to suburbs. Performers like Jay-Z were as likely to wear a business suit as a hoodie. Hip-hop evoked many things. It could be baggy jeans and oversize rugby shirts, but it could also be a fur-trimmed balmacaan or a four-ply cashmere turtleneck.

The *urban* designation had little to do with geography and everything to do with race and class. Black celebrities whom luxury companies simply didn't want styled in their clothes were "urban." *Essence,* a glossy lifestyle magazine that had a devoted readership of Black women and struggled to win over high-end advertisers, was "urban." "Urban" was emphatically not luxury. And frankly, some executives believed *urban* was a red-flag descriptor of a brand that could attract the wrong sort of customer—unruly, uncouth, undesirable—if retailers weren't careful.

Seventh Avenue used the term to categorize Combs. He came into the industry through hip-hop. But he was styling himself as a Black Cary Grant or a modern-day Jay Gatsby, crafting a soft-focus image filled with lavish parties and extravagant yachts in the same way that Ralph Lauren had remade himself from a Bronx dreamer into a lord of his own manor. Combs was putting suits and ties and cashmere overcoats on his runway and infusing them with the swagger and braggadocio of hip-hop. His models were beefy and muscular men of color. And his soundtrack was loaded with hip-hop rather than Frank Sinatra.

The industry couldn't conceive that fashion might be changing. It couldn't reckon with the notion that Combs was suggesting an entirely new way of looking at sportswear, at consumers, and at aspiration—at what it meant to be a creative director at the highest level. Instead, fashion used *urban* as a lazy way of distinguishing Sean John from Gucci or Hugo Boss or Ralph Lauren.

"*Urban.* I was always insulted by the word," Combs said. "I would get insulted when they put us into [that] classification, because they didn't do that with other designers. . . . That 'street, hip-hop shit.' That's what was said behind closed doors."

Combs persevered. And if his influence was boiled down to a singular, profound action, it was his bold representation of young men of color reveling in fashion—not just any kind of fashion but luxurious fashion. For his efforts, the Council of Fashion Designers of America named him best menswear designer in 2004. It was the first time since the awards began in 1981 that a Black designer was honored in menswear, womenswear, or accessories.

Yet even after that victory within the fashion industry, hip-hop culture continued to be stigmatized as wholly violent and lawless—so much so that in 2005, National Basketball Association leadership stepped into the fractious debate about the way hip-hop was influencing men by instituting a dress code. The new rules required players to wear business casual when on team business off the court.

Coaches were already wearing suit jackets on the sidelines. Pat Riley, the longtime coach of the Los Angeles Lakers, was well known for his affection for Armani suits, and he set a fashion standard for his colleagues. "When I came to L.A., there was a sort of image to uphold," said Del Harris, who coached the Lakers from 1994 to 1999 and was dressed by Donna Karan. "Coaches tried to look as business professional as possible."

Chicago's own Michael Jordan was also a suit-and-tie guy, as were Alonzo Mourning and Patrick Ewing. Other players got buttoned up, especially when they headed to the NBA All-Star Games. Players turned to tailors to help them refine their image, others connected with personal shoppers for guidance, and a few were approached by design houses to be ambassadors for their brand—which essentially meant they received free clothes to wear in front of fans and photographers. "All-Star weekend you have to look nice," said former basketball player Chris Webber. "You cannot come down there slipping."

But in the early 2000s, a struggling NBA was also home to a host of young Black men overflowing with disposable income and a fascination for hip-hop. Many of them had adopted the aesthetics of the early era of the music, as well as the gangsta motif. When they weren't wearing their uniforms, they were dressed in baggy jeans, sneakers, gargantuan T-shirts, gold chains, and sometimes do-rags.

But the NBA's image concerns went even deeper than merely gold chains. In 2003, player Kobe Bryant was charged with sexually assaulting a young woman who worked at a hotel where he was staying in Colorado. The prosecutor eventually dropped the case, noting that the accuser declined to testify, and Bryant and the woman reached an undisclosed settlement. But a dark cloud lingered over Bryant and the league. Then, in 2004, a brawl erupted during a game between the Detroit Pistons and the Indiana Pacers at The Palace of Auburn Hills in Michigan. The fight began on the court, ostensibly over a foul, but quickly spread into the stands after a spectator threw debris at one of the Pacers. Soon, it seemed as though the entire lower bowl erupted in violence, with players and fans pummeling one another. Security couldn't contain the mayhem, the game was called off, and the announcer declared the entire spectacle "a disgrace."

As it all unfolded, it was impossible not to notice that the majority of the players were Black and the fans were White. Some fans hurled racial epithets at the players. When the athletes finally left the court, they walked through a gauntlet of anger and a deluge of beer and soda tossed from the stands. In the aftermath, groups of players and fans were charged with assault and battery.

The sight of NBA players attacking one another and their fans, along with the racial undertones, left the league reeling. Commissioner David Stern announced the new dress code and a public service initiative—both aimed at giving the NBA a new image. Neither would necessarily help with anger management, misogyny, or the racial imbalance between players and spectators. But the goal was much less ambitious, yet far more personal. The dress code would expunge hip-hop's gangsta aesthetic from basketball. "We have a minimum standard that we set that reflects on the professionalism of our sport," Stern said. "I think as it's properly understood, it will be embraced by everybody."

The code was specific in its prohibitions: headgear, chains, pendants, medallions, and sunglasses while indoors. It was just as precise in its requirements: dress slacks or dress jeans or khakis; collared shirts or turtlenecks; dress shoes or boots. Initially the players balked. The change was perceived by some as an attempt to exert control over the Black men who dominated the league, particularly Allen Iverson. He was one of the game's biggest stars, and he styled himself with cornrows, tattoos, diamond earrings—essentially all the gestures of hip-hop. The league had already made its discomfort with Iverson's appearance plain. He'd been fined for his long, baggy shorts. A few years earlier, Iverson had been photographed for the cover of *Hoop* magazine, which was an official NBA publication. The picture was airbrushed to remove Iverson's neck tattoo, as well as his jewelry. "They're targeting my generation—the hip-hop generation," Iverson said.

The league's dress code was intended to cloak the players in White middle-class respectability. Instead it opened the doors to a much broader array of styles—far beyond traditional suits and ties. Players explored the full offerings of menswear designers. And those designers began responding to the lifestyle needs of the players.

Ultimately, the new dress code transformed the corridors of sports arenas into catwalks and the players walking through them into fashion trendsetters. Hoop stars hired fashion stylists— sometimes the very ones they'd worked with for a glossy magazine cover—to help them build an aesthetic vocabulary. These stylists brought them along to menswear shows and took them backstage to meet the designers. And menswear designers happily dressed basketball players, who had the perfect physique for showing off the slim-cut suits, form-fitting jackets, luxurious track pants, and streamlined sweaters that had taken center stage.

Players who might dodge reporters wanting to question them about a losing streak or an injury were happy to talk about the clothes in their closets and on their backs. Fashion became a game of one-upmanship. It was about pride and confidence and batting down stereotypes about young Black men having rough edges and a lack of sophistication and artfulness.

With the new dress code, basketball player Latrell Sprewell, whose athleticism was overshadowed when he violently attacked his coach in 1997, spent upward of $350,000 on custom tailoring after his brand strategist introduced him to the work of New York designers Ron and Ron. The young athletes of the hip-hop generation—LeBron James, Dwayne Wade, Tyson Chandler, Amar'e Stoudemire, Russell Westbrook—showed off their *individuality*. They weren't mimicking corporate executives. These Black men, for whom style was always a kind of currency and shield, brandished Thom Browne's shrunken suits, Yohji Yamamoto's billowing black frocks, Rick Owens's romantic goth aesthetic, Ozwald Boateng's technicolor tailoring, and Tom Ford's sexy Gucci sportswear. They wanted their playing style reflected in their personal style. And where athletes went, their fans followed. In 1975, only 25 percent of men bought their own clothes; women were doing apparel shopping for them. By 2005, 75 percent of men were putting together their own wardrobes.

The Council of Fashion Designers of America took advantage of fashion's newest influencers. The trade organization engaged football player Victor Cruz and baseball player Matt Harvey as ambassadors for its week of menswear shows in New York City. Their job was simply to show up and look good. Quickly enough, basketball players such as Wade and Andre Iguodala were sitting in the front rows of fashion shows. Athletes were pondering the launch of their own fashion brands. Their publicists were pitching stories about their style. They were guest-editing fashion stories. And their male fans hovered at a distance, playing it cool while absorbing every detail of their idols' attire through sidelong glances. Women still turned to models and actresses—most often, White ones—for style inspiration; men looked at athletes—at their clothes and at their sneakers.

With athletes—that is to say, Black men—now serving as universal fashion icons, thanks to their embrace of everything from sneakers to European designer brands, the *urban* moniker faded away, its racial overtones ultimately deemed unseemly. *Streetwear* became the new classification for what was essentially a new version of business casual.

Streetwear took its inspiration from the modern world rather than from history or mythology or fairy tales. But *streetwear* was a broader term than *urban*. It had enough space for sneakers, hoodies, T-shirts, and track pants—all the things that athletes loved to wear. It included many of the elements from the hip-hop vernacular, but also from the world of skateboarding and surfing. It had multiple birthplaces: New York, Los Angeles, Tokyo. A lot of different subcultures could live under the term *streetwear*. Because it was so expansive, it had more cultural heft and greater commercial possibilities.

And yet. Once again, fashion had created a term to separate a new generation of designers from their predecessors. For many, the term was frustrating. Why was it even necessary? Sportswear was sportswear. For others, the term was racially charged. Once again, Black sportswear designers were tucked into a separate category.

But in this case, aficionados of streetwear, with its broad reach and international appeal, had financial clout. *Streetwear* might have been a segregating term, but the clothes had the potential to be incredibly lucrative, far more lucrative than urban gear. Black men still faced daily racism, but the world loved the culture they'd created and disseminated, whether on the basketball court or in the recording studio.

IN RESPONSE TO MEN'S rising interest in fashion, *Cargo* magazine, a shopping glossy for men, landed on newsstands in 2004. *Men's Vogue* launched a year later. Both magazines lasted only a few years. The lesson learned was that men were interested in fashion and style, but old media weren't the format in which they wanted to consume news about it. Instead, guys were online, reading blogs and opining in chat rooms. Abloh was reading *The Brilliance,* a quirky, low-tech blog that posted sassy, droll missives about clothes, music, furniture, food, and pretty much anything that captured the imagination of its Chicago-based founders. They wrote about music producer Pharrell Williams, Japanese denim, Malin+Goetz facial cleansers, artists Kaws and Takashi Murakami, streetwear brand A Bathing Ape (BAPE), and a website selling vintage furniture called Porch Modern.

The difference between the print publications and a blog like *The Brilliance* wasn't so much content as a matter of intimacy and accessibility. *The Brilliance* was created in 2005 by Benjamin Edgar Gott, who later founded Boxed Water Is Better, and artist Chuck Anderson. It read like something written on the fly by an inquisitive, smart, and slightly scatterbrained friend who didn't bother to check for spelling errors or grammatical mistakes. One of the earliest posts, in March 2005, concerned the pleasure of eating edamame.

"You know how you pull a jolly-rancher out of its wrapper with you [*sic*] teeth? Same way you eat edamame, except you look WAY more important. Bring your girl back to the condo (your dorm room), serve some steaming edamame, email THE BRILLIANCE with the results. . . . Drop-drop-drop it like it's hot!"

Abloh was in his second year at IIT when *The Brilliance* launched. He was so captivated by it that he emailed the creators and asked if he could contribute. Despite an initial rejection, Abloh stayed in touch and was eventually welcomed on to the team as the blog's popularity grew. When Abloh was introduced to its readers, the founders underscored his focus, even then, on cultural connections.

"What can I say . . . change is good. Really good in this case. For the last 1.5 years that Chuck and I have been running THE BRILLIANCE its [*sic*] been a 2 man show, and we kind of always thought we would keep it that way . . . but the winds of change blew. Introducing our latest (and only) addition to the writing staff—Virgil Abloh. Chuck and myself are pretty excited about this. . . . Virgil will bring a fresh, always articulate, flavor to our site in the everyday posts as well as some new interviews on the way . . . and who knows what else. Dude is a futurist and a visionary. . . . He truly represents our culture, an ambassador of sorts you know? So yeah, welcome aboard man. . . . Let's have fun with this!"

During Abloh's run as a writer, he offered admiring notes on the Bravo reality show *Project Runway,* about aspiring designers competing to win a place at New York Fashion Week, and on an e-commerce business that was selling ultrasoft sweatshirts whose production he described in detail. One of the most telling posts was about an open-air market in a vacant lot across from his Chicago apartment building. His description of it was an assessment of creativity, civic responsibility, global economics, and entrepreneurship all packed into one idealistic paragraph.

"During the week it looks just like any other vacant lot except its [*sic*] got banners branding it as 'The Lot' a streetmarket outlet for Chicago's creative community. I like the sounds of that. On the weekends different vendors inhabit the space each week trying to recoup their $325 fee. It's a mix of random art hipster stuff . . . tee shirts, skateboards, records and collectibles curated by the two founders. I like this concept a LOT . . . its [*sic*] nothing crazy new either (remember Vacant?) but so simple and tons of possibilities to make them very unique for low key vacant spots around the world. Actually, visit any 3rd world country and the space between cars is a place to make money . . . but there is so much under used space in 1st world cities its [*sic*] just refreshing to see people take advantage of it. So show some love to your local starving artist or start one of these up."

The Brilliance posted links to Abloh's many Chicago ramblings and musings. He led a tour of the Wicker Park neighborhood during which he was wide-eyed and everything was "dope." He highlighted a skate shop, a bookstore, and a T-shirt and sneaker boutique. He was remarkably free of both sarcasm and cynicism.

Of course, the blog covered sneakers. The influence of sneaker culture cannot be overestimated. During the early 2000s, one could glance down the front rows of menswear fashion shows in New York City and see nothing but sneaker-clad feet only occasionally interrupted by a woman's stilettos.

CHICAGO WAS WHERE this perfect storm of cultural influences engulfed Abloh. It's also where he met Kanye West. The producer and rapper was riding the wave of attention generated by the success of his 2004 debut album, *The College Dropout,* and its 2005 follow-up, *Late Registration.* Early in his career West rapped about faith, educational inequality, personal insecurity, political protest, and family. His subject matter made him stand out—as many of his contemporaries delved into street violence, braggadocio, women, and partying—and his skill as a producer garnered praise.

West also demonstrated that he could be impulsive and raw, fearless and vulnerable. In September 2005, he participated in a telethon to raise money for the victims of Hurricane Katrina. The storm surge from the hurricane had overwhelmed the levee system in New Orleans that held Lake Pontchartrain and Lake Borgne at bay. When the levees failed, almost the entire city of New Orleans was submerged. The mostly Black residents who couldn't or wouldn't evacuate were left in dire circumstances. Some were screaming for help from the rooftops. Others were stuck in the hellish bowels of the city's Superdome, which had been designated a shelter of last resort but had transformed into an inhumane encampment. Black people struggled to survive as help from the federal government was slow to arrive or didn't arrive at all.

Wearing a rugby shirt and chinos, West walked on stage with comedian Mike Myers. With images of wrecked homes and floodwaters flashing behind them, Myers read his thoughts and prayers remarks from the teleprompter. West, visibly agitated, launched into a personal commentary. "I hate the way they portray us in the media," he said. "If you see a Black family, it says they're looting. If you see a White family, it says they're looking for food." He then took himself to task for initially turning away from the painful images on television. Then the camera turned back to Myers, who continued to read his prewritten script. When it was time for West to speak again, he delivered a devastating assessment of the president and, by extension, the keepers of power in this country: "George Bush doesn't care about Black people."

It's not often that a graduate student serendipitously meets a rising rap star who's confronted the president on live television. But they did meet, and West drew Abloh close and thrust him into the center of an electrifying web of audacious ambition, searing confidence, and creative synergy. Their friendship was one of deep affection, loyalty, mutual ambition, and competition.

The two connected as Abloh was finishing his master's degree in architecture. His tenure at IIT had drawn out his creative impulses, especially his love for graphic design. He had a young assistant professor, Thomas Kearns, who taught a class called "Network Technologies." It highlighted the cultural shifts and technical innovations to which architects should be attentive. Kearns encouraged his students to harness the power of the burgeoning digital world. His lessons were about more than just building websites and searching the internet. He wanted them to learn how the very art of communication was changing through social media. He taught Abloh that "being online" was not merely a tool. It was a place; it was a lifestyle. And he encouraged Abloh to learn Adobe software.

Abloh designed his first T-shirt using Adobe after a trip to New York City and a foray downtown where he took in the sights and sounds of retailers selling skate brands. His earliest ideas about fashion had been formed through companies such as Santa Cruz and Droors, brands rooted in skateboarding and graphic art. Fashion was a T-shirt that connected the wearer to a tribe. "I was into fashion that intersected with the niche cultures I was into," he said.

Abloh returned to Chicago, and with a childhood friend created FORTHOME. It wasn't so much a company as an idea. He made business cards. But the T-shirt was the thing. It was simple: The name FORTHOME on the front in Edwardian script—a swirling, fussy style of cursive—and a large X on the back that foreshadowed one of Off-White's signature design elements.

Throughout graduate school Abloh nurtured his growing interest in fashion. Like a lot of people his age, he was a fan of Leaders 1354, a seminal streetwear boutique in Chicago. Founded in 2002 with a mission that combined capitalism with community service,

Leaders was a hub for the diverse group of young people who were in the thrall of skate brands, athletic gear, and hip-hop style. It was one of the rare stores in Chicago selling Billionaire Boys Club, the fashion brand created by Pharrell Williams and Nigo. The store also sold a small amount of private label merchandise, and Abloh went there hoping he might be able to do a bit of graphic design work. After all, he was Adobe literate.

Vic Lloyd was the general manager of Leaders. He didn't have a budget to hire Abloh, but Lloyd was part of a group of Black entrepreneurs in the city who were willing to give opportunities to young people with an idea and a passion. Leaders happened to stock the Nike "Eire" SB Dunk sneaker, an iteration of the classic sneaker that commemorated the Easter Rebellion—an uprising of the Irish against the British—and incorporated the colors of the Irish flag in the design. With Abloh's help, Leaders produced a T-shirt that paired with the shoe and that acknowledged the city's mayor, Richard Daley. It read: "Daley Making Dollars."

Abloh worked on another shirt for Leaders, one that featured the outline of medallions around the neckline, but it never panned out. The shirt was ultimately created in collaboration with the Paris boutique Colette.

T-shirts epitomized everything about the new era of fashion. They were informal, gender neutral, infinitely malleable, and readily accessible. T-shirts were this generation's foundational garment, a blank canvas awaiting their creative impulses. T-shirts were Abloh's side hustle, which was also his main passion.

Leaders worked with a company called Custom Kings to produce its private-label merchandise. And when Lloyd heard that the owners of Custom Kings needed help, he decided that Abloh was just the man for the job.

In Chicago, Custom Kings was not merely a local shop heat-pressing and silk-screening T-shirts—although it did a fine job at that. Custom Kings was a fashion house with a do-it-yourself ethos; it was a community gathering spot; it was a de facto school for aspiring designers. "If you had an ounce of creativity, you could come in Custom Kings and stay from opening to close," said founder Jay Green, who was known around town as Jay Boogie. "I believed in urban youth. . . . I just wanted to give people an opportunity. An opportunity could change anything."

Green grew up in Chicago's public housing and was a self-described hustler. As a kid he sold candy and had multiple paper routes. He ran a recording studio that opened its doors to local artists, producers, and folks who simply wanted to be part of the music industry. As an adult, he spent time in prison, a period that made him ruminative rather than bitter.

He was drawn to fashion. He was influenced by Barbara Bates, a Chicago designer who outfitted celebrities such as Michael Jordan, Whitney Houston, and Mike Tyson. Green spent huge sums of money buying Bates's designs and was ultimately inspired—by his personal creative impulses and his dwindling bank account—to make his own clothes. He made the rounds of fabric shops for materials and then found a tailor who realized his ideas. Green eventually bought industrial sewing machines, hired a team of seamstresses, and produced his own designs, many of which incorporated leather.

Custom Kings lived in several locations before it began operating in the early 2000s from suite 511 in a building just north of Chinatown on Chicago's South Side. Green owned Custom Kings with Dante Beals. Anthony Mason, the late NBA player, invested more than $250,000 in the shop. The business grew into an in-demand supplier of clothing to entertainers, rappers, sports figures, and people in the know. Custom Kings was booming and the shop needed help.

When Lloyd introduced Abloh to Green, the business owner was impressed with Abloh's technical know-how. Abloh understood the complicated requirements for silk screening. He wasn't particular about the shape or cut of the T-shirts he was making, but he was obsessive about the graphics. He knew how to map out the desired design, how to separate the colors, how to make sure the resulting print was aligned properly. Abloh could create the film positives required for high-quality work. Green quickly hired Abloh as sort of a supercharged intern and set him up in a back office. There he became part of the Custom Kings team, which included more than a dozen sewers who produced jogging suits and leather varsity jackets from the fifth-floor studio.

Custom Kings also happened to be where John Monopoly printed souvenir merchandise for a group called Sa-Ra Creative Partners. The trio was composed of Taz Arnold, Shafiq Husayn, and Om'Mas Keith; they were signed to Kanye West's label GOOD Music. Monopoly was one of the music nerds who hung around Green's recording studio. Monopoly wasn't a producer or performer; he was a business guy, an organizer, a hustler. And he was working with West. Green assigned Abloh to work on the Sa-Ra project with Monopoly, and the two holed up in a back office to confer on designs and production. Abloh quickly impressed Monopoly with his skills.

Soon Abloh was invited to meet West. The introduction was facilitated by Don Crawley, who used "Don C" professionally and was another of West's cohorts. This was a time of relatively easy accessibility, when a neighborhood print shop could be the gateway to a rapper's inner sanctum, and when Crawley could be found on a freezing street corner in Chicago in a nondescript parka and a ski cap watching as a production team collaborated on a West video. It was during the nascent days of West's career, after he'd shifted from behind-the-scenes producer to center stage performer. He was a success, but he was not untouchable. He was a young man with a short Afro, a wide jaw—which had been broken in a brutal car accident—and a penchant for preppy attire.

West was pulling in creative souls who intrigued him, people he believed could help him achieve a vision, as well as those who had their own powerful ideas. His circle was diverse, in race and in age. West had a world of ideas and responsibilities. He needed help with concert production, souvenir merchandise, and album graphics. He also had ambitions of pouring his overflowing creativity into groundbreaking projects that would transform the broader culture from filmmaking to healthcare and fashion.

West threw himself fully into his passions. He latched on to people, part barnacle and part bulldog. He'd decide that someone had the answer to a question that bedeviled him, and he'd pepper them with queries and possibilities. He remembered every detail of a conversation. And if he was engaged with a subject, time was not a concern. He'd talk and talk and talk—especially about fashion. For his first *GQ* magazine cover, he spent nine hours just trying on clothes. He revered designers; he studied them; he put them on a pedestal. He wanted to be one.

In the crush of academic work for his final year of graduate school, Abloh put together a portfolio of ideas and flew to New York for a meeting with West at the Gansevoort Hotel that went by so quickly it felt as though it lasted less than one minute. West challenged Abloh to design a collection based on a convergence of the streetwear brand A Bathing Ape; the elaborate embroidery used by the London-based brand Maharishi, whose oversize trousers had gained traction within fashion; and the nineteenth-century Japanese woodblock print *Under the Wave off Kanagawa* (*The Great Wave*).

The request encapsulated Abloh's attraction to West. He was a cultural figure mixing diverse and surprising elements in an attempt to make something new. Abloh's ideas were impressive enough that he left Custom Kings and began working with West as a creative assistant. "All this stuff happened in a span of six months," Lloyd recalled. Abloh had barely even been put on the Custom Kings payroll before he was scooped up into the West whirlwind—and put on the rapper's books.

After Abloh graduated architecture school in 2006, his first and only job at a firm was with Studio Dwell in Chicago. The young company, situated in an industrial neighborhood, specialized in modern, residential design. Their work featured open floor plans, plenty of wood and glass, and a tendency to embrace the urban environment as part of the lived experience rather than shield their clients from it. Abloh walked in off the street with his résumé. He didn't have an appointment. He had no letter of introduction or reference. He just walked in. "He said he liked our work," said Studio Dwell's Mark Peters. Abloh didn't have any experience, but he made it clear that he was willing to learn, and he was willing to do whatever it took to succeed. He had nerve and confidence in abundance. Peters hired him that day.

"I'd never done that before and I haven't done it since," Peters said.

Abloh worked at Studio Dwell for about two years, in marketing and project management. The last two months of his tenure, however, he was mostly part-time. He'd started to move deeper into West's world, into his dreamscape. Peters once marveled at how quickly Abloh's creative responsibilities with West had grown. Abloh laughed: "I'm the only one who knows Photoshop!"

Abloh became the point person in the center of a creative storm that was eventually called Donda. That was the name West gave to the project that represented his cultural manifesto. He named it after his mother. Donda West, an English teacher, who died in 2007 at only fifty-eight, had been West's compass and his support.

At Donda, Abloh became part of a community that had a simple but profound core belief: nothing was impossible. Theirs was a radical rebuke of a historically divided city, a fashion business that insisted on putting Black designers in a separate category, and a broader political system that didn't seem to value the mind and spirit of Black people. West refused to take no for an answer. He wanted to work with the best in any field that captured his imagination. Often, Abloh was charged with reaching out to those people on West's behalf, a task at which he became so adept that he would cold-call people *he* admired, sometimes to work with them, sometimes simply to express his awe. And most often, they would respond with an open mind.

"Virgil had the best social IQ of anyone I know," said Dirk Standen, who was the editor in chief of Style.com, as well as the founding editor of Condé Nast's creative agency 23 Stories.

In the beginning, Abloh was the protégé. He was the guy with the laptop feverishly taking notes, scouring the internet for ideas, using his software skills to create digital mood boards at the behest of West. It was impossible to be in West's circle and not feed off his sense of limitlessness. While Abloh was inspired by the world that he saw as a seventeen-year-old, West was, to some degree, motivated by the fourteen-year-old version of himself growing up in Chicago. He saw the inequality in the city in the early 1990s. He loved the stores of the Magnificent Mile that sold designer merchandise, but those clothes were far beyond anything he could afford. He was an in-between kid—not wealthy enough, not cool enough, not gritty enough.

When he found his initial success as a performer, he took the stage in preppy golf shirts, sport jackets, and pocket squares. He adored Polo Ralph Lauren. As his taste became more eclectic, he looked farther afield to Paris-based designers such as Martin Margiela, with his masterful deconstruction, and Rick Owens. West adored the urbane minimalism of Helmut Lang and, of course, Raf Simons. The in-between kid made himself the center of all that he loved. He was determined that no one would beat him when it came to music, fashion, and the magnitude of his audacity. West wanted to transform an entire generation's understanding of style.

In the beginning, Abloh believed that he was at the starting line of a collaboration that would change the nature of hip-hop. But he connected with West through more than just music. They had a shared curiosity about culture: music, yes, but also visual art, fashion, and architecture. West could talk for hours about these subjects, sometimes in the most esoteric ways, and Abloh had both the interest and the stamina to keep up with him but not overshadow him.

It can be hard for young Black men whose interests lie beyond music and sports to find their circle, their tribe—to connect with people who take their avocations seriously, who are ready not just to listen to what they have to say but to challenge their ideas and engage in intellectual improvisation. West found that with Abloh. It wasn't unusual for West to spend ninety hours in a week working to develop his latest ideas about the packaging for an album or hammering out the technical problems in creating a fully immersive film or simply dreaming out loud about fashion.

At the top of West's list of creative projects was his desire to launch his own fashion brand. He had many starts and stops along the way. He left a trail of could-have-beens, sort-of-weres, and capsule collections. One of his earliest projects was 2008's Pastelle, which Abloh worked on, along with designer Kim Jones, among others. It was, perhaps, the outing that most closely reflected West's fascination with Polo Ralph Lauren, graphic design, and the pop-art vividness of Japanese street style. It was vaguely preppy, in keeping with his "College Dropout" persona. But despite the effort West expended developing it, Pastelle never attained liftoff. The only item that the public ever really glimpsed was a varsity jacket, worn by West at the American Music Awards that same year. The jacket, which snapped up the front, was cobalt-blue wool, with insets of red leather at the shoulders. The brand name was written in jagged yellow lettering across the left front.

DW, which followed Pastelle, was West's high-fashion gambit

that was years in the making. Because he came from the world of music in which sampling was an art, he applied that same theory to fashion. He solicited dozens of opinions, a million bits of data, and then tried to assemble them anew into his own work of genius. He sought out Professor Louise Wilson at London's Central Saint Martins, the art school that had produced some of the most renowned designers working in contemporary fashion. West thought studying fashion design would be a route to success—and a signal to the industry that he was serious about his aspirations—and she was one of the most influential fashion educators in the modern era.

Wilson, who died in 2014, was a tornado of a woman. She dressed almost exclusively in black, adorned her fingers with thick silver rings, and doled out criticism with unflinching clarity. She oversaw the master's degree program in fashion and worked with Alexander McQueen, Stella McCartney, Craig Green, Simone Rocha, and others. She was not an instructor who demanded perfection; she demanded inventiveness and imagination. She encouraged her students to break boundaries. Wilson did not believe in remaining hostage to the way things had always been. She advised West against adding a fashion degree to his résumé. In many ways, design school was where students found their voice and learned to be fearless. Neither West nor Abloh could stitch up a suit, but they knew what kinds of jackets and trousers they liked. In Wilson's mind, fashion didn't need more technicians, it needed more visionaries.

IN 2009, while DW was percolating, Abloh married Shannon Sundberg in Chicago. They'd met at a soccer game when they were growing up in Rockford and attending different high schools. She was a seventeen-year-old junior when he was an eighteen-year-old senior. They stayed together as undergraduates, when she studied marketing at Edgewood College in Madison, and through his time at IIT and those first years when he began working for West. Abloh proposed at O'Hare airport as she was dropping him off for a flight.

They had a purple-hued wedding, which was her favorite color. The bride wore a pale pink gown by Amsale, and her blond hair was swept into a French twist. Abloh wore a classic tuxedo.

She built a professional life at tech companies. They started a family. And Abloh drew a line of demarcation between home and everything else.

"He would do crazy flights just so he could get home to be with me and the kids," Shannon Abloh said. "He would get the last flight he could take out, and then he would stay up and take the first flight back home to see the kids before school or be there when they got home from school."

That same year, Abloh also made his formal entry into the Paris fashion show scene alongside West. In January 2009, street style photographer Tommy Ton snapped a picture that became infamous within fashion circles and beyond. It captured West and Abloh arriving in Paris for their first round of shows. They were outside the Comme des Garçons Homme Plus show, a Chicago posse of multi-hyphenates in fashion and music that included Don Crawley, Taz Arnold, Fonzworth Bentley, Chris Julian, West, and Abloh. There were no crowds of influencers and hangers-on posing for battalions of street style photographers that day. Fashion had yet to explode onto social media. "I saw Kanye and his posse walk from their car towards us and there was no paparazzi. They saw me and the one other photographer there and just stopped to assemble in formation in front of us," Ton said.

The six men were dressed like characters from a Hollywood caricature of a fashion show. They were a technicolor, live-action cartoon. As Abloh would say, they were eager tourists at an event intended for fashion purists.

West stood in the center of the picture. He was wearing a Black-watch tartan car coat over a navy blazer and dark-wash dungarees, along with reddish-brown leather gloves. He was also holding a Goyard briefcase, as if he were headed to a boardroom in the land of Oz. Abloh stood on the end. He too was wearing a visually chaotic ensemble. His thick eyeglass frames were fire-engine red. He'd paired a sky-blue Moncler down vest over a black-and-white marble-print shirt designed by Raf Simons when he was working for the Jil Sander brand. Abloh added a bow tie, gray flannel trousers, and butter-yellow sneakers. His hands were stuffed into his pockets, and he was slouched forward as if he was trying to fit into the frame with his shorter friends.

The earnest and outlandish image eventually reverberated through popular culture and served as fodder for mockery on an episode of the animated comedy *South Park*.

These pals obsessed over designer labels—Louis Vuitton, Raf Simons, Prada—and paid close attention to the way those brands were packaged, marketed, and sold. A friend once gave Abloh a book from an exhibition celebrating designer Miuccia Prada. Abloh admired the book, but, like a child captivated by the ribbons and wrapping paper on Christmas morning, he was mesmerized by the bag in which it came. And it *was* an unusual bag for a luxury company. Constructed from a sort of stiff, opaque bubble wrap and shaped like a FedEx mailing envelope with a short handle, it was a perfect example of Prada's signature aesthetic triumph: elevating the mundane. Abloh carried his laptop in the bag until it finally fell apart.

In that photograph, taken just before a presentation by one of fashion's most self-consciously intellectual brands, one of its most respected labels, there's determination and certainty, along with naiveté. The young men might as well have been wearing fanny packs and flip-flops and clutching a Fodor's travel guide in their hands. In later interviews, Abloh recalled how they'd only managed to access a little over half the shows that were on their wish list. He posited that as evidence of their outsider status. But in truth, theirs was a pretty good batting average. An anonymous fashion student or fan, without a critically acclaimed rapper in their midst, would have faced dismal odds of gaining access to a single Paris runway show. An editor from a modest publication with limited readership would have faced ego-bruising hurdles—just turning up at the entrance to a show would risk a crushing dismissal.

Abloh felt like an outsider, but he had extraordinary access because he was with West. And West was known to fashion editors and stylists and executives—and the publicists standing watch at the entrances. He'd made inroads in fashion by leveraging his fame and his incessant curiosity. West had access because by 2009, hip-hop was no longer an outlier culture; it had become the dominant popular culture thanks to its record sales and diverse audience. Black men had style chops recognized by the fashion world. West was valuable currency. He greased the wheels and opened doors.

That photo was telling for another reason. West wore distinctive sneakers, in a patchwork of burgundy, pink, and tan suede. Originally retailing for about $960, the sneakers had sparked that group trip to Paris. West worked with Louis Vuitton to design them. Marc Jacobs, the American designer who invented Louis Vuitton ready-to-wear, was inspired by the visual arts, hip-hop, and street style. He welcomed all those elements into the world of luxury fashion, collaborating with Stephen Sprouse, Takashi Murakami, Richard Prince, Pharrell Williams, and West.

The seed for the relationship between West, Abloh, and Louis Vuitton had been planted three years earlier. West had just released *Late Registration,* and Abloh was fresh from graduate school and still juggling his work at Studio Dwell.

Tokyo was a hot spot for streetwear, sneaker culture, and men's fashion. One of the primary instigators of Tokyo's importance in this realm was an entrepreneur named Tomoaki Nagao, better known as Nigo, who founded A Bathing Ape. The name was a truncated version of the phrase "a bathing ape in lukewarm water," which referred to a person so overindulged and coddled that they lounged in the bath until the water turned cold. The brand name mocked privileged youth, who were, in fact, its primary customers.

Nigo launched A Bathing Ape in 1993, shortly after opening the streetwear shop Nowhere in partnership with another Japanese designer, Jun Takahashi. BAPE was known for its graphic designs, its American retro sensibility, its celebrity fans—which included Pharrell Williams—and its recognition that scarcity breeds obsession. It purposefully produced far less than it could sell, turning its fans into rabid treasure hunters and its merchandise into gold. Its signature was the silhouette of an ape's head—like a headshot from *Planet of the Apes,* the 1968 science fiction film in which gorillas and chimpanzees sit at the top of the animal kingdom and humans are caged and enslaved. Nigo didn't invent Japanese streetwear culture, but he transformed it into a commodity that was glamorous, fashionable, and in (artificial) high demand. He turned streetwear into a luxury, which made Japan a beacon to young men around the globe flexing their new fashion muscles.

"Tokyo was, for menswear back then, really the place to be. That's where street really met luxury, and Nigo was the leader of that aesthetic," said Michael Burke, who was a longtime executive at LVMH. "Everybody worshipped him, including Kanye and Virgil. Everybody went to Tokyo the way Catholics go to the Vatican. And they would all go worship at the altar of Nigo."

Burke wasn't a Nigo acolyte, but he checked in with him regularly and listened closely to what he had to say. It made good business sense to do so. And Burke, a veteran of the fashion industry, knew that companies didn't grow and prosper by playing it safe.

Burke could be an amiable and chatty executive. An American who was born in France, he'd worked for LVMH from its beginnings. He started as an employee of Groupe Arnault, the investment firm founded in 1978 by Bernard Arnault. Burke entered the luxury fashion business when he took the helm of Christian Dior USA after the French brand was purchased by Arnault and became the first fashion brick in his luxury conglomerate. Burke later moved to Rome to run Fendi, which LVMH acquired in 2001. He went on to lead Louis Vuitton. As a fashion boss, Burke was constantly on the alert for shifting winds. Thoughtful and intentional risk-taking was part of his job.

As the chairman of Fendi, Burke was preparing to travel to Tokyo for the 2006 launch of a new accessories line, one that represented the brand's early and tentative foray into a streetwear sensibility. Silvia Venturini Fendi, whose grandparents had founded the company in Rome in 1925, had played with the brand's double F logo and its signature color palette of tan and brown for a collection called B.Mix. Using bags stitched out of cotton jacquard as her base, she manipulated the Fendi Fs to mimic the ostentatious style that bootleggers used on their fake Fendi products. Fendi took a cue from the very street merchants who cribbed their intellectual property and transformed the exercise into a statement about outsiders and self-creation. It was the perfect collection to launch in Tokyo, where streetwear was treated as a luxury product rather than a mass market one.

In preparation for the launch, Fendi rented Tokyo's National Stadium, which had hosted the 1964 Olympics. The stadium caught Fendi's attention because its multi-tiered, open design recalled Rome's Coliseum. Fendi flags flew from the stadium in anticipation of the launch. After taking in all the hoopla, Nigo contacted Burke and asked whether he'd be interested in hosting a concert in conjunction with the launch. "Who do you have in mind?" Burke asked.

"Kanye," replied Nigo.

"Sure," Burke responded.

The night before the concert, Nigo invited Burke to meet the rapper. An unlikely group gathered at a local restaurant: Burke, West, Nigo and members of his band Teriyaki Boyz, an anonymous squad of fashionable Japanese youth, and Abloh.

"I'm the only White guy. So I'm the proverbial outsider. They were looking at me as an insider on the fashion business, but at that moment, I was totally the outsider," Burke recalled. "I could barely understand what they were talking about. They were the insiders in music and in a certain aesthetic and I was an insider from traditional fashion. Virgil riffed on that a lot: every insider is an outsider, and every outsider is an insider. We were both insiders and outsiders at the same time during that dinner."

Burke didn't talk much. Instead, he listened and he watched, admiring the group's willingness to invite him into their circle, to trust him in their space. The fashion executive expressed humility; he knew he was the odd guy out. Preconcert giddiness and excitement filled the room that evening. West talked animatedly, leaping from one topic to another. He was the star of the evening, but he was willing to share the billing with a brand he admired, even going as far as shaving the Fendi "F" into his hair. He'd turned his skull into a fashion billboard. The evening went on until the wee hours of the morning, with things wrapping up sometime around 4 a.m.

Through it all, Abloh was reserved. Not shy, bashful, or aloof. He simply wasn't pounding his chest.

"I was very impressed by the silence of Virgil," Burke said. Abloh had resisted any urge to perform or to try and outshine all the bright lights at the table. "It was a moment in time. It was quite magical," Burke said. "It clicked; everything clicked at that moment."

Several years passed. West worked on his Louis Vuitton sneakers. Then, in 2009, a few months after he and Abloh stormed the fashion gates in Paris, West unleashed another startling speech on live tele-vision. This time, it was during the MTV Video Music Awards. He interrupted Taylor Swift as she accepted the trophy for best female video. West climbed on stage unannounced and took the micro-phone in front of a flabbergasted Swift. He declared Beyoncé the rightful winner and a camera panned to the singer, who was sit-ting in the audience, to reveal an expression of shock and horror. The declaration astonished viewers. West's actions led President Obama—when an interviewer brought up the incident—to call West "a jackass." Shortly after, while West was still being roasted over the fires of public outrage, he called Burke, who was running Fendi, and asked to be a fashion intern in Rome.

Burke explained that fashion was unlike music. Designers were tethered to a seasonal schedule that was demanding and unrelenting. They couldn't hold on to a collection until they deemed it ready for public consumption. They didn't choose a new cast of collaborators with each collection. And they didn't just design the clothes. They had to deal with production and marketing, advertising and retail.

"You just can't show up one day and become a designer over-night," Burke told West. "It's going to take years and years."

West assured him that he understood, but he was insistent. He wanted to start training, and he wanted to start at Fendi.

It took a certain kind of executive to do what Burke did next. It took someone with confidence and nerve and a sense of possibility. It required a realization that the old ways of doing things were not always the only way or even the best way. Perhaps it took someone who had known their boss for more than twenty years, had known that boss before he had become one of the richest men in the world, and knew how much faith and trust that boss had in him.

It took someone who understood that menswear was changing, someone who'd spent an evening in Tokyo being a fascinated, eaves-dropping outsider.

Burke said yes.

He warned West that he had only $500 a month allotted for an intern. Fendi was on financially rocky ground; that's why Burke had been asked to take the reins. West arrived in Rome with Abloh, the reserved dinner partner whom Burke admired. So Burke doubled his budget. He got two interns for $1,000. They promised to do whatever was necessary. They'd make coffee. Pick up pins. Fetch fabric.

The team at Fendi was aghast. They couldn't believe Burke had hired a rapper and his sidekick. What on earth would the atelier do with them? Mostly, they thought Burke was nuts.

"That seems to be a leitmotif throughout my life," Burke said. "Most of the time it means I'm doing something right."

Burke installed the duo in the studio with Sylvia Fendi, a place full of history and artistry where three generations of Fendis had worked and a fourth generation was on the cusp of joining. Abloh and West brought themselves, their ideas, and a lot of music. Very loud music. The Fendi studio was located in the center of Rome and surrounded by residential buildings filled with neighbors who didn't hesitate to complain about the boom-booming disturbance. At one in the morning, the lights of the studio would be shining bright, and music would be blaring.

In Italy, business deals began with a relationship. People did business with those they knew, people with whom they were on good terms, Burke said. In France, it was almost the opposite. A business relationship *might* lead to a friendship. It might not. Either way, it didn't matter. Business was business. In America, everyone was your friend . . . until they weren't.

West was often caught up in his own ambitions and ideas. He was living in his own world of music, ego, and the fallout from his self-generated controversies. Abloh was consummately present. He was easy to like. He got to know Sylvia Fendi, as well as her mother and aunts, and she kept an open mind as she got to know the unorthodox intern. Then Burke invited Abloh to his home for dinner.

"When that happened and all the Romans saw that—nothing is private; it's not like Milan, in Rome everything's on the streets—when everybody saw that he was close to the Fendis, he was close to Michael, [the whole team] started working with him," Burke said.

When Abloh talked about his ideas, he did so with a pen and paper nearby. The skills he had learned at IIT helped him communicate visually. He sketched as he spoke. His drawings weren't exacting—he wasn't a fashion illustrator, after all—but they were clear. They were part of the universal language of the studio. Abloh moved patiently from task to task. West swung for the fences. By the time the internship finished, Abloh had a friend in Burke.

In the fall of 2011, West decided he was ready to debut DW and he wanted to do so in Paris. He'd treated previous fashion seasons in the city like an all-you-can-eat banquet, and he'd consumed the aesthetics, the point of view, the signatures of countless other designers.

Since his false start with Pastelle, he'd collaborated on sneakers at Louis Vuitton and interned at Fendi. He'd gotten advice from educator Louise Wilson. He'd pinballed between cocky and panicked. His fame was both a blessing and a curse, opening doors for his fashion aspirations, and making him someone to be taken down a peg for daring to dream so expansively.

When he presented his DW collection on the runway, he did so in front of an audience that included designers; photographer Terry Richardson; Mary-Kate Olsen and Ashley Olsen, who'd successfully made the leap from actors to fashion moguls; and Lindsay Lohan, who'd had a brief, gimmicky, and catastrophic stint as an artistic adviser at Ungaro.

DW by Kanye West, a nod to his late mother, was the last show on a day that included presentations from Comme des Garçons and the lyrical work of Haider Ackermann. West's musical soundtrack dazzled—he was an award-winning producer after all—but the clothes did not. They didn't fit. They didn't make sense for how people lived. There was only the tiniest hint of streetwear, the style of dress that was on the cusp of exploding and that spoke to the sensibilities of the same generation that was drawn to West's music. Instead, the collection was a watered-down version of a thousand other perspectives. West had gorged himself on fashion and then spat it back out.

Backstage afterward, West was visibly uncomfortable and seemed skittish and overwhelmed as music blared in the background despite his having implored anyone within earshot to lower the volume. Still, he took questions from assembled journalists. When asked about his inspirations, he whiffed. Then he bluntly admitted: "I'm so scared. I'm so distracted."

There was something compelling about his honesty and vulnerability. It was a trait that Abloh had and one that people admired. Abloh didn't shy away from admitting what he didn't know. He wasn't embarrassed to ask questions and to reveal an eagerness to learn. He could be vulnerable. In an industry that prided itself on swagger and mystique, earnestness was a rare and valued find.

But by the time West appeared at his after-party—because in fashion there was *always* an after-party—he'd regained his footing and his bravado. That awful show? It wasn't awful at all; it was just misunderstood.

When it was time for his sophomore effort, West called in reinforcements. He brought in Michael Rock. Or to be more accurate, Abloh did.

While in New York, Abloh had walked past the new Prada epicenter on Prince Street in SoHo and noticed the interior wall murals. They stretched across an entire floor and registered as a kind of digitized dream. The shapes were abstract but invoked images from nature—birds, flowers, insects. They referenced people and garments and shoes, but only obliquely, never directly. Mostly what stood out was the enormous mural that dominated the interior of the clothing store. It had little to do with clothes.

When Abloh, now working full-time with West, learned that 2 x 4 was responsible for the wallpaper, he recalled the signage and icons inside the campus center of the Illinois Institute of Technology, and he remembered Rock. So Abloh fired off an email asking if Rock would be willing to meet with West.

"That was one of the strangest meetings I've ever had. It just spiraled from originally thinking about a fashion show to healthcare, education, security systems, world travel," Rock said. "It was kind of like the megalomania period of Kanye. And they wanted to put together some infrastructure so that they could start to kind of apply this methodology, however inchoate that methodology was, to all these different kinds of social problems.

"It was kooky," Rock said, "but at the time, everything was kind of kooky."

The community around West as he sought to redeem himself after the disastrous DW debut grew to include a cast of personalities who shared an interest in music and fashion and the ways in which popular culture knit them together. As West prepared for the second outing of the DW fashion collection, Rock met with West and this creative hive in London. Rock was the forty-something baby boomer listening as a klatch of guys in their twenties and thirties huddled in a wood-paneled suite at the St. James Hotel near Hyde Park and brainstormed ideas for how the show might look.

"They were all sitting around with laptops, and then someone would be like, 'It'd be cool if all the girls' hair were on fire!' And then everyone would be on the internet searching. And then they would turn their computers around with different pictures of that and be like, 'Oh, dope! Yeah, that's cool.' And then another idea would get thrown out and then they were furiously googling. It was this crazy idea-generation thing that was going on," Rock said. "It ultimately led to a roller coaster and then it was going to be a go-kart thing. There were just a million things that were being thrown around.

"For me, I kind of tend to work in the world of reality and rationality. There was a certain aspect which I thought was really interesting: Could you let yourself go into flights of fantasy and see what happens?" he wondered.

"I oftentimes felt like I was completely the wrong person in the room because a lot of it didn't make sense to me," Rock said. "But I was also willing to go and explore that aspect of it: maybe not making sense was a good idea."

The result of all that spitballing and frantic online research was a Paris fashion show in March 2012 that ended with a fleet of go-karts whizzing around the audience—a finale that left fashion editors, the few who had gone back to see another DW collection after the disappointing freshman effort, dumbfounded. Why go-karts? West had fond childhood memories of them. But there was no narrative thread on which to hang those memories. West had treated a fashion show like a concert. And while concertgoers were accustomed to watching performers sing in front of video montages that were more stream-of-consciousness thoughts than a direct representation of lyrics, fashion was built on storytelling, on layers of references that collided on the runway.

"The example I always use is Miuccia Prada saying to me one time, 'What's an idea in fashion? An idea is a little twenties, a little sixties, a little Russian woman on a horse,'" Rock said. Everything builds from that seed of an idea: the hairstyles, the makeup, the music, the set, the lighting. West was freestyling, and fashion didn't know what to make of it.

West's fashion failures and his often antagonistic relationships with editors were important early lessons for Abloh. West fought back against negative critiques by belittling the fashion industry and its denizens. He stoked the fires of animosity. West was a disruptive force during fashion weeks as he scheduled last-minute shows that conflicted with those of other designers who'd been meticulous in their planning. West developed a reputation as a petulant music star who insisted on making a place for himself within a fashion establishment that accepted him grudgingly—if at all. He was the frustrated creator who would lash out defensively; he was the guy who declared that he was bringing creativity to an industry that was simply too lazy to use its imagination. West exuded anger and aggrievement. He felt White publications used *rapper* in a derogatory manner when writing about his fashion. He felt belittled.

Abloh was there through it all. Watching. Taking note. He was the conduit between West and reality, West and reason. He was getting things done, making sense out of complicated notions.

In the beginning, Abloh's work with West could be summed up as "Hey, come over here and bring your computer." But Abloh eventually applied a kind of rigor to West's process. There'd be regular briefs detailing West's goals. Instead of it being a building, that goal could be a graphic for a T-shirt, an outline for a video, or simply a note about "buying flowerpots." Abloh created visual studies of ideas, and he did so fast and furiously on his computer. And he quickly realized, "We are two sides of one brain."

Abloh understood how important it was to West to create a mood and not simply a product. "Kanye calls it emotionalism," Abloh said. "He is a minimalist at his core: he believes if you cut right down to the essential, you'll get to something pure and honest.

"When I first met him, being an architecture grad student, I would have these long explanations for [the] littlest things, and he would be like, 'Why are you talking so much?' He used to call me

Steve Jobs. And I would launch into this long blah, blah, blah, and he would cut me off and tell me, 'Just let it speak for itself,'" Abloh said. "Kanye's only five years older than me but I'm much younger than him in terms of our references. He's more nostalgic about classic hip-hop, for instance. I'm more immersed in youth culture. He dedicated himself to the art of making music. . . . I bring street culture to Kanye's matrix."

Abloh was the lead researcher and notetaker. He took advantage of the speed at which information could be googled, absorbed, and reimagined. He exploited the ability to interact with established designers as well as kids on the street to get a lickety-split understanding of what was cool and what was old hat as of last week.

"I have a kind of add-on function with Kanye. I'm more approachable and I listen to what someone is actually saying, so I can provide the feedback that helps the conversation move forward," Abloh said. "Enabling people is the most satisfying aspect of this job. . . . I get more gratification out of corralling the right people, getting them on the same time zone, and making a project come to fruition than actually brainstorming the actual creative idea."

Around 2011, West's ambition expanded to film. He wanted to create a multiple-screen cinematic experience for the Cannes Film Festival. Rock had been giving lectures on this immersive technology, and he gave West a minicourse in the history and possibilities of motion pictures that incorporated more than one screen. West envisioned a movie using seven screens: three in front of the audience, one on either side, one on the ceiling, and one on the floor. It was a massive undertaking that required specialized cameras, a dedicated space for the screening, and an incredible amount of money. West filmed *Cruel Summer* in Doha, with the help and guidance of Rock and the organizational skills of Abloh. It was received as a curiosity, a way of connecting the pop-cultural dots between music, art, technology, and cinema.

"The story is secondary to the pyrotechnics, with new music from West and a thumping surround-sound quality that makes a 3-D Michael Bay effort feel like an iPad short," wrote Steven Zeitchik in the *Los Angeles Times*.

Abloh was the person who sorted out the complexities of the project. He spoke the language of architects, designers, and filmmakers so that each contributor was able to do their bit of the work and reach the end goal. Abloh had the soft skills that so often are undervalued: sending thank-you notes, engaging in small talk, being genial. He was vulnerable, not volatile. While West was constantly trying to imagine a distant future, Abloh was reconfiguring the present. Abloh surprised the fashion industry, but he didn't confound it.

In the swirl of activity stirred by West, Abloh began racking up air miles. He honed his ability to work in multiple time zones at once and to conduct entire business meetings via the text-messaging service WhatsApp.

West turned his attention to another fashion project, Yeezy. Abloh began to consider his own ambitions. What did *he* want to do?

"I realized I have an identity too. I was forgetting what my own vision was," Abloh said. "It takes a lot out of you to do that kind of trail blazing [with Kanye], being away 365 days a year, just barreling through at this amazing pace and doing all this crazy work. It's hard to remember sometimes what your stake is in all this."

The Outsiders

ABLOH BEGAN BUILDING a community of like-minded men who supported one another as they focused on their own dreams and pressured the fashion industry to be more expansive in how it defined a designer and how it articulated luxury. Matthew Williams, Heron Preston, and Jerry Lorenzo all had their own creative desires. All of them chipped away at the traditions of the fashion industry. They fed off one another, creating an environment of support and comity—something previous generations of designers often lacked—that helped them all soar.

In the early 2000s, Heron Preston Johnson left his hometown in California and traveled across the country to study marketing and business at Parsons School of Design in New York City. Along the way, he remade himself professionally as simply Heron Preston.

Born in San Francisco, Preston moved to the North Bay and the town of Fairfield—home to the Jelly Belly candy company—when he was in the eighth grade. He came of age in the nineties and as a teenager loved skateboarding, music, and movies. It was only a matter of time before he landed in New York. That was the mecca for all his passions.

Tall with cocoa-brown skin, Preston had close-cut hair that framed a long, narrow face. His high forehead was punctuated by a widow's peak. His garrulousness was a measure of his enthusiasm and a reflection of the frenetic energy of his adopted home. Yet his richly tattooed arms remained still when he spoke. He didn't talk with his hands. West Coast informality was embedded in his languorous body language.

Preston arrived in New York full of ambition and with a set of important skills. First, he was computer literate and extremely online. For his junior and senior years, he attended New Technology High School, an experiment in education focused on making technology fundamental to students' lives. As a result, Preston was not simply a digital native; he knew how to construct a digital village. He was adept at coding and building websites and thought his future would be behind a computer. But naturally restless, he soon realized he didn't want to spend his days staring at a flashing cursor.

His second skill was in making T-shirts. Preston started screenprinting them when he was in high school and continued while attending community college. A friend discovered a print shop in Hunters Point that had an old, unused screen printer pushed into a corner. The owners were willing to let Preston fire it up for his creative endeavors, and Preston began producing a line of T-shirts. In recalling this moment, this beginning of his career in fashion, he didn't describe the look of the shirts; instead, he described the logo. "I developed these woven labels that said *Heron Preston*. I wanted to have a fancy-sounding brand, and the first logo was in cursive."

Preston also worked in retail in the Upper Haight district in San Francisco at stores called Red Five and True. The former sold mixtapes, books, T-shirts, incense, and the like. The latter was a haven for sneaker fans. Preston soon learned about line sheets—the barebones product descriptions used to wholesale goods—and the basics of production. In no time, he had a small business.

"I had my little filing cabinet in my little desk in my bedroom, and I was invoicing and boxing up shirts, getting them made and shipping them on my own," Preston said. "I started selling to stores in Japan, and I started selling to some local stores in San Francisco. And then I got into Parsons."

Eager to find his way in the city he'd always idolized, Preston ventured online to find community. He became fascinated by *The Brilliance*, the same blog that had captured Abloh's imagination and welcomed him as a contributing writer. Preston struck up conversations with the writers with the instant familiarity that social media allows. They considered him someone to watch if you wanted to be plugged in to the next cool thing. Soon Preston had his own blog, which *The Brilliance* promoted. He was writing about his life in New York, describing for his friends back home what it was like being a student in the chaotic East Coast city. In Preston's imagination, he envisioned New York as a teeming high school. The streets were the hallways where the cool kids clustered around a group of downtown stores like Supreme, Marc Jacobs, and Stüssy; the taxis were the school buses; and La Esquina was the cafeteria.

La Esquina opened in 2005 on a drab corner in Nolita. At street level, it was a reliable taqueria. The real attraction was the subterranean lair that was accessible only through a doorway marked "no admittance." In its earliest days, La Esquina had no listed telephone number, yet a reservation was required to get past the sentinel guarding its door. Frank Bruni, the *New York Times* restaurant critic, described La Esquina as "sort of like Studio 54 with chipotle instead of cocaine." It was a place that attracted actors and musicians and preternaturally hip people, and they, in turn, transformed La Esquina into a buzzy scene. It wasn't unusual to find black Mercedes-Benz Maybachs parked outside and Jay-Z or Bono dining inside.

La Esquina mimicked the sexy subterfuge of a speakeasy. To reach their table, guests walked down a narrow staircase, through corridors lined with cooking supplies and through the kitchen itself. For a time, some of the best people-watching in the city was against a backdrop of commercial stoves and dishwashers. Preston worked at La Esquina as a runner during summer break from Parsons. He spent his evenings shuttling food from the kitchen to the tables in the dimly lit, cave-like dining room.

One night, as Preston waited to pick up orders, he caught sight of a Black man not much older than himself walking through the kitchen and into the dining room. The man looked familiar. Preston did a cartoon double take and realized it was the fashion, music, skateboarding, street style fan with whom he'd formed an online acquaintance: Virgil Abloh. Preston called out to Abloh, and that serendipitous meeting started a real-world friendship. It would be a fortuitous relationship.

Preston finished his degree, dabbled in brand consulting, and finally landed at Nike, where he became a coolhunter, tasked with finding the newest subcultures and helping the company make sense of them.

"Nike was really smart at understanding people and culture and communities and getting under their skin," Preston said. "I remember one of the marketing VPs spoke to us about getting under people's skin: '*Get under their skin*. Get under the skin of the community, of culture. Who should we connect with? How do we connect sports to community and culture in authentic ways? Who are the kids in the streets of New York City that are interesting, that are cool, that are creative? We need to find them.'

"So, at that point," Preston said, "I started really taking community seriously, obsessing over community and obsessing over people."

Fresh out of college, Preston struggled to balance work and play, a particular challenge when so much of his work revolved around understanding precisely what interested and delighted a generation of young people, essentially his peers. He logged into Tumblr for clues about what was on the horizon. He attended events in Central

Park—meetups that allowed folks who were online friends to connect in person. Often these gatherings would transform into makeshift marketplaces—Etsy in the wild—where young people who were creating T-shirts or music at home brought their products to sell or simply to elicit feedback.

"They were all bedroom creatives," Preston said. "They're all the coolest, freshest kids from a style standpoint. I would go; I would learn about the meetups, and I would just go by myself and put myself in their midst."

In many ways, Preston was doing what Abloh was doing: listening to what kids had to say and figuring out how to give them what they desired. Preston was doing that in quirky meetups. Abloh was doing it as a deejay and as the approachable one in Kanye West's crowd.

Preston absorbed kids' fascination with brands, fashion, and style. The market research was the easy part. Preston fumbled as he got used to the corporate nature of Nike—a company that, despite its focus on youth culture, still demanded regular conference calls, planning sessions, and prepared presentations. Preston learned that even when the company hosted a boozy off-site meeting in Atlantic City, there was no excuse for turning up late for the next morning's meeting. Preston endured a head-throbbing walk of shame on his way to learning what it meant to exist in the corporate world.

One day, while Preston was working on programming at the Nike store on Bowery, where customization of sneakers was the big draw, Abloh walked in fresh from touring with Kanye West. Abloh explained that he and a few other guys were joining forces and throwing parties. Did Preston want to participate in their latest project?

Abloh had become an experienced party impresario and deejay. He drew on his connections and his connections' connections to populate his parties with entertainers, sneaker fans, fashion obsessives, and style aficionados. His mix of music—hip-hop, rock, electronic—bound the eclectic group together and injected an inclusive, freewheeling energy into the room.

"Ever since college, I have this knack for hosting, for making sure that everything is smooth. So I was naturally drawn to deejaying because you curate people's experience," Abloh said. "It's a very intense form of hosting. My style is to play Joy Division next to Wu-Tang next to an obscure Miles Davis song. In the right room, people's minds will open.

"Having these different outlets to express these small ideas," Abloh said, "leads to more ideas."

Even as Abloh was traveling the world working with West, he kept a foothold in Chicago. His family was there. And it was his home base, his cultural community, and his proving ground. Partnering with Don Crawley, the two opened a boutique in Wicker Park called RSVP Gallery. Situated underground, with the name plastered across the squat building's basement windows, the store featured the brands that delighted and intrigued Abloh during his travels. Customers entered through a glass door and stepped down into a neon-lit space whose wares reflected Abloh's fashion interests: high-end labels such as Comme des Garçons, street brand A Bathing Ape, and artists including Kaws. The store aimed to bridge the divides between art, music, and fashion in all their iterations. The sheer audacity and breadth of the shop was its calling card, and it inspired the young men and women who crossed its threshold.

"Don C and I started the shop as a creative outlet and to bring pieces of what we have seen around the world back to Chicago," Abloh said. "Along the way, it's been rewarding to see it as a brand and a platform for kids to be creative and learn under us. We actually [sic] all learning as we self-taught ourselves how the business works. Boutiques like these are in my mind modern museums."

To celebrate the shop's grand opening in 2009, the owners hosted a party at the Harris Theater's Rooftop Terrace overlooking Millennium Park. With a line of guests snaking beyond the entrance, the event drew Chicago-born rapper Common and the British singer Mr. Hudson, who was a Kanye West collaborator, among others. Abloh arrived wearing a black T-shirt and a gold necklace. He wasn't deejaying that evening, but he held his own among an audience of music producers and performers. He wasn't a rapper or a singer, but he was Chicago famous and an integral part of West's creative team.

Abloh's love of deejaying begat an entertainment brand called Super Fun. And Super Fun parties at JBar on North Rush Street in Chicago were a magnet for a racially and ethnically diverse crowd who came for the atmosphere, the cocktails, and the mix of music that, because it was Abloh, ranged from hip-hop to techno to European pop. Super Fun was an expression of Abloh's ability to create a community that was drawn together by its interests rather than the tribal affiliations that tend to segregate dance parties into Black or White, gay or straight, city or suburbs. Super Fun parties became a place for fashion debuts, as well as birthday bashes, including a memorable one for West's tour deejay Million Dollar Mano.

Advance marketing warned guests to arrive early rather than risk being boxed out of the small, narrow lounge with its mirrored walls. As revelers danced and drank, Abloh's Ray-Ban-style sunglasses were perched on his nose as he held a bottle of Hennessy Black cognac aloft. Behind the deejay booth, reflected in the club's mirrors, were prints of artist Takashi Murakami's jellyfish eyes floating amid the Louis Vuitton logo—a collaboration initiated by Marc Jacobs.

Super Fun parties—and the ethos behind them—turned them into a point of connection. Like most deejays, Abloh understood what moved a crowd. Music had always been the connective tissue that joined disparate groups of people; it was a delivery system for art and politics; it was a source of ecstatic release. Music was a form of currency, drawing people close and making them fall in love with whatever was wrapped in the beats and rhythms of a song, whether it was a model sashaying down a runway or an art project unfolding against a penetrating soundtrack. Super Fun parties weren't simply about music and dancing; they were emblematic of a particular mindset. Party promotion, deejaying, if done well, became a kind of human alchemy. Being able to bring together the right folks in a place that broke down inhibitions and fired up the senses was a superpower that translated into constituent building. It gave those who were adept at deejaying an understanding of what excited people, what created a spark that leapt from one person to the next until an entire room was aglow.

The answer was sometimes as simple as a particular song, or just a few beats of a song, that thrilled a crowd. More often, the answer was more complicated, more nuanced. It meant tapping into emotions in a way that felt unforced and organic. Party promotion was the art of wooing customers with the possibility of pleasure. The product being sold was a vision of themselves belonging to something bigger than the individual.

Abloh also deejayed under the pseudonym Flat White. And as his reputation grew, he transformed from an aural Wizard of Oz, an almost hidden figure orchestrating the mood and energy of a party from a distant corner or a platform looming above the dance floor, into a personality working in the thick of it all. During a set at the EDITION Hotel in London, fans hovered around Abloh—acolytes watching a mad scientist at work. They weren't dancing. They vibrated hypnotically to his rhythms.

It was a funny thing to watch the crowd as it watched Abloh. Distant from the dancers and swaying revelers, a group of young men would gather around him, listening but also mesmerized, as he manipulated technology, that is to say his blending of genres, in a way that sounded effortless and inevitable. Their presence was marked by their studious intensity. They found pleasure in the music. But there was also a single-minded focus—as if they were memorizing precisely how one beat merged into another. They collected these moments of delight for future examination and rumination instead of consuming them on site. Abloh was their teacher as well as a contemporary. His students were in awe of him.

ABLOH WAS MAKING T-SHIRTS TOO. At the time, there were few T-shirts with as much audacity and impact as the ones that grew out of Abloh's newest party project, the one that Heron Preston was invited to join that day in the Nike store. It was called Been Trill.

The idea for Been Trill began as a lark, a goof, a confection. It was a distraction born out of endless brainstorming sessions and data collection in service to the creative demands of West. It was a brand built on a font.

Abloh had settled into the long hours and constant travel that his job required. He had a friend on the road, someone else who thrived amid the creative cacophony: Matthew Williams. They were both intensely curious and engaging background players in a world of center stage performers.

Abloh and Williams, despite having been raised in different parts of the country, were kindred spirits. Williams was born in Evanston, Illinois, but grew up in Pismo Beach, a town on the central coast of California, halfway between Los Angeles and San Francisco. Williams had been a top-notch high school soccer player who loved fashion, skate culture, and music. Like almost everyone growing up in the nineties, Williams loved rap, but he'd also been introduced to techno by a cousin who lived in Los Angeles and partied at raves. But it wasn't until Williams went to Europe to play soccer that he really saw the way techno could move a crowd. He was sixteen when he attended his first massive rave in Norway. Everyone was in the public square, drinking beer and dancing. Williams had never seen anything like it. It was so distant from his comfort zone of skate parks and beaches. The scene defied the notion that America was the center of the cultural universe; it informed him; it dazzled him.

Williams came home and enrolled at the University of California Santa Barbara, where he continued to play soccer and also studied art. He left within a year. He wanted to focus on fashion. He applied to Parsons School of Design, but when he wasn't admitted he set out to get a job in the field to which he was drawn. Like Abloh, he came to fashion by a circuitous route.

"Fashion is so multidimensional; you get to work in music and architecture and there's a performance aspect to it," Williams said. "When I started, you'd see great, great fashion out at night. Or if you went to a runway show, it was like this secret window.

"It wasn't as instantaneous as it is now," he said. "It was like this really awesome happening where you would see people and meet people and hear music you maybe hadn't heard before."

Fashion was serendipitous.

When Williams began to work in the field, he was only nineteen. When he moved from Pismo Beach to Los Angeles and then off into the wider world, he established connections with people who had similar interests and aspirations. They weren't his competition; they were his inspiration.

Among his many jobs, Williams worked as an assistant to the art director Willo Perron. The Montreal-born Perron designed American Apparel stores and, after moving to Los Angeles, began a long professional relationship with Kanye West that began with an edit of his closet and soon led to Perron collaborating with Abloh on the artwork and packaging of West's album *808s & Heartbreak*.

In the early 2000s, a musician still needed to have the star power of Madonna or Elton John before high-end brands would dress them. It was an additional challenge to convince most designers to lend clothes to hip-hop performers. Groundbreaking stylists such as Misa Hylton and June Ambrose were de facto designers, often creating the looks worn by their clients rather than borrowing them from preexisting fashion collections or commissioning them from luxury firms. Williams found his niche creating clothes for musicians who wanted a distinctive style. He worked with Erin Hirsh on a jacket with LED lights for Kanye West, and the musician wore the otherworldly ensemble when he performed "Stronger" at the 2008 Grammy Awards. The song made mention of West's many fashion loves, from his own label Pastelle—one of his earliest attempts as a fashion designer—to A Bathing Ape (BAPE) and Louis Vuitton.

Williams worked with—and dated—Lady Gaga, crafting the costuming that she wore both onstage and on the street. He learned how to help musicians articulate their style sensibility, and he became a reliable source for one-of-a-kind designs. Soon enough, Williams had become a permanent part of West's creative circle, working on Pastelle, album covers, and the like.

Williams was a striking presence. He had a slim, athletic build and sandy-colored hair that he wore slicked back, platinum tipped, buzz cut, and chopped into a Flock of Seagulls–meets–Mohawk asymmetrical sculpture. His most distinguishing feature was a tattoo of a black cross that ran down the nape of his neck. He was most often seen dressed in black, as if he was rebelling against a childhood of sunshine and beaches. When his face settled into a resting expression, it had an intense, almost brooding mien. But when he was animated, those same features softened, turning almost impish.

He and Abloh became globe-hopping pals touring with West, working relentlessly, and settling into a rhythm of making the impossible possible.

"We were traveling around the world, and there were still these microuniverses in each city. London's creative and music community didn't feel like Paris, which didn't feel like Tokyo. It didn't feel like L.A. It didn't feel like New York," Williams said. "We were able to travel the world before social media was as it is, and online marketing, and really be a part of all these cities for a few months. And that was just super inspirational."

This was a time before everything was available everywhere. The clothes one could buy in Los Angeles were different from those in Paris. The sense of discovery was tremendous. They made connections in a way that felt intimate and organic. Later, social media would connect all those microuniverses. But for the moment, each new city was a revelation of people, fashion, and music. Their learning curve was steep, but it was firsthand and intimate.

Williams and Abloh even deejayed together in Brussels inside the Atomium. The modernist structure, created for the 1958 World's Fair, was modeled after an iron crystal that had been magnified 165 billion times. Its shiny steel orbs towered 335 feet over the city and served as an exhibition space, as well as a vantage point for sweeping views of the city. The Belgian photographer Pierre Debusschere had rented the space for his birthday party.

Wherever they were, whatever new city or physically discombobulating time zone they woke up in, there was music. They'd pull up a song on their laptop and try to impress one another with their eclectic curation.

London was the birthplace of Been Trill. During West's 2011 tour for the album *Watch the Throne,* when Williams and Abloh and a group of friends were holed up in the Lanesborough Hotel, they decided to deejay together. They wanted to play the music that they loved but that they weren't hearing when they went to clubs. The name was meant to suggest a band; the specific words were a merging of *been,* as in not recent, and *trill,* a portmanteau of *true* and *real.*

But Been Trill was not just a group of any friends. These were folks who'd forged connections with musicians, fashion editors, and style savants. Each of them chose a stage name. Preston took Maserati Flamez. Williams was Pretty Blanco. Another member, Justin Saunders, founder of the blog *JJJJound*—a visual clearing-house of stylish imagery—who was also working with West, was JRS Rules. Florencia Galarza, a former star soccer player turned fashion editor, simply went by Flo. Abloh chose Pyrex Vision. And West was a kind of shadow member.

"We started throwing parties together, but as we're all creatives, we started making T-shirts to deejay in. We thought it was really funny to kind of appear like a boy band," Preston said. "We all got our own hats, and we customized them with our own deejay name."

It wasn't long before Been Trill was a subculture sensation, a hashtag, and a fashion line. Been Trill had a tremendous run. The collective deejayed backstage and at afterparties during West's "Watch the Throne" tour, which was a collaboration with Jay-Z. Been Trill performed in Cannes, France. They were one of nine "non-headlining bands you must see" at Coachella in 2013. They were a collective of connected creatives, most of whom had little experience as professional deejays, a lack that didn't give Abloh a moment of hesitation. The crew would learn how to deejay simply by doing it. Their shameless chutzpah was part of their allure.

"There was something so interesting and fascinating," said Julie Gilhart, a fashion talent scout. "They were stylish, and they were daring."

When the friends turned to fashion, their approach was simple. They made T-shirts emblazoned with the words "Been Trill." And the font? It was a sort of "Rocky Horror," dripping, fun-house style. They'd dug up the font as an option for one of West's projects, but he'd rejected it. They resurrected it for their off-the-clock pursuit.

To be clear, there wasn't anything special about the T-shirts themselves. Been Trill was a brand more than anything else. It offered fans bragging rights about their insider knowledge, creative affiliations, and appreciation of a different kind of luxury—one that was defined by a diverse youth culture and street style, rather than some European legacy brand. By traditional measures, there was nothing that made a Been Trill T-shirt worth its $100 price other than the people associated with it. The brand didn't connote status as much as it meant connection. A customer buys Chanel because it signifies wealth. People bought Been Trill because it identified them as part of a group. The buy-in was expensive, perhaps even absurd, but it wasn't prohibitive. And instead of a fan base of skateboarders or sneaker enthusiasts or basketball fans, it was creative individuals who spanned music, fashion, and art.

"Been Trill was an open source idea," Abloh said. "It was inclusive. It was the opposite of elitist. Usually a downtown community based in, sort of, streetwear or skate culture, usually has this air of 'We're cool and you're not.' That collective of us, we preached fun."

The established fashion industry didn't really know what to make of Been Trill. Some just saw it as a line of amusing, overpriced T-shirts. Others viewed it as part of a seismic shift in fashion, a change that meant design didn't matter as much as affiliation and branding. Would Been Trill spark the kind of breathless desire that Supreme stirred among its fans who were willing to pay a premium for anything emblazoned with its logo? Would it take on a meaning and value that could transfer to anything it touched—even a discarded brick? Or was Been Trill merely an entrepreneurial gambit by savvy young people with famous friends?

It was all those things, including a fortuitous blend of timing and buzz. Been Trill burned white hot and then quickly burned out. The business was sold to the mall brand PacSun in 2015 and in a postmortem by StockX, the online reseller with an expertise in streetwear, the assessment was biting: "The brand itself is a perfect example of what influencer marketing could do for those who had the connections. With little to no substance to hold the brand up, the collaborative project was still able to thrive early on through the unrealistic level of hype the brand portrayed."

Members of the collective took the experience—and the knowledge gained from it—and poured it into individual projects. A single seed planted in the ground might go unnoticed, but when an entire field starts to blossom with saplings and seedlings, it's hard to deny that a new season is at hand.

IN LOS ANGELES, another deejay with a love of fashion was dabbling in a similar kind of voodoo as Abloh. Jerry Lorenzo had been throwing parties and blending music across genres with a goal of creating a social scene that broke down the usual walls. Now Lorenzo wanted to force fashion to rethink the role of Black men in both the back office and the atelier.

Although Lorenzo lived for a time in Chicago, he'd gotten to know Abloh in Los Angeles, which Abloh frequently visited in service to West and his ongoing fashion dreams.

"When I would go back to Chicago, I would hit [Virgil's] parties, and when he would come to L.A., he would hit my parties," Lorenzo said. "The connection was not necessarily deejaying at the time, but it was more like 'Hey, I like the community that you built in Los Angeles.' 'I like the community that you built in Chicago.' It was more mutual respect for one another."

Lorenzo, who is Black, straddled multiple worlds. Born Jerry Lorenzo Manuel Jr., he's the son of a former Major League Baseball player, coach, and manager. Lorenzo attended a high school with a mostly White student body, and the music that dominated the scene was grunge, rock, and metal. But he also worshipped at a Black church. His Black friends loved hip-hop. A multitude of different cultures overlapped in Lorenzo. He brought them all into the parties he organized. He had a great deal in common with Abloh, who often described himself as a Black kid obsessed with skateboards, BMX bikes, Nirvana, and hip-hop.

Lorenzo had dreamed of a career in sports, but after assessing his own abilities he decided that the likeliest route to that goal would be in an office rather than on the field. So he studied business in graduate school at Loyola Marymount University and worked in retail at The Gap, Diesel, and Dolce&Gabbana.

Lorenzo was neither tall nor bulky. He was medium size. He had a honey-colored complexion, a full beard, and long dark hair that was often braided into cornrows or pulled back into a man bun. He could just as easily slip unnoticed into a room full of hip-hop devotees as into a commune of peaceniks or the latest Hollywood members-only club. His look was simultaneously nonchalant and meticulously studied.

Lorenzo was a pool of calm. He spoke quietly in moderated tones, never getting too animated, yet never slipping into a monotone. Abloh exuded eagerness; Lorenzo oozed self-assuredness. They found common cause in the realm of fashion.

"I never intended or desired to be a part of an art community," Lorenzo said. "I love beautiful things and I'm blessed with good taste. I'm blessed with the ability to know how to present myself. I'm more so into finding solutions through clothing to help me become the best version of myself—to relieve the preconceived notions others may have of me."

During one of Abloh's visits, he and Lorenzo discussed their pet projects. Abloh was thinking about what he would do after Been Trill. Lorenzo was working on the first garments in his Fear of God brand—a name that reflected his Christian faith rather than any sense of secular irony. He had a family and he'd decided to try his hand in the fashion business as a way of removing himself from the late-night, all-consuming grind of organizing and promoting parties. He was tired of looking out over the crowd and noticing how many of the guests had their own fashion companies—not just guys silk-screening T-shirts on the side, but guys with full-fledged collections that fell under the umbrella of streetwear thanks to their heavy reliance on hoodies, cargo pants, and, of course, T-shirts. Lorenzo believed he had a better sense of style than all of them. He knew he had an eye for proportions and shapes.

So he made some T-shirts. They were the business plan, the marketing proposal, and the communications pitch all in one. Lorenzo was ready to build equity for himself. He knew that founders of brands such as Crooks & Castles, Black Scale, The Hundreds, Diamond Supply Co., and Supreme were making far more money than he was, and it didn't seem as though they were laboring into the wee hours. These were not stylistically innovative clothes. What mattered was the graphic designs on them, the branding, and the sense of identity that their consumers found by purchasing them.

"I just honestly, narcissistically, felt if I can dress better than these guys, I should be able to figure this out," Lorenzo said.

So Lorenzo invited Abloh to come to his house and see what he'd cooked up and had stored in his garage. Lorenzo gave Abloh a few pieces from the collection, and Abloh passed them to West. A few weeks later, West asked Lorenzo to come to Atlantic City to show him the entire line. Lorenzo arrived with his samples and a book of photographs showing the collection on models. One of his T-shirts spoke volumes about how Lorenzo planned to distinguish himself. West saw how much thought and precision had gone into its actual design, a sensibility that some said reminded them of Rick Owens, who merged sensuality and gothic romance in his work. So West did what he had been doing ever since he set his sights on fashion. He latched on to Lorenzo, asking him to fly to Paris to help him with a fashion project—*yet another fashion project, always another fashion project*—that he'd taken on in collaboration with the French brand A.P.C., which focused on minimalist basics with just enough flair to distinguish them as relevant to the times without being trendy. It was France's version of The Gap. Lorenzo agreed.

"I was brought into that conversation, into that group of creatives, because of my knack for clothing at the time. Although I was just self-taught and learning how to communicate through clothing, Kanye still saw the perspective; he understood the perspective. And he respected the perspective more than he respected the craft at that time," Lorenzo said.

Lorenzo stepped into the creative circus that was West's enduring desire for fashion greatness. They were young men figuring out the fashion industry as they moved through it together. Lorenzo stayed with West for a handful of years, working on A.P.C., on tour merchandise, and finally on West's partnership with Adidas, which became Yeezy—a monochromatic sportswear collection of streetwear-inspired basics with a luxury price point.

In all of this, Abloh was the ringmaster, keeping order and meeting deadlines. But he had plans for himself. That same day that he saw the beginnings of Lorenzo's Fear of God, he shared that he'd just finished a short film to introduce his own solo stab at fashion.

"We were just trying to get to the best product no matter what we were working on. We were continuing to throw things against the wall and see if it stuck. How do we get it to stick?" Lorenzo said. "We loved sneakers. We loved fashion. We loved music. We loved all these things, and we wanted to express ourselves through each of these different platforms and mediums."

Lorenzo admired luxury fashion: the fabrics, the construction, the way it made one feel. He wanted to build a luxury brand that reflected his style, an easy athletic sensibility combined with polish and informality. Abloh loved unexpected juxtapositions, clothes that bridged the divide between cultures—and that had the emotional pull of the biggest luxury brands.

"I think our strength is that we're brand fanatics," Abloh said. "We're brand loyal and we fight for them. We believe in them." And what Abloh had planned for his next project was one of the most audacious acts of branding that the fashion industry had seen.

The Art Project and Something for Himself

IN THE FALL OF 2012, Abloh introduced the world, or basically anyone paying attention to his social media feed, to Pyrex Vision. He referred to the New York presentation, titled "Youth Always Wins," as an art project.

Pyrex Vision didn't debut with a runway show, but rather was a live tableau in service to the creation of a film. As artist Jim Joe spray-painted "time wounds all heals" and "don't save money take a taxi" on a blank wall, a diverse group of young men—members of the burgeoning hip-hop collective A$AP Mob—moved with a nonchalant swagger as they sat and posed on a single bench in a plain white loft, a makeshift workspace for Donda. In the background, a soundtrack blasted music. Instead of contemporary hip-hop, Abloh chose "Heart and Soul" from the 1980 album *Closer,* by the British rock band Joy Division, which blended a postpunk sensibility with electronic music.

A pair of large windows on the models' left offered a view of . . . nothing. Overhead industrial lighting plunged the models' faces in shadow and left much of the clothing—in basic hues of red, blue, yellow, and black—in shadow too. It was just as well. There was little nuanced or subtle about the cut or fabrics of Pyrex Vision.

The points of interest were the music and what was printed on the clothing, and that was clear from fifty paces. The clothing consisted of Champion sportswear—hoodies and T-shirts and long shorts. Abloh described the scene as depicting a team without a sport.

On the front of the hoodies, Abloh reproduced Caravaggio's *The Entombment of Christ*. The painting, completed in 1604, depicts the body of Christ, having been removed from the cross, being carried by his followers who gently place him on a slab. Caravaggio's poetic use of light and shadow are evident. And it's almost as if Abloh attempted to recreate that drama with the harsh lighting and murky shadows in his film. The painting also called to mind the *Closer* album cover, which was designed by the British art director Peter Saville and featured a black-and-white photograph of a carving depicting the body of Christ on a funeral altar.

On the back of the Champion hoodies and on the shorts and T-shirts and flannel shirts, Abloh silk-screened "Pyrex," along with the number 23. Pyrex 23.

"I branded it to death," Abloh said.

The Pyrex name recalled a 2006 song by Clipse, the Virginia Beach–based hip-hop duo made up of Pusha T and No Malice. Their song "Mr. Me Too," which featured Pharrell Williams—and was also produced by Williams as part of the Neptunes—was a braggadocious rap about personal style as well as a reprimand to those who copied the chosen luxuries of others. The music video highlighted private planes, Lamborghinis, and Cristal champagne. It objectified women. The lyrics referenced A Bathing Ape, Ice Cream—a line founded by Williams and Nigo—Louis Vuitton, and Versace. It also included the line "Pyrex stirs turned into Cavalli furs," meaning that the lucrative work of crack dealing had financed the purchase of designer furs. (Pyrex was the glassware of choice for heating cocaine to transform it into its smokable form: an off-white rock of crack cocaine.) And, of course, the "23" was a reference to basketball legend Michael Jordan's jersey number with the Chicago Bulls.

"My first encounters around Virgil were surrounding Hawaii while working on [West's album] *My Beautiful Dark Twisted Fantasy*," recalled Pusha T. "Virgil was very quiet, often on a laptop off to the corner. He was this guy that Kanye seemed very interested in what was on his laptop. We could be in the middle of verses or trying to crack the code on a beat, but he would always stop to see what Virgil had going on on his laptop. Virgil was the one who could break the flow of the music with whatever was going on with his laptop. I noticed that quickly. You would get a glimpse of [Virgil's laptop], and it could be a hoodie, a desk, a table, or architecture."

Abloh "was very open in speaking about Clipse music to me," he added. "I remember it from the laptop, like the actual word and font on the screen. He was like, 'Yo, check this out. Pyrex Vision? Understand, this comes from you.'"

The film and the clothes reflected Abloh's obsession with cultural touchstones, his catholic tastes, his liberal cross-referencing, his disregard for orthodoxy, and his comfort with appropriation. The graphics served as a form of gatekeeping, with each level of understanding getting a person further and further "inside" his growing group of collaborators and their hierarchy of cool. They reflected his belief that fashion could appeal to both the tourist and the purist—the person who just admired a graphic for its color or shape, and the person who was keenly aware of every reference and innuendo. At its most high-minded, Pyrex Vision offered a counterargument to the limitations too often felt by young men without means. The route out of poverty was not only through drugs, sports, or rap. Art was an option too, a viable one—and a cool one.

The film was personal. Abloh described the collection as a convergence of his youthful obsessions: Pusha T and drug raps, Champion brand gym clothes, Michael Jordan as a god, Kurt Cobain and grunge rock and Caravaggio paintings. It was a mood board of "a Black kid with White tendencies."

Brands such as Gucci and Louis Vuitton that have transformed their origin stories into a form of mythmaking had nothing on Pyrex Vision. Abloh's art project was steeped in its own mythology, tribal references, artful flourishes, and whispers of intrigue.

Pyrex Vision was also audacious. Been Trill ruffled feathers with its $100 T-shirts. Abloh charged five times as much for flannel shirts—ones that he had neither designed nor manufactured. But he *had* created a graphic with an emotional pull.

He'd purchased the flannel shirts from Ralph Lauren's Rugby line. The division, established in 2004, was marketed to customers in their teens and twenties. And while it aligned with the company's signature preppy sensibility, it had a tad more of a boisterous, rebel edge. But it wasn't a success story. The company announced Rugby's closure in 2012 and Abloh scooped up discounted, discontinued merchandise. Rugby Ralph Lauren originally sold the shirts for $79.95, then discounted them to $35.99. Abloh sold his screen-printed versions for $550.

The writer Jian DeLeon noted this 700 percent markup in a story for *Complex* magazine. "There's no arguing that often 'luxury goods' get by more on brand cachet than craftsmanship," DeLeon wrote in 2013. "While the streetwear world has long played on the convention of flipping high-fashion imagery and re-contextualizing in a cultural cool context, Abloh and company's hustle consists of a different sort of swagger jacking.

"Should Abloh be called out for blatantly ripping people off? Or is this absurdity reflective of the current status of the hype game?" DeLeon wondered. "Yes, it's egregious that these Rugby shirts became such a coveted streetwear item, but what's worse is that they *sold out*."

The success of those Pyrex shirts forced a consideration of how the traditional rules of fashion were breaking down and how Abloh was relating to the industry with a sense of nonchalant privilege that, coming from a Black man, landed like a thunderclap.

The cotton shirt as designed and manufactured by Ralph Lauren originally sold for $79.95. That wasn't the intrinsic value of the shirt. That wasn't a measure of the creative effort, the cotton fabric, the labor, and the marketing. It was the sum of all of that, plus, most significantly, the value of the Rugby Ralph Lauren imprimatur. That was composed of the company's reputation, the experience of shopping in one of the Rugby stores, the feeling of walking out with a tastefully packaged purchase and the knowledge that people might look at that shirt with its recognizable label and be impressed. Ralph Lauren was, after all, a beloved brand in the broader culture as well as within hip-hop and street style. With a $550 price tag, Abloh proposed that *his* imprimatur was worth more than Ralph Lauren's. Or at the very least, that when his mark was combined with Lauren's the sum was greater than the individual elements.

This wasn't just wishful thinking; it was lucrative. The numbers added up. If one were to make a back-of-the-envelope estimate of operating profit, Abloh's was in the ballpark of $400 versus Ralph Lauren's $20. Customers assigned a "cool value," a desirability rating, to Abloh's Pyrex 23 flannel shirts that was twenty times that of the shirts in their original state. Abloh didn't yet have a fashion company, but he already had a clear sense of his own value in a changing fashion ecosystem.

"If he didn't charge what he had charged for those pieces, I don't think it would have been as controversial. I think that was part of it. Having those high prices really just got people talking about it," DeLeon said. "No one could really foresee the value in saying, 'My ideas are worth how much my ideas are worth,' which I guess is the statement."

The market might have reeled, but it didn't cave. It was no longer outrageous to see T-shirts priced well over $100. Back in 2006, Abloh mused about this in one of his posts for *The Brilliance*. He'd wandered into a Gucci shop and noticed that the company was selling T-shirts that riffed on the Gucci knockoffs that street vendors once sold on city corners or at flea markets. "Gucci is now making real versions of their heavily bootlegged tees. Of course, they are $200 something. Yes $200 bucks for a tee shirt . . . and no I didnt [*sic*] buy it. I am not rich, but I am immune to sticker shock these days. Hence why I still think the idea is awesome."

By 2011, Givenchy designer Riccardo Tisci was selling a black T-shirt with the giant face of an open-mouthed rottweiler printed on the front for $265. The shirt debuted in his men's collection, and it was immediately embraced by celebrities from Liv Tyler to Kanye West. There was nothing special about the shape of the shirt or the material. The graphic, combined with the cachet of the French brand, combined with the community of boldface names who immediately embraced it, sold it to everyone else. The rottweiler shirt was a fashion moment—one of those unexpected instances when a particular garment becomes *the* garment for a small window of time. It's often impossible to discern what lit the fuse that sent something skyrocketing into desirability. It's an alchemy of timing, concept, and the right messenger. Models walked down the runway wearing that graphic print just when menswear was beginning to drive the fashion conversation, and editors, celebrities, and fashion lovers were taking notice. Good fashion no longer meant trying to reinvent the shirt; it could be as simple as a good screen print.

To be clear, Tisci had the traditional training of a designer. He'd graduated from London's Central Saint Martins. He'd briefly had his own label before he joined Givenchy. But the simple graphic T-shirt made him a lead protagonist in luxury's shift toward streetwear. It was also an implicit acknowledgment of a rising skepticism about

FAR LEFT: At Boylan Catholic High School, Virgil Abloh was a devoted soccer player and snagged jersey number 23 on the varsity team.

LEFT: At Boylan Catholic High School, Abloh was a minority among minorities.

Abloh's time studying architecture at the Illinois Institute of Technology in Chicago informed his understanding of graphic design, structure, and organization. He presented his work during a studio review in 2006 to Susan Conger-Austin, who is partially hidden; and (r to l) David Chipperfield, the visiting Morgenstern Chair at IIT; and Martha Thorne, who is the former dean of the architecture school at IE University in Madrid and was the executive director of the Pritzker Architecture Prize.

One of Abloh's early side projects was BeenTrill, a DJ'ing collective that transformed into a T-shirt business and fashion industry phenomenon. Abloh is pictured in 2013, during New York Fashion Week, behind the turntable with (l to r) Matthew Williams and Heron Preston.

ABOVE: After years of rejecting attention to his race, designer Ozwald Boateng (center, in green), who broke ground as the first Black creative director for Givenchy menswear, mounted a 2019 fashion show in Harlem that celebrated his African roots.

RIGHT: Trailblazer Edward Buchanan worked with Abloh at Off-White. The two are pictured in Paris in March 2019 at a presentation of PIECES, a collaboration by Andre Walker and Maison Yves Salomon.

In a few short years, Abloh went from competing for the LVMH Prize to judging it alongside (l to r) designers Marc Jacobs, Stella McCartney, and Kim Jones.

PHOTO:
STELLA McCARTNEY

Virgil Abloh was deeply influenced by the work of graphic designer Peter Saville and considered him a mentor.

PHOTO:
FLO KOHL

Abloh's introduction to Paris Fashion Week was alongside his employer, mentor, and friend Kanye West (center, with briefcase). Their technicolor ensembles left an enduring mark on the industry and pop culture.

PHOTO: TOMMY TON

PHOTO: COURTESY NIKE, INC.

Abloh's collaboration with Nike blasted his name and reputation around the world.

RIGHT: Nike asked Abloh to reimagine some of its most popular sneaker styles in a project referred to as The Ten. Abloh deconstructed the sneakers and added his beloved quotation marks.

ABOVE LEFT: For his womenswear, Abloh was inspired by Princess Diana, who died in 1997, when Abloh was seventeen, a year he described as pivotal to his design sensibility.

ABOVE RIGHT: In his Fall 2019 Louis Vuitton show, Abloh highlighted Michael Jackson's pop culture influence. The timing unexpectedly coincided with the release of a documentary that accused the singer of inappropriate relationships with children. Direct references to Jackson were pulled from the Louis Vuitton collection.

RIGHT: Hazard stripes were one Abloh's favorite branding marks— these are from his Spring 2019 Off-White men's collection.

PHOTOS: JONAS GUSTAVSSON

ABOVE LEFT: Quotation marks introduced irony and a whiff of intellectualism. These boots are from his Fall 2019 Off-White collection.

ABOVE RIGHT: This sweater, with the silhouette of Dorothy and her friends, was one of the most whimsical elements in Abloh's Louis Vuitton debut.

LEFT: Abloh's harnesses from his Louis Vuitton debut found their way to the red carpet worn by Timothée Chalamet and Michael B. Jordan.

PHOTOS: JONAS GUSTAVSSON

When Abloh took his first bow at Louis Vuitton, it was an emotional moment and the culmination of a journey that began with a T-shirt.

PHOTO: JONAS GUSTAVSSON

The Miami Louis Vuitton menswear show in November 2021 became a memorial to Abloh and included a building-size statue of the designer.

expertise. Expertise—technical skills, draping experience—was losing its value. Hypercreativity was still admired, but it was no longer the driving factor. It was becoming a specialized part of the fashion sphere rather than the reason fashion existed at all. Fashion was betting heavily on buzz and group dynamics to sell its products.

After all, fashion doesn't exist in a vacuum. It isn't immune to the winds of social change or politics. Musicians no longer needed to play an instrument, read music, or have perfect pitch. Graffiti was art, and a urinal could propel an aesthetic movement. Then why should fashion be tied to design degrees, lengthy apprenticeships, and deep experience in retail, publishing, or public relations? The editors and critics who looked at fashion from the front rows of shows were decreasing in number and clout. While they still had the ability to decide whom to feature on the cover of a magazine or place fashion into the broader cultural context, they competed with social media influencers for the attention and fealty of shoppers.

AS ABLOH'S CAREER in fashion blossomed, he'd often talk about his belief in a do-it-yourself approach to design and entrepreneurship. Transparency was part of his philosophy. He was the magician who believed in revealing just how he'd pulled off his tricks.

"Can you still be the wizard but give people a look at the inner workings of Oz?" DeLeon wondered.

Abloh and his friends regularly spoke of their admiration for legacy luxury houses such as Louis Vuitton and a raft of traditionally trained designers. Indeed, Louis Vuitton was a point of bonding between Abloh and Benjamin Edgar of *The Brilliance*. When the two first met in New York City after getting to know each other virtually, they indulged in a shopping spree. "We met at the airport arrivals, jumped in a cab and headed to Hotel Rivington, dropped our stuff, and headed out to our first stop, a shared personal favorite . . . the Louis Vuitton store in Soho," Edgar wrote on the blog. "That first time Virgil and I hung for a weekend in NYC, in 2006, at the Soho Louis Vuitton store . . . we each purchased a Wapity. I bought a classic one, which I still have, and he bought the white Murakami design of course."

The Wapity was a small Louis Vuitton clutch with a hand strap. It could hold a few essentials—a mobile phone, keys, a credit card— and not much more. It was a starter purchase, a way to lay claim to fashion as status.

Even as he admired trained designers and could sometimes be awestruck by the clothes and accessories they produced, Abloh did not let his lack of technical training hinder his ambition. And the truth was that myriad well-known designers were, in fact, self-taught. It was not that uncommon for a designer to have found success in fashion without a degree from Central Saint Martins or Parsons or the Fashion Institute of Technology. Some had a background in architecture or industrial design or retailing and then shifted their attention to building their own fashion brand. Indeed, Raf Simons, whom Abloh lionized, studied industrial design before he became entranced by fashion after attending a Martin Margiela show. Simons went on not only to design his own menswear collection but to hold the top creative jobs at Jil Sander, Dior, and Calvin Klein, with each chapter in his career hailed as a creative—if not financial—success. Each chapter was also profoundly influential.

Abloh was an outsider, but so were a lot of other designers until they made their way inside. Giorgio Armani originally planned to go into medicine but then worked in fashion merchandising. Tommy Hilfiger began his fashion career by reselling bell-bottom jeans from the trunk of his Volkswagen Beetle in his hometown of Elmira, New York. Tory Burch worked in public relations. American designer Thom Browne, whose shrunken gray flannel suits transformed the silhouette of trousers and jackets for an entire generation of men, had a degree in business. Tom Ford studied architecture while at Parsons and essentially talked and fibbed his way into his first fashion apprenticeship.

Long before Abloh and his cohorts came along, fashion had lowered its barriers to entry. It just hadn't lowered them for everyone. No Black American outsider had ever broken through to the highest circles of fashion. Edward Buchanan had a degree from Parsons before his job at Bottega Veneta. Lawrence Steele, who worked in Milan for decades, spent years as a design assistant at Moschino and Prada before launching his own brand and then becoming creative director of Aspesi in 2021. And in 2004, California-born Patrick Robinson became creative director of Paco Rabanne, after having graduated from Parsons.

They found success, but none had tried to do so while maintaining such an intellectual disregard for industry traditions. Abloh didn't bluff his way into salons and boardrooms by pretending he was something that he was not. He convinced fashion that it needed him just as he was.

PYREX VISION WAS SHORT-LIVED, but so much about it tested the boundaries of fashion. How far could the rules be pushed before they simply gave way? How did the industry define originality? What did it even mean to be a designer? Abloh insisted that Pyrex Vision was an art experiment, but retailers purchased the clothes. Editors eagerly photographed the collection. "It was very, very cool. I *had* to get my hands on it for the magazine," said Jim Moore, who was the creative director of *GQ*.

And everyone mused about the legitimacy of it all. Abloh had a convincing way of speaking about his work. He made it sound important. It was his "practice." He'd harken back to midcentury architecture, his beloved Mies van der Rohe, Helvetica typeface, minimalism, and brutalism. He focused on what was silk-screened onto his work and the emotions it inspired.

His creative rhetoric, as it applied to fashion, began to take shape with Pyrex Vision. Here were the first clear examples of how he thought about creativity and ownership. Everything was source material—clay that he could mold to his liking.

Abloh explained and excused his borrowing and riffing—something that was common in hip-hop and deejaying and street culture but was considered verboten in fashion—by referencing Marcel Duchamp and ready-mades. Put simply, the idea was to take preexisting objects and insert them into the realm of fine art. The act of moving the object from one context to another was the creative gesture—as when Duchamp placed a urinal in an art gallery.

But that notion was misguided in the context of fashion. "When [Duchamp] takes a urinal and presents it as a sculpture, it's not that he wants us all to look at a urinal and say, 'Isn't that a beautiful thing?' It's only about the change of categories. It's changing a category from nonart into fine art. That's the really crucial thing that happens," said art critic Blake Gopnik. "When it happens in other contexts, it doesn't have the same meaning. It's not the same thing as taking streetwear and using it for high fashion. That's mostly a change in status, in money."

Despite his references to Duchamp, Abloh wasn't taking objects and moving them into a new category. He was merely shifting ideas from one corner of the fashion industry to another, something that designers had done for eons, going at least as far back as Gabrielle "Coco" Chanel, who took the striped sweaters worn by the fishermen she encountered in Deauville and placed them into the context of womenswear for privileged ladies.

Abloh described Pyrex Vision as an art project, but he didn't need to justify or gussy up his choices by claiming an affinity to fine art. Fashion had its own power to shape society and challenge conventional wisdom. Besides, designating something as "art" wasn't up to him anyway. Art provokes a multitude of questions, often unanswerable ones. It proposes a stream of what ifs and why nots and whys. The main question most people had about Pyrex Vision was "Why are these shirts so expensive?"

"What makes me a little bit nervous about Virgil Abloh's move, and lots of fashion designers' moves, in their effort to get cultural recognition, cultural status—all of which they deserve—they want fashion to inhabit this other world of fine art, which I don't see as superior in any way," said Gopnik, author of the *Warhol* biography. "I'm perfectly willing to say that fashion is actually *more* important than fine art. We all wear it. It touches every one of us. Why turn it into this other thing? Why aspire to turning it into this weird little, tiny corner of culture? And the reason to do that, is because—for bad reasons—fine art has high status."

Fashion too often relies on collaborations with fine artists—or fine arts verbiage—to give it cultural significance. What Abloh was doing was significant without referring to art or music. He was changing fashion.

The most powerful element of Abloh's Pyrex Vision collection was rooted in his use of Ralph Lauren flannel shirts. As a style, Pyrex Vision wasn't especially inventive. But as a sociological proposition, it was tantalizing and inspiring.

Abloh bought discounted Ralph Lauren shirts. That meant something. The Polo Ralph Lauren brand stood for the American Dream. The story of its founding by a young man from the Bronx with a love for old movies and vintage cars was a fashion fairytale. The company's advertising highlighted Western vistas, East Coast cottages, Wall Street might, and preppy conservatism. The designer outfitted the U.S. Olympic teams, creating the closest thing the country had to a national uniform. Indeed, in 1998, the company donated $10 million toward the restoration of the Star-Spangled Banner. The thirty-four-by-thirty-foot flag flew after the battle of Fort McHenry during the War of 1812, and the sight of its having endured inspired Francis Scott Key to write the poem that became the national anthem. Lauren salvaged Americana.

The brand celebrated a WASP sensibility even as it portrayed a diverse America. The Ralph Lauren brand represented America as a melting pot rather than a mosaic. Its founder—né Lifshitz—was Jewish. For more than twenty years, Black models had starred in the company's advertising. Tyson Beckford became the rare male model, perhaps the only one, to achieve pop cultural name recognition thanks to his work with Polo Ralph Lauren beginning in 1993. In 2022, the brand partnered with Morehouse College and Spelman College on collections inspired by the style on these historically Black campuses. Still, the brand's touchstones of privilege and accomplishment remained inextricably linked to a White world. Its signature logo, after all, was a polo player. For Abloh to have claimed Ralph Lauren flannel shirts for his own purposes and to have valued them at a premium because of his creative touch spoke to the power of diversity in a way that resonated beyond fashion. A Black man—a son of immigrants—didn't simply lay claim to the American Dream; he announced that the Dream was more valuable because of his contribution to it.

Abloh placed young Black men in the center of the American story. And it wasn't just that they wore the clothes or personalized them with their own style flourishes, as men of color had been doing for years, Abloh presented this reimagined story as a business proposition. It was a blend of high and low: a statement about the added value of Blackness and a merging of past and present, a convergence that would point fashion toward its future.

"With Pyrex, the first thing I thought was: brilliant," said Peter

Saville. Abloh described Saville as a mentor, a designation that sat uncomfortably with the British graphic designer because he would never claim to have taught Abloh or counseled him on anything. Nonetheless, Saville's impact runs throughout Abloh's work—both visually and aurally.

Saville, who was born in Manchester, cofounded Factory Records in 1978. It was the home label of Joy Division, which later evolved into New Order. He also helped to establish the Haçienda nightclub in his hometown. The Haçienda was a revered temple of dance music, specifically acid house with its burbles and bleeps flitting atop basslines. The Haçienda, designed by architect Ben Kelly, opened in 1982 in a former yacht builder's warehouse. It was striking because of its airy interior interrupted by metal columns that Kelly covered in yellow and black hazard markings. Those diagonal lines became a visual shorthand for the postindustrial club whose energy and prominence helped to transform Manchester from a city of heavy industry to one with a vibrant media, music, and entertainment community.

Saville looked more like an earnest graduate student than the foundational source for some of music's most innovative visual language. His brown hair just brushed his shoulders. He wore dark-framed eyeglasses in a soft rectangular shape. The frame was delicate, not the thick, heavy-rimmed variety that has long been the default aesthetic of fashion designers, architects, and off-duty actors. He spoke slowly and precisely, comfortable with long pauses as he edited his thoughts so that they unfurled in considered paragraphs unmarred by verbal fillers.

Abloh was a student of Saville's confident blending of disparate cultural references to create something wholly new, to disrupt assumptions about what was important and what was frivolous.

Saville had used one of artist Henri Fantin-Latour's still lifes of flowers as the cover art for a New Order album. It wasn't an enormous leap for Abloh to select another classical painting—one by Caravaggio—to use on his Pyrex Vision T-shirts. Following Saville's lead, Abloh incorporated irony into his work.

The man Abloh claimed as his mentor considered irony fundamental to understanding contemporary culture. "All the things that I was drawn to and appropriated into my work, all of them, demonstrated an inflection of irony. If I took a piece of eighteenth-century typography and put it on a new-wave album in 1980, that had to be seen through a frame of ironic juxtaposition. That was the point. When I put Fantin-Latour's oil painting of roses on the New Order album *Power, Corruption & Lies,* that was a knowingly ironic gesture. That was the point of it. And, of course, that sense of slightly cynical irony pretty much has been, in a way, the most defining characteristic of our engagement with culture," Saville said. "There's nothing particularly sinister about it. It's just more worldly. It's society growing up.

"We don't expect fashion or pop music to change the world. We know it can comment; we know it can make a meaningful contribution or gesture. But we don't place unrealistic expectations on it," he said. "In a way, the most pertinent work is the work that knows what it is.

"The fashion industry continuously presents untruths, and it seems guileless in doing so," Saville added. "Virgil was very good at cutting through that."

The reluctant mentor and the exuberant mentee hadn't met when Abloh unveiled Pyrex Vision. But Abloh's name was buzzing in Saville's ears because Saville knew Kanye West. *Of course he did.* The aspiring fashion designer sought out Saville, who was based in London and widely considered one of the best graphic artists in the world—both for his work in the music industry and for his contribution to fashion brands such as Jil Sander, Burberry, Yohji Yamamoto, and Stella McCartney. Saville and West met in Paris for coffee not long before West's 2013 album *Yeezus* debuted. Saville presumed West wanted him to design an album cover, something that he was not keen to do. He'd taken a reprieve from music. Eventually, West got around to what he wanted. It wasn't help with an album cover; it was input on his fashion project.

Once inside West's orbit, Saville began to hear a constant refrain: *Have you met Virgil?* He had not. Finally, in New York City, "Our paths crossed in the lobby of the Mercer Hotel a few years later. But I didn't know they had. I went up to my room and then I got an email from the mysterious Virgil, 'Just saw you in the lobby.'" Saville recalled. "I said, 'Well, we must meet sometime when you're in London.' He said, 'I'm there this weekend.' So suddenly Virgil was here. And he turned up one Sunday afternoon in the studio. And he was just immediately lovable and engaging."

It didn't matter that the two men were so different. Saville was twenty-five years Abloh's senior. He was a White man who'd grown up middle class in northern England. But Saville was taken by Abloh's intelligence, his charm, and his easy manner.

"I would struggle sometimes to talk with Kanye. . . . He was a really lovely man who would at some point just go off on a dogmatic tangent where it became difficult to then reconnect," Saville said. "Virgil did not have that weird tangential [manner]. I always used to be quite amazed by Virgil's ability to frame things. He was very, very good at putting language together. He was a very smart guy.

"So, I might have been, like, a kind of mentor to him. Fine," said Saville as he hesitantly took on the title. "But I can tell you, whenever I had a half hour with Virgil or even five minutes, *I* was more than happy to listen to *him*."

Abloh had a "willful spirit," Saville said. "Virgil used the medium of clothing as his channel to speak to people. He wrote things on it. It was about communicating ideas."

The two never had the chance to collaborate on a project, but they were in each other's world of associates and friends. Abloh even encouraged Saville's partner to launch her own fashion line. In some ways, that initial visit was a mission of gratitude. It was a chance for Abloh to meet a hero.

PYREX VISION WAS Abloh's first significant foray into fashion on his own, but he hadn't gotten there by himself. He was part of a rising generation of creative men who had an easy relationship with fashion and who in practice blurred the lines between fashion, music, and art. Each discipline inspired the others—but they were on equal footing. Music told a story about politics, race, and capitalism. Art challenged assumptions and posed questions. Fashion was a form of identity—a statement of affiliation, success, and tenacity. Expertise in one area gave you bona fides enough to be viewed as a formidable presence in another. And of course there was money to be made in the expanding world of menswear.

This generation of young outsiders had confidence and impatience that pushed them to become entrepreneurs rather than to wait until some preexisting company saw the wisdom in their vision. They had each other. They were each other's expressions of what was possible—and what was cool.

"It was competitiveness, but it was motivating," said Matthew Williams, who went on to launch his own brand 1017 ALYX 9SM and design for Givenchy. "It was as if you're skateboarding with a friend and they just did a nine-stair handrail, so it makes you believe that you can do it. I think naturally that's what happens with areas of creatives or athletes or musicians. They just feed off one another. And I was just lucky enough to meet the people that I met during that time."

Williams, Jerry Lorenzo, and Heron Preston, who launched his own brand in 2017, were fashion renegades. To varying degrees of success, they were creating a world of their own that fashion wanted to infiltrate. They'd begun speaking to shoppers who loved fashion, who loved designer brands, but whose connection to those brands was tenuous and impersonal. So they anointed smaller brands and more affordable labels that catered to their interests as desirable, influential, and collectible. The traditional fashion industry expended an incredible amount of intellectual capital trying to reinvent the wheel—or in this case, the business suit—when there was a whole world of potential customers who weren't moved by such formal aspirations.

They lived in track pants, T-shirts, jeans, and sneakers. They wanted them to have the same aesthetic clout, the same aura of luxurious legitimacy, as a tailored suit. They didn't want to reinvent them; they wanted them to have meaning.

The impact of Pyrex Vision, the uneasiness it stirred and the attention it attracted, made it clear that Abloh was on to something. And he had access to the spotlight and the bullhorn of fame and social media to exploit it.

AFTER YEARS OF being the assistant, the creative director for someone else's vision, Abloh decided to start his own fashion company. And from the very beginning, he said it was going to be a designer brand, on the same level as the ones he grew up coveting. The clothes wouldn't be the same. The mission wouldn't be either. But it would be luxury.

In 2013, he founded Off-White c/o Virgil Abloh. The name said everything about his background and his temperament.

"Off-White was just a shorthand phrase for me to always remember that I don't have to be polarizing. I don't have to be Black or White," he said. "I like Diet Coke sometimes. I like matcha sometimes. It's the shades in between. To be human is to change your mind. . . . What kind of music you listen to, what your political views are today, it doesn't mean that you have to stay that way through your whole life. That's not human; you grow and you learn and then you adapt.

"I named my label Off-White as like my own measure. It's like my own ruler," he continued. "It's okay to have two answers to a singular question. It's okay to be in between.

"Don't let anyone put you in any box," he said. "It allows a conversation to happen without you even speaking. . . . The world puts me in a box, yet I don't see any box. That's my freedom."

Off-White boasted a celebrity fan base before the first garment was ever produced because of Abloh's work with Kanye West. It was a fashion curiosity before there was ever a show because Pyrex Vision had piqued the interest of editors and stylists. They wanted to know what was next. The Off-White launch was, as new brands go, not a heavy lift. Publicists didn't have to cajole anyone into previewing it. Off-White generated coverage on Style.com and in *The New York Times*.

Abloh had fans who followed him as a deejay. He talked to his customer base as if they were all part of an intimate social media friend group. He positioned himself as one of them: a young person who aspired to big luxury logos but who didn't see a way into that world. Technically, Abloh was born during the last gasp of Generation X—a generation removed from the tribes to whom he spoke. That was okay. In public, he often described how he *felt* like a kid. That was what mattered.

Abloh invested less of his time into West's projects as he built Off-White. While West always sought out a multitude of opinions before making a decision, Abloh was decisive. He was fast. He knew what he liked, and he knew what he wanted. He wasn't one for displays of frustration or outrage. If he was aggrieved, he kept those feelings private. His social media didn't document grievances—nor was it a place of raw truth telling. It traced his travels, his accomplishments, his merchandise.

Abloh presented an optimistic attitude on the subject of race. And this was no small thing. Optimism went down easier than outrage. It was more palatable. There was something sepia-toned about Abloh's expression of race and diversity. He made people feel comfortable and good. He was the child of immigrants and shared their belief in what was possible, rather than what was improbable. He had wide-ranging interests that allowed him to connect with an equally wide range of people. He had the armor of education and the knowledge that of course he was talented. Of course he was twice as good.

He was the approachable one, the notetaker who relished collaboration and getting people to do their best work. His temperament was a combination of nature and nurture, and it worked to his advantage. He'd also seen how often West's volatility and impetuousness had derailed or muddied a goal.

Unlike West's myriad fashion schemes, Off-White wasn't a collective with a million cooks in the kitchen. It wasn't a side project. Abloh partnered with a group of Italian entrepreneurs, the leader of whom he'd met through West, who pitched his fashion ideas to anyone willing to listen—as well as those who weren't. Year after year, West pounded on fashion's walls with the battering ram of his personality; Abloh moved calmly through the resulting cracks, sidestepping the fallen bricks.

Off-White was produced by New Guards Group, which licensed the trademark from Abloh. It was manufactured in Italy—a country revered for manufacturing high-quality garments, particularly knitwear, and its belief in menswear as a form of aesthetic self-creation. *La bella figura* was not a cliché. It was a philosophy espoused by men from all walks of life, from the cabbie to the chairman of the board. Abloh no longer bought blank T-shirts from Champion or sought out dead stock at discounted rates. He crafted garments.

He wanted to present the collection in Paris because it remained the center of global fashion, a marketplace for ideas born everywhere from New York to Tokyo. A Paris presentation would underscore Abloh's intentions to build a serious luxury brand. Abloh engaged fashion's establishment. He didn't go around them; he wooed them. He didn't take up arms; he engaged in diplomacy. "Virgil had a gift," fashion editor Jim Moore said. "He could talk anyone into backing him."

The first Off-White collection, spring 2014, launched online and drew heavily from what Abloh had done with Pyrex Vision. It was inspired by Mies van der Rohe's Edith Farnsworth House—the glass box residence built in Plano, Illinois, between 1945 and 1951. At least, that's what Abloh said. Essentially, the collection—jeans, work jackets, hoodies, oversize shirts—had lots of graphic lines. The clothes had a design reminiscent of the Haçienda night club's interior. It had a modernist's obsession with function. Its very existence seemed to have grown out of Abloh's earnest belief in his own abilities and the industry's need for what he could offer, which was an open line of communication to an eager generation of consumers with whom fashion was stuck relating to in ways both awkward and muddled.

"My premise is to create a brand that's immersed in this young fashion customer," Abloh said. "Me, as a designer, that's what I draw from, that's the culture that I'm a part of: the music, the restaurants, the Chateau [Marmont] to the Mercer [Hotel]."

Hazard lines, recalling the Haçienda as well as road construction, were printed and stitched on T-shirts, hoodies, shorts, baseball caps, and backpacks. The number 23 figured prominently, and another classical painting appeared on T-shirts: Caravaggio's *Saint*

Jerome Writing. The bearded, gaunt Jerome was hunched over an open Bible, a swirl of fabric surrounding his torso. A skull—or memento mori, a reminder of the inevitability of death—rested on the table. The collection included an olive camouflage jacket with "White" stitched on the back along with hazard lines. The garment became a familiar sight on influencers and a signature piece from the brand.

"The one thing that I think the luxury market needs to understand is that culture has changed," Abloh said. "I don't know if there's any way to underline that any further. This should be in bold writing—that luxury by a seventeen-year-old's standard is completely different than his parents'. His version of luxury is streetwear."

Off-White quickly found its footing with retailers—customers wanted items with the hazard markings and the Off-White name—and a few seasons after its virtual debut, Abloh met with editors in a Paris showroom just off Place Pigalle in Paris's red-light district. He was backlit by windows and racks of clothes were pushed off to the side. He wanted the dozen or so assembled editors sitting on folding chairs to ask him questions, ones that weren't fashion related. And he had questions for them too. Then one writer arrived late with his thirteen-year-old son, who was bedecked in Off-White socks. Abloh beamed.

"You know my style of clothing is basically a discourse between me and the kids. That's what the premise of the brand is," he said. "A 17-year-old can be more advanced and often is more advanced than a 45-year-old, so my design theory and the culture that surrounds Off-White is nontraditional." Abloh saw fashion as his blank canvas—his off-white canvas—where he could communicate his thoughts about everything: music, art, architecture, youth, design.

When he finally put the collection on the runway, as audience members arrived and searched for their seats, a voice on the sound system discussed the advantages and disadvantages of not fitting neatly into a creative box and about the financial challenges that come from having wide-ranging interests and not being considered an expert on a given subject. "I thought, 'Who the fuck is that? It sounds like the sort of silly things I'd said,'" recalled Peter Saville. "And then I listened a bit more. Oh my God, it *is* me!" His existential musings welcomed guests—something he discovered when he happened to stumble across a video of the presentation. Saville was flummoxed and flattered.

"Because of the nature and the context of my work, it gets reproduced in one way or another and bootlegged all the time. And even though it's slightly unsettling, . . . I was quite taken by the fact that an interview I did with Show Studio, that I probably thought about two people listened to, was suddenly being played to a room full of people in Paris," Saville said. "Instances through which your work is kept alive and kept relevant to a generationally shifting sea are not altogether bad."

As Off-White quickly expanded and opened its first store in Hong Kong in 2015, its visual language became cemented in fashion. The hazard stripes were joined by quotation marks around, well, anything. The punctuation turned the entire brand into an exegesis of irony. As Saville said, irony was the language of youth. Everything was nestled inside air quotes. The garments themselves were familiar: distressed jeans, cargo pants, motorcycle jackets, workman jackets. Almost everything had some form of branding on it: stripes, quotation marks, patches, or the words Off-White. Abloh's collection wasn't recognizable by cut or quality—both of which were fine. His clothes were recognizable because they said "Off-White," either literally or symbolically.

Abloh became even more committed to his belief in a 3-percent principle—the idea that an object altered by 3 percent becomes something wholly new. The work of many other designers could be detected in an Off-White collection. It had whiffs of Helmut Lang in its exploitation of utilitarian tropes and Raf Simons in its references to youth culture.

Off-White did not impress Simons, who bristled at Abloh's liberal use of others' work as source material for his own. "He's a sweet guy," Simons said of Abloh. "I like him a lot actually. But I'm inspired by people who bring something that I think has not been seen, that is original.

"It's not always about being new-new because who is new-new? And of course you have to have people who inspired you," Simons continued. But he expressed frustration over the degree to which Abloh, and others, relied on ideas midwived by him or Phoebe Philo or Marc Jacobs and so on. "Fashion doesn't exist if we don't exist," Simons said.

This is true. Contemporary sportswear was built on a foundation established by earlier generations—whether it was a polo shirt, a crewneck sweater, blue jeans, a sport coat, loafers. But the measure of a designer's skill had always been what they did to make those building blocks uniquely their own, what they did to make them feel new. By touting his 3-percent philosophy, Abloh spotlighted fashion's reliance on reiterating what had come before. Yet how had Abloh made fashion's building blocks his own? He hadn't. But he absolved himself—and anyone following in his footsteps—by claiming creative transparency when he used the work of others as his raw materials.

Abloh typically refrained from calling himself a designer. He was a creator, a maker, a director. He put his energies into creating logos and graphic designs that could be trademarked. A particular garment—a pair of slouchy cargo pants or an oversize hoodie—has no copyright protection under U.S. law. Off-White assembled a healthy collection of trademarks, from the name of the company itself to "for walking"—a phrase that appeared on footwear and was finally approved by the U.S. Patent and Trademark Office two years after Abloh's death. Indeed, one of Abloh's generic T-shirts emblazoned with his company's name had more legal protection in the United States than Diane von Fürstenberg's famous wrap dress, which landed her on the cover of *Newsweek* magazine in 1976.

As Off-White expanded, Abloh and his cohorts made it clear they wanted their work to hang alongside other designer brands, the brands they'd long admired. They did not want to be shunted into a ghetto called *urban* or *streetwear* or *athleisure* or anything else. They wanted to go into the world of luxury.

But what did that mean? It had once implied something quite lofty.

"If someone is allowed to participate in luxury, not even own it, but to look at it, your heart opens up and your spirit is lifted," said Thomaï Serdari, who studied the meaning of luxury and advised businesses on the subject. Serdari sometimes told corporate chieftains that if they wanted to know if theirs was a true luxury product, they should ask themselves whether they could envision it in the Metropolitan Museum of Art someday.

In a more practical sense, luxury once meant a revelation in craftsmanship or human imagination. Robert Chavez, the former U.S. president of Hermès, described the mindset behind the company's products. "We make things to be repaired," he said. His point? Luxury lasted. It could be handed down. It was a generational investment.

In contemporary fashion vernacular, the term was overused and diluted. It was applied to anything that was expensive. The modern challenge was to find meaning in that expense. If luxury wasn't enduring or heart-lifting, what set it apart? Luxury had become a measure of branding audacity. But it was becoming something else too: a measure of one's cultural worth.

AS OFF-WHITE WAS GROWING, Jerry Lorenzo was in Los Angeles building his brand Fear of God—the bits and pieces of which Lorenzo had shown Abloh in his garage. Lorenzo became the brand's best advertisement, often photographed swaddled in its $800 sweatpants, $700 hoodies, and $2,800 oversize wool coats. Celebrities Justin Bieber and Jared Leto acquitted themselves nicely in the line too.

"I'm trying to redefine how people see and view and feel luxury," Lorenzo said. "Our fight is to be seen. We want to be *seen*. We don't want to be recognized. I want you to really see the nuances and details and understand what's gone into my work. I don't want to be recognized for the sake of you said you recognized someone of color."

Lorenzo would become somewhat leery of the term *streetwear*, not because it didn't capture the roots and point of view of the work but because it was limiting and artificial and not equated with luxury.

For Kim Jones, streetwear had always been essentially whatever a person wore on the street—and if they chose to wear haute couture, well then, that was streetwear too, wasn't it? An earlier group of mostly Black designers who emerged from the hip-hop community had seen their work labeled with a limiting term: *urban*. They too had pushed back. But streetwear had an easier battle. Streetwear had roots in hip-hop but also in skate culture and Japanese youth culture. From its beginnings, it was global. As its fans matured, they didn't want to set aside the clothes they loved. They wanted better versions of them. They wanted versions that could be worn with blazers and cashmere overcoats: Versions that they and their peers understood to be meaningful. Versions that made them feel as empowered as a business suit made older generations feel.

To accomplish that with Off-White, Abloh surrounded himself with talent. He reached out to untapped creatives, experts who were in the shadows, experienced designers who had not quite gotten their due. He reached out to Edward Buchanan.

WHEN BUCHANAN LEFT Bottega Veneta, he began consulting for others—Iceberg, Max Mara, Sean John (which was founded by hip-hop entrepreneur Sean Combs), and singer Jennifer Lopez's Sweetface. He was never interested in the world of celebrity despite his working for Lopez and Combs. What impressed him most during his tenures there was that the person who hired him was a person of color. That meant something to Buchanan. He wasn't alone, as he so often was in Italy.

The years he spent working with celebrity brands provided him with a glimpse into fashion's future. He saw what it meant when the person who was the creative head wasn't a trained designer but simply someone with a point of view. He witnessed firsthand the power of fame and a fan base and how both offered advantages that mere design expertise did not.

"I understood what it meant, celebrity and marketing, and creating a collection that you don't necessarily have to sell. Instead, you're creating an image that in return is going to sell a fragrance or is going to sell a bracelet," Buchanan said. "It was that aspirational aspect that I learned."

Away from the glare of the spotlight, in the backrooms of design studios, Buchanan perfected his craft. His reputation as a knitwear master grew, and eventually he started his own brand, Sansovino 6. He started selling it out of a Milan showroom run by Roberto Grassi, a Tuscan businessman who helped to establish retail distribution for brands such as Maison Martin Margiela, Katharine Hamnett, and Antonio Marras. Retailers visited his showroom and others like it to see new collections and make buying decisions. Showrooms like Grassi's provided an opportunity for smaller brands to be viewed in the broader context of a season's offerings and freed individual designers from having to finance their own brick-and-mortar spaces with salespeople, assistants, and models. Group showrooms allowed busy merchants to see as much product as possible in a limited amount of time. A showroom also offered a seal of approval for lesser-known brands. A showroom, after all, was only as good as the designers it represented. And Grassi's showroom was better than most.

One of the other collections Grassi brought into his showroom was Off-White. And that's where Buchanan and Abloh eventually met: the knitwear wizard and the man who wasn't a designer.

The two became friends. They traveled in the same circles, went to the same parties. Each man admired the business the other was building. They were also Black men in Italy.

"When you see a Black man working in the same space in Italy, my first instinct is grab on, to know what the hell is going on here," Buchanan said. "When I'm walking on the streets in Milan and I see a Black person across the street, I give them a nod. It's like, 'I see you. I acknowledge that you're here. I don't know you, but I see you.'"

Buchanan knew Off-White as a business of T-shirts and sweatshirts—that's what was selling in stores—but Abloh spoke about elevating the collection and turning it into a more fulsome expression of a new kind of luxury. Doing so required technical skill and connections with Italian mills. Buchanan had a wealth of that knowledge from his time at Bottega Veneta, his work consulting for brands such as Sean John, and establishing his own knitwear label. Abloh was in his early thirties; he'd traveled the world. Elevating the collection wasn't just a reflection of ambition, it was also a reflection of his growing up.

"He was like, this is where I want to go. He was always interested in luxury as an idea and as a concept," Buchanan said. "He wanted to fuck up the idea of what luxury meant."

Abloh approached Buchanan with some trepidation. He wasn't sure if the veteran designer, a decade his senior, would want to work for him and with him. After all, West had tried to entice Buchanan into his camp, but the designer had resisted.

"Nothing could ever be really formulated—in that Kanye way," Buchanan said. "At that point, I was a proper adult. I don't want any drama. If I'm going to work for you, we're going to have a schedule, we're going to do things. I'm not going to be running into factories just saying, 'Make some knits for Kanye.'"

Abloh collaborated, communicated, and edited on his phone using WhatsApp. He respected Buchanan's position as a knitwear designer. He gave him the space to work. And perhaps most important, he gave Buchanan his trust. And each year, Buchanan produced some two hundred designs for Off-White.

It was possible to track the evolution of Off-White through social media. Abloh flooded the digital world with images of his work, with behind-the-scenes glimpses into his process, with announcements about his growing list of collaborations, with invitations to just turn up at his fashion shows. He monopolized his followers' social media feeds until it seemed that he was doing everything everywhere around the clock.

"I was impressed with how fast [Off-White] grew," said Kim Jones. "With fashion, it's all about timing."

Jones had known Abloh since about 2007. Jones was a round-faced, bearded designer whose resting expression of sober intensity and whose many highfalutin brand appointments belied his generous, populist attitude toward fashion. He had graduated from the Central Saint Martins master's program in fashion with a love of hoodies and T-shirts and the technical expertise required for tailoring and haute couture. He swooned over the craftsmanship of Martin Margiela as well as the branding genius of A Bathing Ape.

Jones launched his own collection soon after graduating and took on odd jobs as a consultant, including for Kanye West. Abloh, ever the organized, right-hand man, sometimes stayed at Jones's flat in London, doing research and soaking up whatever knowledge he could. And as was typical for anyone who worked with West, there were late nights on the road for Jones. He remembered sitting on the floor of the Grand Hyatt in Tokyo, like some scene out of *Lost in Translation*, brainstorming and strategizing with Abloh. "We'd sit in a corner and have conversations," Jones said. "He worked very fast; I like to work fast. I'd insist that some people had to leave the room so we could concentrate, and then it would just be Virgil and me and Kanye. It wasn't that chaotic; it's just that time was always working against us."

By the time Abloh launched Off-White, Jones had made multiple leaps in his career. He'd closed his brand after taking on the role of creative director at Dunhill, where he'd injected youthful vigor into its men's tailoring. In 2011, he moved to Louis Vuitton to lead the menswear team. He was hired by Marc Jacobs, the American designer who'd been tasked with establishing ready-to-wear at the historic house.

Jones was influenced by the aesthetics of skateboarders, clubbers, and hip-hop fans. He'd grown up fascinated by the different subcultures he read about in magazines. He reveled in getting to experience them firsthand in clubs. And in Jacobs, he had a boss who was keen to break rules, someone who found inspiration in both fine art and street culture. "I was seeing him working with artists," Jones said. "He was very open to stuff."

For his spring 2001 collection, Jacobs brought in street artist Stephen Sprouse to transform the Louis Vuitton monogram into a version of a graffiti tag. For a 2003 collection, he collaborated with

Japanese artist Takashi Murakami, who added his colorful, cartoon sensibility to the Louis Vuitton monogram. Jacobs worked with Pharrell Williams on sunglasses and with Kanye West, who called himself the "Louis Vuitton Don," on a sneaker collection.

With Jacobs's free-range approach to creativity as encouragement, Jones proposed his collaboration with Supreme in 2017. The partnership further blurred the lines between streetwear and luxury. The collection featured bright red hoodies covered with the LV logo and the Supreme name, along with belt bags, backpacks, jerseys, duffels, and even a storage trunk for a skateboard. When it launched, customers lined up for the opportunity to spend scandalous amounts of money for the merchandise. Prices ranged from almost $500 for a T-shirt to more than $45,000 for the dedicated skateboard case. (Five years later, Sotheby's auctioned that case and the accompanying skateboard. It sold for $75,600. A skateboard deck from that collaboration had a winning bid of $21,420.)

It was impossible to determine which company contributed more of the magic to the collaboration. Louis Vuitton was the fetishized French label that exuded privilege and financial wealth. Supreme was the company that young men had turned into a signifier of community. The combination was a powerful statement about a new cultural hierarchy.

Abloh built Off-White within this context. The fashion industry, specifically menswear, was changing. The door was cracking open for Abloh, and he was pushing hard to open it even wider. He wasn't just building a brand of clothing, he was constructing a launchpad for his further ambitions.

"I have a litany of ideas that bring modern relevance, but also a financial vision, on how these brands can be more successful in the space of luxury," he said. "Off-White is sort of my résumé, and it's my laboratory to experiment with these ideas to see which ones are valid."

One of Abloh's goals was the LVMH Prize. LVMH, the world's largest luxury conglomerate, owns Christian Dior, Givenchy, Louis Vuitton, Céline, Kenzo, and a host of jewelers, winemakers, and perfumers. LVMH wraps all its commerce in the patina of good taste and *savoir faire*. Its annual fashion award provided money and mentoring to talented designers and gave LVMH the opportunity to interrogate some of the most creative new minds in the industry.

Thomas Tait won the inaugural LVMH prize in 2014, and finalists that year included Simon Porte Jacquemus, Simone Rocha, Julien Dossena, and Shayne Oliver. Among that creative freshman class, Oliver was an outlier—one who helped clear a path for Abloh.

Oliver didn't have a fashion school pedigree and hadn't apprenticed in major design houses as the other finalists had. He launched his New York–based brand Hood by Air with a graphic T-shirt featuring an enormous logo that could be seen from fifty yards. Originally, Hood by Air was a collective of sorts, but it eventually distilled into a focused brand helmed by Oliver. For him, streetwear wasn't just hoodies and jeans, it was the glue-gun glamour that dreamers pulled together on the fly. He believed that his iteration of streetwear could be reimagined through the lens of luxury apparel even though he readily admitted that he'd only recently started to concern himself with the fit and tailoring of his clothes. Still, the power of his ideas was undeniable. Abloh took note. He contributed graphic designs for the collections.

Oliver's aesthetic came from "me being a queen around a bunch of downtown skater boys. . . . [I'm] noticing the difference between social backgrounds, but people who are rich and people who are not wealthy are digesting the same ideas." Oliver's aim was to create a new archetype for a luxury brand.

Oliver didn't win, but the LVMH judges awarded him one of two special prizes that came with the equivalent of $130,000 and a year of mentoring.

Abloh owed a debt to the upheaval Oliver wrought. Oliver proved that a brand could come to life around an idea, around a group of people, rather than some pristinely constructed garment. He'd shown how hungry luxury fashion was for something that seemed to have emerged from an authentic community instead of being invented in front of a sketchpad.

One of the people Oliver enthralled with his point of view was Julie Gilhart. She'd been impressed by the ideas at the root of Hood by Air. She'd also seen the tiny shoots of a fashion collection that Been Trill represented. "It was just all the things that you're always looking for, you know? And my training at Barneys was, you don't wait for the press to endorse something. You're out there seeing what smells good. And it just had this great energy; and it was constantly being validated by other things. And they were also really accessible, nice people—every one of them," Gilhart said.

For years, Gilhart was the fashion director of Barneys New York, one of retail's foremost agenda setters. Tall and lanky with long sandy hair, she brimmed with energy and thoughtful enthusiasm. Even in her criticism of a designer's work, her slowly unwinding assessments, tinged with the languid vowels of her Texas roots, were wrapped in kindness and respect for the sheer emotional effort that was required to enter the fashion arena. At Barneys, she learned how to trust her gut, suss out new talent, and nurture that talent into a mature brand that retained its creative spirit while navigating commercial demands. She was one of the last of the great fashion directors who were once synonymous with their stores.

There were few dilapidated warehouses, stuffy lofts, or far-flung performance venues that Gilhart hadn't ventured into searching for a creative spark. Over the years, Barneys contracted; in 2020 it closed. Before its ignoble demise, Gilhart recreated herself as a talent scout: someone with deep roots in the industry and an eye for the next great creative mind.

So as the window opened for applications for the 2015 LVMH competition, Gilhart met Abloh for lunch at the Standard Grill in New York's Meatpacking District. Gilhart had been working with LVMH on the fashion competition since its inception. She had a wide view of all the talent that was percolating, not just in New York, but internationally. The two settled into a booth and Abloh asked for her counsel. Did she think he should apply for the LVMH Prize?

Gilhart remembered this moment clearly because she was so astonished. She knew that even though the prize was only in its second year, judges received thousands of unsolicited applications. Certain promising young designers were invited to apply. The judges, who worked for brands under the LVMH umbrella, were among the top designers in the world: Karl Lagerfeld, Phoebe Philo, Raf Simons, Marc Jacobs, Nicolas Ghesquière, Riccardo Tisci. These were people with formal training, people who had apprenticed at other fashion houses, people who studied fashion history and the role their forebears played in contemporary style. Gilhart was doubtful but wanted to be encouraging and open-minded.

"I was like, 'Yes, I think you should apply.' And at the same time, I was thinking, 'It's going to be a different kind of application!'" Years later, she would chuckle at the memory and at her hesitation compared to Abloh's confidence. "He was not a designer. And the purity of the prize has always been about really good taste, good talent, and design," Gilhart recalled. "But then, I felt like it's also a fashion prize. And he *did* have his finger on the pulse; and he had created this brand, Off-White, that was really getting a lot of buzz.

"I had gone and taken a look at the clothes and everything, and I was like, 'It's cute.' But it wasn't designed," Gilhart said. By this Gilhart meant that Abloh wasn't offering innovations in proportions or silhouette. He was adding graphics, choosing color palettes, selecting fabrics, and slicing up garments. But he wasn't altering the fundamental nature of the clothes. A varsity jacket was a varsity jacket was a varsity jacket, no matter how many patches had been stitched on it.

After their meeting at the Standard, Abloh sent Gilhart flowers. And he plowed ahead. He was seemingly filled with the belief that the system would work in his favor. His optimism was impressive. If he politely knocked on fashion's front door, he fully expected to be welcomed in. And if he was not, he simply knocked again.

"Every no is perfect for me," he said. "I thrive off of no."

In March 2015 at the start of another Paris fashion week, guests arrived at LVMH headquarters to meet the semifinalists in the luxury conglomerate's second annual fashion competition.

The twenty-six upstart brands were all assembled inside the sleek gray building at 22 Avenue Montaigne in the city's fancy eighth arrondissement, home to the Grand Palais, the Arc de Triomphe, and fashion boutiques known as much for their high prices as their high style. LVMH dominated much of this block, from Dior's adjoining gray and white townhouses perched at the corner down through the endless glass display windows of the Louis Vuitton store.

On this evening, the scene outside number 22 resembled a posh nightclub with a virtual velvet rope. Black Mercedes sedans idled in front of the stone façade, and men and women holding digital tablets checked guests' names before directing them to the glass entryway.

Inside, each striving young designer displayed their work in a small makeshift boutique. It was impossible to see the actual contours of this large, open room because it was packed shoulder to shoulder with editors, retailers, and other industry professionals all trying to get a look at these anointed few: young entrepreneurs that LVMH had designated as simmering with creativity. The champagne was flowing liberally, and the ascetic hors d'oeuvres that regularly turned up at fashion events in Paris—bits of cucumber spread with chèvre—were laid out and untouched on tables by the main bar. Guests moved with urgency because this was only one pit stop on an evening filled with presentations, openings, and runway productions.

Toward the center of the maze-like floorplan, the crowd was denser and the video cameras jostled more aggressively for the optimal position. The evening's energy concentrated in front of the display for Off-White. Abloh had made it to the semifinals. His work was a continuation of a conversation that Oliver had started the previous year.

There wasn't anything special about Abloh's booth. Like all the others, it was tiny, with his modest collection hanging on racks. It wasn't as if he'd conjured some interactive installation or intellectualized the evening with an artsy mural. Abloh, himself, was the draw.

He stood in the center of his small booth. Getting to him was a challenge, not because he was being standoffish or because he was distracted from the task at hand, but because his chum, fellow aspiring designer and buzz generator Kanye West, was in the way. West had been making the rounds at the cocktail party, loping from one booth to the other, trailed by video cameras. "Is this the god of London?" he yelled upon arriving at the booth helmed by Craig Green, a British designer specializing in menswear.

When West got to Abloh's stand, he began pulling Off-White jackets from the racks and trying them on, marveling at the aesthetics and chattering away to the cameras about why *he* thought Abloh was important and the beauty of *his* relationship with Abloh. A person had to struggle past this gregarious hype man who seemed to be luxuriating in the reflected glow of Abloh, but also in the goodwill so eagerly lavished on him. West could always capture the fashion industry's attention. Its affection, however, too often eluded him.

Abloh wasn't a visual braggart. His personal style that evening was discreet; frankly, it was a blur. He was one of twenty-six semifinalists. But he exuded calm and confidence. He was eager to discuss the nitty-gritty of his designs and his belief in the way his customers related to fashion as a form of identity. Everyone in the room seemed to know and like Abloh, not just by reputation but also through their various interactions with him. He seemed to have encountered every fashion editor in attendance that night at a previous party, a show, a something.

Abloh was charming but he wasn't smooth. He didn't act like he had all the answers to everything that ailed the fashion system—and to be clear, there was so very much wrong with fashion. The industry was obsessed with influencers but still struggling to form authentic connections with those up-and-coming shoppers in their late teens and early twenties. It hadn't figured out precisely what luxury meant to a generation that lived in hoodies and sneakers. All the industry knew was that the meaning of luxury had changed.

Luxury conglomerates were dominated at their highest levels by White men even as the world of luxury consumers became increasingly diverse. Fashion remained stubbornly, suffocatingly Eurocentric at a time when its largest and most influential customer base was in Asia and North America. Abloh was an outsider, to be sure, but if he felt any uneasiness that evening, it didn't show.

About two weeks after that crowded fashion week showing, LVMH announced its eight finalists. It was a prestigious group: Arthur Arbesser, Coperni's Sébastien Meyer and Arnaud Vaillant, Craig Green, Simon Porte Jacquemus (again), Marta Marques and Paulo Almeida of Marques' Almeida, Faustine Steinmetz, Demna Gvasalia of Vetements—and Abloh.

The winner was announced at a Paris news conference in June by actress Natalie Portman—who was a spokesperson for Miss Dior fragrances. Marques' Almeida took the top prize. The brand's designers experimented with proportions and reinterpreted streetwear—particularly denim—using tailoring, corsetry, peplums, and a good amount of slashing and fraying. Their work was forward-looking, but the brand was born in the most traditional way. The two founders had met as fashion students in Portugal and later launched their brand after moving to London and studying at Central Saint Martins under the late Louise Wilson.

For Abloh, making it to the finals was a true victory. He'd spent time within the milieu of fashion's agenda setters, gatekeepers, and headhunters. In a room bursting with examples of what tradition could foster, Abloh proved what community, ambition, and imagination could muster. His presence raised several questions: What is a designer in the modern era? And if we want our designers to be diverse, doesn't that also mean they should have diverse talents?

"When we were going through the applicants to decide on the semifinalists, we had long discussion about that," Gilhart said. "He wasn't really a designer. But this guy's creative. He knows style. He knows how to create a posse around him, not an entourage, but more a creative community. . . . It was really kind of a benchmark year."

When Abloh didn't win, he wasn't sad; he was shocked. "You know, I've had to deal with people that I've supported and have them not win. And it's tearful many times. With Virgil, it was like, 'How come I didn't win?'" Gilhart recalled and then laughed at the memory. "It wasn't a thing of like: *woe is me*. He was just more perplexed, like, 'How come I didn't win?' It was a question, and then on to the next thing. That's who he is. I don't think he belabored it at all."

Abloh arrived at this pivotal moment believing that the system would eventually work in his favor. Progress came slowly, in fits and starts, but it came. Indeed, shortly after he lost the LVMH competition, Abloh was sitting on the judging jury, alongside the likes of

Jacobs, Ghesquière, and Dior's Maria Grazia Chiuri, assessing the potential of other young hopefuls. His swift ascent was improbable.

Abloh had wanted it to be even faster.

He wanted to be a creative director of a major fashion house, and he saw an opportunity. In February 2017, Givenchy announced that Riccardo Tisci, who'd helmed the brand for twelve years, was leaving. Tisci transformed Givenchy into a twenty-first-century emblem of bittersweet romance and streetwise élan. Now the company, owned by LVMH, was on the hunt for a new creative director. And Abloh thought it should be him. Why not? Luxury fashion needed to speak to young consumers. And that's what Abloh had been doing all along—talking to the seventeen-year-olds and listening to them.

Soon after the announcement that Tisci was departing, the night before Abloh's Paris fashion show for Off-White, he was having dinner with friends at the Japanese restaurant Takara, a Fashion-Week favorite. Nonetheless, when Gilhart walked in, she was surprised to see him. She was accustomed to frazzled designers locked in their studios the day before their show, working late into the wee hours and fighting off anxiety. But Abloh was confident that his creative team had everything in hand. Besides, he had his phone and Whats-App. Texting was as good as being there. He was happy to see Gilhart and he had a question.

"Virgil said, 'I want Givenchy. Who do I talk to?' And my first thought was, going back to the design thing, Riccardo is a designer. He's a creative director, but at the end of the day, he's a designer," Gilhart said. "And I was thinking to myself, 'Oh my gosh. That's over your capabilities.'" She hedged, not sure what to say. Finally, she promised to think about it and get back to him.

"It was my ignorance," she said. "In my small mind, it had to be a designer.

"But he understood his talent."

Abloh's signal creative gesture—his persuasive thesis on youth culture and what it meant to rewrite the definition of luxury—was ultimately not any garment he produced for Off-White. It was a collaboration with Nike. In 2017, he unveiled his reinvention of ten of the sneaker giant's most consequential styles. Abloh deconstructed them and redesigned them. He sprinkled "fine art fairy dust" over the Air Jordan 1, the Nike Air Force 1 Low, and others.

He had an audacious goal for these shoes. He didn't want to build a better sneaker; he wanted to construct a sneaker that could be in the Museum of Modern Art. He wanted sneakers that made a case for a new form of luxury that was equal to—and maybe even better—than the past.

Sneakers

BY THE TIME NIKE noticed Virgil Abloh, revenue from the global sneaker market was more than $48 billion and was steadily climbing. The customer base fueling those sales was dominated by young men in the United States, who transformed what had once been a business focused on performance footwear that boasted incremental advances in technology into a cultural phenomenon featuring star athletes and musicians, a steady flow of limited-edition products and partnerships, a generous helping of designer flourishes, and a thick layer of emotional gamesmanship. Young men turned the business of sneakers into a brotherhood.

Nike played a central role in this world of hypebeasts—those who hunted the trendiest and hottest kicks—and sneakerheads—the obsessive collectors who prided themselves on their knowledge of sneaker minutiae and the sheer quantity of shoes in their closet. Nike helped move the sneaker industry toward this paradise of profits by being more than a merchant. Nike functioned as an anthropologist, a therapist, and even an evangelist. The brand's success was directly connected to its astounding ability to tap into the human desire to feel like a high-flying individual all while remaining deeply rooted within a collective. Being part of a team was everything.

Nike was established in 1964 when Phil Knight, a former member of the University of Oregon track team, and his coach Bill Bowerman set out in search of a better running shoe. Together, they created Blue Ribbon Sports, which by 1972 had been refashioned as Nike, Inc. As Nike expanded, it placed athletes at the center of its marketing, focusing on both the heroic nature of sports achievement and the emotional complexity of triumph and failure. Nike's narratives were not simply about winning the trophy; they told stories about the breathtaking effort required to reach one's goals. Nike's star athletes were not depicted as monumental marble gods; they were sweaty, panting, sprinting, and jumping icons of possibility. They were mighty, but they were human, and if they were human, then there was the slightest possibility that you could excel too. With the right shoes.

By 1984, Nike had won plaudits for its running shoes, the core of its business. But its basketball division struggled. Converse and Adidas were far more popular among both professional players and weekend dabblers. Converse, in particular, won over fans with a nonskid, rubber bottom that allowed players to make quick starts, stops, and turns on the basketball court. During the 1930s, the canvas Chuck Taylor All Star became the dominant shoe in the game. In the 1970s, Converse swapped canvas for leather; the Pro Leather was born, and it soon became the shoe of choice. The 1980s brought The Weapon, which boasted a sole with cushioning foam and attracted stars such as Larry Bird and Earvin "Magic" Johnson. Adidas entered the basketball market in the 1960s, and a decade later, players had fallen in love with its Superstar shoe.

To better compete and to improve its fortunes, Nike set its sights on rising basketball standout Michael Jordan, who was just entering his rookie season with the Chicago Bulls. After frantic cajoling— and a promise of royalties—Nike signed Jordan to a five-year endorsement deal for $2.5 million. The following year, when the company introduced the first red, black, and white Air Jordan basketball sneakers, Nike's position significantly improved. It sold more than $100 million worth of the high-tops in the first year.

By 1990, the company's annual revenue had grown to $2.23 billion, an enormous leap from $270 million in 1980.

The Air Jordan 1 begat an entire family of basketball sneakers for men, women, and children, along with countless iterations in the ensuing years. That single shoe grew into the Jordan Brand, a billion-dollar division of Nike that has its own ethos and aesthetic separate from that of its corporate parent. The soaring silhouette of the basketball legend—the jumpman logo—is as recognizable as the swoosh. With the Jordan Brand, Nike transformed what it meant for fans to salivate for a pair of sneakers.

Before the Air Jordan 1, sneaker collectors were mostly an underground faction of young men who obsessed over gym shoes. This subculture included skateboarders who sought out particular sneaker styles because of their grip and feel. And certainly, there were those who turned to specific basketball shoes because of the way in which they facilitated a jump shot or allowed a player to pivot with precision. Sneaker culture had an enormous fashion vernacular that reflected its ever-shifting aesthetics, trends, and stylistic rules. Sneaker-ville was a place where skaters and surfers met hip-hop fans. It was an overwhelmingly masculine space where young men bonded and competed, where outcasts were finally part of the in-crowd.

"We don't consider sneakers to be feminine," the curator Elizabeth Semmelhack said in 2015. An exhibition she'd organized on the history of sneakers at the Bata Shoe Museum in Toronto was preparing to open at the Brooklyn Museum. The show looked to the early part of the twentieth century, when sneakers first took on an element of status. Some of the first sneakers worn by nonprofessional athletes were those donned by the leisure class for games of lawn tennis. Modern sneaker culture retained its connection to status, with young men selecting sneaker styles to match their ensembles. They wanted certain styles in specific colors. The more difficult they were to find, the more valuable they were. Sneakerheads preferred their shoes spotless, valuing a fresh-from-the-box aesthetic rather than worn-in comfort and familiarity. Wearing them was not always the point—simply possessing them was what mattered. Certain stores catered to these connoisseurs by prohibiting customers from trying on those styles that might appeal to collectors. An errant imprint from the foot of a shopper just trying to determine if they were a size 8 or a 9 would devalue the gym shoes in the eyes of a sneakerhead.

"Sneaker collecting, done by many men, is in the tradition of other male collecting, like baseball cards and fine wines," Semmelhack said. "It's about having every single one in every single model."

Finding a limited edition or being privy to an impending sale was akin to being a hunter tracking and nabbing an elusive prey. Sneaker collecting was a sport.

The sneaker hunt remains a mostly masculine pursuit. And even though there are women who adore sneakers, collect them, and wear them, a glance at the vast style offerings directed at men versus the limited numbers aimed specifically at women reveals a bias toward the male consumer. Sneakers are deeply embedded in the culture of boys. Sneakers are their own subculture, and subcultures are a kind of identity.

Air Jordans brought men's sneaker obsessions out of the shadows. In the aftermath of Jordans, sneaker talk became a way of indulging in the pleasures of fashion without directly engaging in a fashion industry that could be oblique, fey, overwrought, Eurocentric, and predominantly White. Sneakers accommodated much of the clichéd discomfort straight men had in their relationship to fashion. When men talked about sneakers, they weren't talking about fashion per se; they were discussing music, sports, and comfort. They were bragging.

Fans found the emotional satisfaction that fashion could provide in self-expression and self-creation while keeping their language free of fashion's usual references to ateliers, accessories, and frippery. With sneakers, men weren't obsessing about something as silly as a pair of shoes. No, no. They were *collectors,* and as such, they regaled anyone who would listen with the technical specifications of every pair of shoes in their closet or on their wish list, reeling off its complicated name—the specific iteration—and noting whether the color combination was part of a limited edition or some quirk of distribution. They spoke of technology and provenance. They could detail which shoes a basketball player had worn when he made the game-winning shot. "There's a showoff factor with guys," said fashion editor Jim Moore. "They're insecure. They need a little story behind things."

A woman might be taken to task by total strangers—folks who had no knowledge of her bank account, for example—when she purchased a $10,000 haute couture confection or a pair of $1,000 stilettos. But men endured little ridicule when they intoned about sneakers with the same self-assured energy they unleashed during conversations about computers, sports, or cars. Men, by virtue of their privileged place in society, imbued sneakers with importance simply because they took the time to care about them. Masculine pursuits had long been afforded respect; feminine ones were dismissed as superficial. Items such as gloves, hats, handkerchiefs, and socks—once common in the masculine wardrobe—were referred to as "furnishings" in the fashion vocabulary. The term afforded them an aura of necessity and solidity. They endured. Jewelry, pantyhose, handbags—more feminine items—were "accessories," which was to say they were superfluous extras. The men who salivated over sneaker releases were hype*beasts.* The women who kowtowed to stylistic fads were fashion *victims.* Men were active participants in fashion. Women were slaves to it.

Female buying was posited as an action predicated on emotion. And that was often true. But as sneaker culture grew and evolved, the emotion wrapped up in rubber, shoelaces, and a swoosh or three stripes became undeniable.

In the modern era, feminine clothing changed rapidly and dramatically. Hemlines rose and fell; shoulder pads were shed and then reinserted. The erogenous zone shifted from the décolleté to the derriere to the legs to the midriff. Western menswear, once gentlemen relinquished their position as the peacocks of the industry, shifted only incrementally. This slow, creeping change was a sign of seriousness and stature. Men were removed from fashion's ebb and flow. Sneakers brought even the most reluctant men, that is to say straight White men, into the fashion space. "Men's fashion is being transformed from the feet up," Semmelhack said. If a designer made an impact in the world of sneakers, it had a legitimizing impact with a broad swath of men. The reverberations in menswear—both financial and critical—were virtually incomparable. Shoes once worn by youthful rebels, disrupters, and antagonists were at the center of men's style.

The strongest drivers of sneaker fashion were Black men and the hip-hop community, whose affection for trainers reached back to at least 1971, when the German company Puma signed an endorsement deal with New York Knicks player Walt "Clyde" Frazier. Frazier wanted a low-rise shoe, and Puma rechristened a suede sneaker that had been in its line since the 1960s, one that had been on the podium next to Tommie Smith at the Mexico Olympic Games when he raised his fist in protest of racial inequality. Puma renamed that shoe the Clyde and reproduced it in almost four hundred color combinations so Frazier could have a different iteration for each game.

Hip-hop's love for sneakers extended to Adidas. In 1986, Run-DMC installed Adidas into pop cultural lore when the group dedicated a rap to their beloved Superstar sneakers. Superstars, with

Adidas's signature three stripes wrapping around the sides, were another streamlined, low-rise sneaker like the Clyde.

> My Adidas and me close as can be
> We make a mean team, my Adidas and me
> We get around together, we down forever
> And we won't be mad when caught in bad weather.

Both Puma and Adidas were founded in Germany by brothers Adi and Rudi Dassler, who, in 1924, were partners in the shoe company Gebrüder Dassler Schuhfabrik. In 1933, the year Adolf Hitler became Germany's chancellor, the Dassler brothers joined the Nazi Party. During the 1936 Olympic games in Berlin, African American sprinter Jesse Owens wore their running spikes when he won four gold medals, each one serving as a rebuke to White supremacy. After a falling out, the Dassler brothers went their separate ways. Rudi Dassler founded Puma in 1948 and Adi Dassler created Adidas in 1949.

For sneakerheads, their footwear represented a lifestyle long before the fashion industry took up that word as a branding and marketing tool. Sneakers were not just an accessory to an aesthetic; they were the main event—a flourish around which an entire community revolved. Sneakers were central to hip-hop, athleticism, and streetwear—all movements that were transforming the way a generation of men thought about their clothes. When men fell for sneakers, fashion outsiders gained the upper hand in fashion. An industry run by White businessmen—from Beaverton, Oregon, to Herzogenaurach, Germany—one with a predominantly White customer base, one that benefited mostly White shareholders—was ruled by Black kids in American cities who drove the conversation about what was desirable and what was cool.

Thanks to the Air Jordan 1, as well as the Air Force 1, few sneakers became as covetable as Nike's. In 1988, the company released a commercial directed by Spike Lee, who'd established himself as a new-generation auteur with his 1986 independent film *She's Gotta Have It*. In addition to directing, Lee played a character named Mars Blackmon who was obsessed with Air Jordans. He reprised that role for the commercial. Shot in black-and-white, with a funky bass-driven soundtrack, the cinematic advertisement firmly planted Nike, Jordan, and Lee in the popular consciousness.

But the shoes' sudden white-hot popularity also connected them to incidents of violence. These attacks led to heartbreaking magazine cover stories, dire network news reports, and outrage from activists. Complicated social pathologies—income inequality, disintegrating family support systems, a thriving gun culture—were explained away by demonizing these objects of desire. Sneakers became controversial, which only made them more coveted.

Still, the violence was a fact. By 1990, reports proliferated of teenagers being mugged and even killed, with the culprits making off with their sneakers. In Detroit, an eighteen-year-old was shot seven times by a group of boys who then stole his Nike shoes. Near Baltimore, a fifteen-year-old was killed for his Air Jordan sneakers. In Anne Arundel County, Maryland, a fifteen-year-old ninth grader was strangled. A seventeen-year-old was charged with his murder and for allegedly stealing the freshman's Air Jordan sneakers and leaving his barefoot body in the woods not far from his school. It wasn't uncommon for some cities to have fifty muggings a month all in the name of cool kicks.

The civil rights veteran Jesse Jackson lamented the pressures put on Black teenagers by Nike to buy and wear the latest sneaker styles. From the beginning, the shoes were expensive. They sold for $65, which would be the equivalent of $190 in 2024. For a blue-collar parent, that was a significant investment in a pair of shoes that an adolescent was likely to outgrow within a year.

Nikes were cool because Black kids said they were. Nike resold a cool factor grown and nurtured in Black communities back to those very same communities. Did Nike transform the sneakers into emblems of belonging? Or did the company exploit desires and symbolism that were already present? Was Nike simply "getting under the skin" of a subculture to improve its bottom line and grow its place in the youth market? Or was it being exploitative? As with most trends in fashion, the currents flowed both ways.

Educators vented their frustrations over the muggings and shootings. They established dress codes, hoping to remove peer pressure to follow sneaker fads. Counselors bemoaned seeing kids come to school in $100 sneakers but without the means to buy lunch. Retailers debated the ethics of knowingly catering to drug-dealing sneakerheads in a bid to enrich their bottom line. And parents mourned the loss of childhood innocence and, in some cases, their dear children.

The violence didn't stop. Decades later there were still reports of deadly fights over Nike sneakers. But the company soldiered on—mostly unscathed.

From the 1990s onward, Nike secured its dominance in the sneaker market, overwhelming Reebok and its pump technology and leaving Adidas, Fila, Puma, and every other brand in the distance. In July 2003, Nike bought a bankrupt Converse for more than $300 million.

BY 2015, while Nike remained the Goliath in the marketplace, Adidas was on the rise. Nike's sales were more than double that of Adidas, which was its closest competitor, but the German brand had made several strategic moves that resonated within streetwear culture and the wider fashion market. It had also been the beneficiary of extraordinarily good luck.

Adidas had a relationship with designer Yohji Yamamoto that dated back to 2005, but in the fall of 2010, the shoemaker got a significant fashion jolt. Céline designer Phoebe Philo stepped onto the runway to take her bows at the end of her women's fashion show wearing a pair of Adidas Stan Smith sneakers. The shoes, which had been around since 1963, were decidedly low tech. They didn't have pillows of air in the sole or a pump system to adjust the fit. They were minimalist shoes with a rounded toe box. At the time, Philo was one of the most influential designers working in the industry. She'd reinvented the French brand Céline, a division of LVMH, as a woman-friendly, spare collection that spoke of comfort, sophistication, and independence. Her clothes were subtle and precise. She could make customers' hearts beat a little faster with a collar placement or the width of a shirt's cuff. Her personal style was widely admired and copied, by both women and men. Philo didn't produce a dedicated men's line for Céline, but that didn't matter. Her oversize tailoring and austere aesthetic drew male customers such as Pharrell Williams, Kanye West, and Abloh, who wore one of her blouses when he spoke at his friend Matthew Williams's wedding.

Philo's embrace of Stan Smith sneakers was an endorsement that rippled throughout the fashion ecosystem. They became the preferred shoe of fashion savants. Raf Simons collaborated with Adidas, creating a version with a punched-out letter R along the side. In 2013, French *Vogue* photographed model Gisele Bündchen wearing nothing but a pair of Stan Smiths. And in 2014, Williams, with his connections to streetwear and hip-hop, worked on a collection for Adidas in which he reimagined Stan Smith sneakers covered in polka dots.

All this hoopla pushed low-tech, retro sneakers into the forefront of fashion customers' desires. And then, in 2015, Williams took on the Superstar—the Adidas sneaker about which Run-DMC had rhapsodized, the sneaker of early hip-hop lore. The collaboration resulted in a reissued Superstar in a rainbow of colors—fifty of them in total. Each shoe looked as though it had been dipped in a vat of paint to create a monochromatic effect. Priced at about $100, they were like sweets for the picking. They were fun and dynamic and accessibly priced at a time when a pair of Air Jordans had ticked up to $145 and the price of designer shoes in general had soared into the $1,000 stratosphere. Williams's version of the Superstar blended luxury fashion with hip-hop and streetwear in a way that was attainable for a mass audience.

The sudden emphasis on retro, lifestyle sneakers boded well for Adidas's balance sheet. The company's sales grew by 20 percent in 2015. Adidas sold eight million pairs of Stan Smith sneakers and fifteen million pairs of the Superstar style.

Adidas had also signed another collaborator from the music world: Kanye West. He'd defected from Nike, where he'd worked on the Air Yeezy 1, which was released in 2009. Three years later, his Air Yeezy 2 hit the marketplace. But the rapper left Nike in 2013 after a dispute regarding royalty payments. West wanted them; Nike wouldn't pay them.

West's last shoe under the Nike swoosh came to retail in 2014—the $245 "Red October" iteration of the Air Yeezy 2. The high-top sneakers looked as though they'd been doused in blood. They also recalled the red low-tops West designed with Louis Vuitton, which were a precursor to Williams's rainbow of Adidas Superstars.

Adidas lured West by giving him a 15 percent share in the profits from their collaboration. In 2015, the first Adidas Yeezy sneakers entered the fray. The Yeezy Boost 350 won shoe of the year at the Footwear News Achievement Awards, the industry's equivalent of the Oscars. The partnership sent sneakerheads into a buying frenzy. It transformed West into a billionaire. And Yeezys soon accounted for 8 percent of Adidas's annual sales. Adidas expected net sales of Yeezys to grow from $65 million in 2016 to $1 billion by 2021.

Nike lost market share to Adidas. In Nike's 2016 annual report, chairman Mark Parker told shareholders the major risk factors facing the brand's growth included competition from Adidas, as well as changing consumer desires. Trends were shifting away from Nike and its emphasis on athletes and just doing it, and moving toward Adidas with its focus on sneakers as a pure lifestyle gambit. Puma also helped push that trend along, thanks to its work with Rihanna on her Fenty line. Nike's sales dominance was for the first time in a long time being challenged.

And then, after more than a decade of being king of the hill, a Nike product did not sit atop the annual list of the best-selling sneakers in the United States. In 2016, that honor went to the Adidas Superstar. Fashion had a new love interest.

"We were in need of some fresh blood; we needed some new partners. We needed to shake things up. Adidas was actually doing well; Kanye had gone over there and that started to kick off," said Fraser Cooke, a Nike coolhunter. "I think Nike just felt like we want to get back to where we're strongest, which is this sneaker community in the streets."

An amiable White man with a modest build and short, shaggy white hair, Cooke dressed in the sort of high-frequency attire that only astute fashion followers recognized. He'd grown up in East London, but his interests and work assignments led to frequent trips to the fashion and nightlife realms of Los Angeles and New York, until he finally settled in Tokyo. His life story overflowed with dabblings and obsessions and a multitude of crisscrossing relationships that constantly had him in the thick of whatever "it" might have been at any given moment. Cooke's peripatetic life wasn't a result of his joining Nike in 2004. He was brought into Nike precisely because of his array of connections and interests.

As a young man in London in the 1970s, Cooke discovered skateboarding. He later developed a fascination with electronic music, specifically Detroit-born techno, and moved into deejaying. He was a hairdresser, which was akin to being a psychologist or, perhaps, an anthropologist. And Cooke was also a retailer. He ran a store in London called the Hideout, which was one of the early purveyors of streetwear brands Stüssy, A Bathing Ape, and Supreme. Young men who were intrigued by skating, streetwear, and youth culture made a pilgrimage to the Hideout when they were in London. Abloh was one of those zealots.

At Nike, Cooke helped the sneaker giant build relationships in industries outside the realm of sports. He connected Nike to fashion, music, and art. He sussed out movements bubbling up from the streets; he identified creative voices often just as they were clearing their throat and beginning to articulate a message. Cooke wasn't a designer. His great skill was in timing and compatibility. He was Nike's matchmaker.

And he wanted to match Nike with Virgil Abloh.

One of Cooke's first memories of Abloh was when he'd accompanied West to Paris during the early days of the rapper's romance with Louis Vuitton. Cooke was at the Comme des Garçons Homme Plus show in 2009 when the group of Chicago friends made their earnest, but ostentatious, entry on the fashion show circuit. They'd arrived bedecked in designer labels and clutching Louis Vuitton and Goyard briefcases—a sight both rare and confounding. Aside from a simple handbag, most regular guests carried nothing more than a mobile phone. Even the most devoted number crunchers from fashion's boardrooms didn't bring attaché cases to runway shows.

"I was looking at these guys thinking, 'What are they carrying these big briefcases for? What's in there—sandwiches or something?" Cooke recalled.

Abloh and Cooke became better acquainted as they swam in the same social waters after West began working with Nike. They saw each other at parties and store openings. Abloh was the friendly one. He said hello in a way that was open and genial. Cooke was more than a decade older than Abloh, but it didn't matter. Abloh chatted up Cooke about their mutual interests in skateboarding, streetwear, and, especially, electronic music. West was mercurial. If he was annoyed or frustrated by something that happened with Nike executives, he would be distant with Cooke even if Cooke had nothing to do with the disagreement.

"I'm not saying that [Abloh] was successful because he was nice," Cooke said. "But I very rarely experienced anybody that was so consistently balanced and never seemed to be flustered in stressful situations. I've not really seen him even get particularly angry. I think he was always very even with people.

"It was very, very, very refreshing and lovely to meet somebody that would be equally attentive to anyone that was around. When we had meetings later on with Nike, he wouldn't be sort of picking out who's the important person, who's got power, and 'I'm going to cozy up to them.' He seemed to be genuinely open and evenhanded with everyone," Cooke said. "I think that made people warm to him and want to work with him. And unfortunately, not so many people are like that. It's very special."

Abloh's career trajectory impressed Cooke. He'd witnessed the curious popularity of the Been Trill merchandise; he knew about the audacious Pyrex Vision, with its riff on the idea of ready-mades and the use of Ralph Lauren rugby flannel shirts. He watched as Abloh established Off-White using his branding acumen, his charismatic community-building, and his acute understanding of how streetwear was becoming a dominant force in luxury apparel.

"It's graphitized stuff and the graphic is signaling to somebody else, 'I'm into this and you're into this and we're friends.' And so, it's community. It's not really down to any incredible design differentiation," Cooke said. "It's quite basic stuff repeated over and over and over again. The same item takes on a different meaning depending on who's touching it."

Cooke understood that the best partnerships were not just a merging of logos but a form of dialogue. Successful collaborations allowed consumers to see the familiar in a new way. Ideally, a fresh product should emerge that neither entity would have been able to craft with such sure-footed ease on its own.

Over the course of his career at Nike, Cooke worked with Undercover's Jun Takahashi, Chitose Abe of Sacai, Kim Jones, and Hiroshi Fujiwara, among others. These collaborations pushed sneakers—and streetwear—deeper into the luxury fashion universe. They also helped to expand Nike's identity as more than a sportswear brand.

Around 2015, Cooke took notice when an anonymous mock-up of a Nike Air Force 1 spliced with Off-White markings began floating around the internet. It sparked so many questions and so much buzz that Abloh publicly disavowed any connection to the image. Nonetheless, the interest confirmed a market for such a collaboration. But Cooke, ever sensitive to the shifting winds of street culture, felt the timing wasn't right. It was too soon for Abloh.

In the meantime, Nike severed its rocky relationship with Kanye West. It reveled in a creatively fruitful partnership with Chitose Abe, whose label Sacai was known for its trompe l'oeil effects, its mash-ups of athletic wear with sportswear, its merging of hard edges and soft flourishes. The company worked with Riccardo Tisci, a relationship that began when Nike loaned him sneakers for his first show out of design school. And it also partnered with Abloh's friend Kim Jones, who was making headlines with his work at Louis Vuitton.

Then–Nike chairman Mark Parker finally balked at Adidas's success. Adidas was winning plaudits for its Stan Smith and Superstar sneakers, which had been given new life thanks to designer fairy dust. The styles were making Adidas central to the cultural conversation, and they were boosting the brand's bottom line—at the expense of Nike's. Parker wanted to exploit the most famous styles in Nike's archives, shoes that had deep cultural resonance—particularly within the overlapping worlds of streetwear, hip-hop, and sports obsessives. That rich history was languishing, so Parker wanted to focus on ten of the company's most storied sneakers. He wanted to reinvigorate them in a way that was modern and exciting to a new generation. He wanted to stir emotions.

To accomplish that, Nike planned to work with two outside creative talents. They turned to one of their longtime collaborators, Hiroshi Fujiwara, ostensibly the founding father of streetwear in Japan. The company also wanted to bring in someone fresh. Each person would unleash their imagination to transform five archival styles. The project was dubbed "The Ten."

Cooke suggested Abloh for the newcomer slot. It was 2016 and the time was right. "To me, he was just the most interesting person that was floating around," Cooke said. "It was something about the way he communicated. I could just sense that he had some momentum already and it was a good time to talk about something."

But Cooke had some convincing to do. Some executives at Nike didn't see the allure. For them, Abloh was merely "Kanye's assistant." The rapper had a growing reputation for combining chaotic creativity with self-aggrandizement and political volatility. Abloh was a plugged-in social media savant who saw his fashion as an artistic practice. They couldn't have been more different. But all the heat emanating from West made it difficult to get a clear sense of Abloh.

"Collectively we had to argue to get Virgil to be quote-unquote *approved* internally," said Sami Janjer, who was part of the marketing team working on the project. "And then, three years later, even if we were to try to stop it, we couldn't because it was so amazing and successful."

Janjer, who's from London, met Abloh through Kanye West. The rapper was on tour in London, and Abloh was with him. Janjer's memory was fuzzy about the timing and location, but one thing was certain: West was the connector. Janjer was working for Nike on the brand's European team. He'd been with the company since 2012, when the city hosted the Olympic Games. Janjer's job was to focus on collaborations, and over the years, he worked with designer Martine Rose and had a hand in rapper Drake's partnership with the sneaker giant. In describing his work, Janjer used terms such as *concepting*, which wasn't designing and wasn't exactly marketing. It really wasn't even a word. Mostly, Janjer, like Cooke, conceived ways for Nike to connect with individuals from other creative fields to build products that enthralled different communities of consumers.

Abloh used to refer to Janjer as the "Clarence Avant of our generation." That comparison mystified Janjer because he'd never heard of Avant (who died in 2023), which was part of Abloh's point. Avant was a behind-the-scenes powerhouse. His life story was the subject of the 2019 documentary *The Black Godfather,* in which presidents Bill Clinton and Barack Obama marveled at his clout. Baseball trailblazer Hank Aaron praised Avant's negotiating acumen. Then-senator Kamala Harris attested to his political savvy. And a significant portion of the entertainment industry, including Quincy Jones, Jamie Foxx, and Jimmy Jam and Terry Lewis, shared their admiring gratitude for Avant's ability to open doors, find additional seats at an already crowded table, and ensure that talented Black folks were fully paid what they were worth.

Janjer, a brown-skinned family man with short black hair, a full beard, and an easy manner, helped make things happen for people. And like Avant, he was often the least imposing guy in the room.

When Abloh visited Nike headquarters in Beaverton in October of 2016 to make his pitch to a skeptical audience, to be the star of his own show and not merely a background performer, he had the same sense of urgency and nonchalant confidence he'd brought to the LVMH Prize and to his independent work in fashion. The final result didn't have to be perfect; it simply needed to have a distinctive gesture. A do-it-yourself authenticity was a powerful selling point. It didn't need to be the best; it simply needed to have an emotional resonance with its target audience. And Abloh understood that audience because he was part of it. He'd grown up idolizing Michael Jordan. He'd sketched his own versions of Nikes and sent the designs off to the conglomerate—which politely rejected the ideas.

"That Jordan 1, that was a childhood dream," Abloh said. "In that golden era of the '90s, when the sneaker brands made sneakers seem bigger than life, they were making these shoes seem like Superman! Like capes!" As a teenager, he saved his pennies and bought his first pair of Air Jordans from Marshalls; he estimated that over the years he'd collected some two thousand pairs of sneakers, most of which were in storage. He kept about thirty pairs on hand to wear. "This generation may value sneakers more than a Matisse because [Matisse] is not attainable," he said. "I hold sneakers as art, to hold on to and be close to."

Nike signed Abloh. And at one of his earliest studio meetings in Beaverton, he came across a cut up Air Max One that designer Shamees Aden was experimenting with for a sort of inside-out shoe. Seeing how she had exposed the sneaker's guts sparked an idea.

Abloh pulled out an X-ACTO knife and deconstructed a pair of black Air Force 1 sneakers to reveal their inner structure. The Air Force 1 is considered Nike's "art shoe." It's the one Nike viewed as a cultural artifact, the one it aligned with museums and galleries. Abloh drew on the sneakers with a marker. He seized the opportunity to *show* Nike what he could do; he didn't just tell them.

Abloh made clear that he preferred a hands-on approach, unlike some Nike collaborators. He wouldn't be satisfied merely suggesting new color combinations. He wasn't planning to look at fabric swatches and treat the endeavor like a multiple-choice exam. In fact, Abloh wasn't particularly interested in colors; he liked the default neutrals of the sneaker prototypes. He adhered to his 3 percent philosophy about alterations, but he made his limited changes count.

Abloh wore his one-off sneakers at Design Miami. That was his way. He didn't believe in embargos. He brought prototypes to speeches. He tossed footwear into the audience for people to examine. Every encounter was an opportunity to connect with his growing fan base and let people in on the process.

He worked fast. Even when he wasn't in Beaverton he was in constant WhatsApp conversations with the design team: sending photographs, discussing materials, outlining silhouettes. His manner of communicating was disruptive. Typically, Nike worked with collaborators in preplanned meetings and through formal emails. Abloh insisted on starting an informal text chain so everyone could chime in from wherever they happened to be. He called in to the factory and reviewed samples on video calls, something that was rare at the time. Nike didn't let outsiders, even ones with whom they were collaborating, participate in their manufacturing process.

Abloh considered how the shoes would look; he also thought about how they could be seeded within the community of sneaker lovers and celebrities. He envisioned how he might introduce them to his millions of social media followers. He was concerned with the follow-through—sometimes two years hence. For most other collaborators, designing captured their attention. The marketing and retailing weren't primary concerns.

"I think one of the reasons he was highly successful was because unlike a lot of people that I've worked with—and there's been a *lot* of people—he seemed to have a very strong sense of the end [point] in mind, where he's trying to go. Not just with the products, but how he wants to 'image' them. He was a marketing guy—big time. Really visionary about the whole story, not just the product," Cooke said. "I don't actually think that the product is the reason he was so successful. I think there are other people that do better individual products—that's just my personal opinion—but not so many of them have that ability to create this community, with ideas of how it's going to come to market. And then garner the support along the way."

When Abloh thought about the look of the shoes, he asked himself, "What would make a sneakerhead stop scrolling?"

Within a few months, Abloh made his vision for the project clear. It was all about irony and DIY. His idea was to suggest that any kid could go into a Nike store and buy a pair of sneakers and take a scalpel to them—use their imagination to reinvent the shoes to their own liking. A Sharpie was Abloh's other design tool. He scribbled quotation marks around words to layer his sneaker designs with irony. Lots and lots of irony. He graffitied shoelaces with the word "shoelaces." The air-filled soles read "air." On other shoes, Abloh wrote "foam." He threaded red zip ties through the laces and eyelets, a flourish that mimicked the antitheft devices retailers used to deter shoplifting. A kid—maybe even a Black kid who might have been followed around by a security guard at the local mall simply because he was "shopping while Black"—could reappropriate that antitheft zip tie and attach it to any sneaker of his choosing—his own DIY version of an Abloh shoe. It wasn't theft; it was creativity. And it made Abloh's shoes recognizable from a distance.

ONCE THE TEAM AT NIKE saw how Abloh had conceived the project, something that Abloh—the ultimate nonperfectionist—

said took exactly one day, they decided to cede creative control of all ten sneakers to him. Abloh was the sole collaborator for The Ten. He worried that failure could end his fashion career. But success? His trajectory could be limitless.

Five of his shoes were part of the "revealing" group, sneakers that had been cut open and their innards exposed: Air Jordan 1, Nike Air Max 90, Nike Air Presto, Nike Air VaporMax, and the Nike Blazer. Another five were described as "ghosting," because of their translucency: Converse Chuck Taylor, Nike Zoom Fly SP, Nike Air Force 1 Low, Nike React Hyperdunk 2017, and the Nike Air Max 97.

Nike unveiled the collaboration in September 2017 with the kind of fanfare that might accompany the arrival of new works by Picasso. It was fitting since Abloh liked to compare Nike's most enduring sneaker styles to Leonardo da Vinci's *Mona Lisa* or Michelangelo's *David*. The reimagined Nike sneakers were treated like works destined for a museum—Picassos for your feet.

Nike crafted the marketing so that the shoes could rise above clichés about sports, hip-hop, and rappers. Abloh didn't disavow those connections, but he didn't want his work to be defined by them. "He was a really, really hardworking, well-educated engineer," Janjer said. "That's the core of who he was."

The first members of the public to see The Ten were sneaker aficionados in London and New York City. They registered for the privilege of attending a multiday conference—a gathering of Nike nerds, collectors, bloggers, and the media that chronicled the changing fortunes in the streetwear economy. Over several days, the sneaker styles were intellectualized, admired, and, if one was lucky enough to be a VIP with a green wristband, purchased. In New York, the three-day summit convened at 23 Wall Street—an elegant, pale marble building that was the former home of J.P. Morgan & Company—in the heart of the Financial District. A bright-red banner hung over the entrance to the building and welcomed attendees. In the center of the sign were Abloh's familiar gestures: quotation marks. "Insert Idea Here," it read. The Nike markings—the famous swoosh and the jumpman—were tucked into the corners.

The dramatically lit interior blended the mood of an airy recreation center with a contemporary art gallery and a designer fashion boutique. A phantom Michael Jordan was posed midjump beneath a basketball hoop. A wall-size video monitor played a stream of chaotic behind-the-scenes images of Abloh at work. Large seating cubes were scattered in front of a stage where an audience gathered for panel discussions, one of which featured Abloh and others who'd collaborated with Nike on shoes: Spike Lee, Don C, and stylist Aleali May. Abloh served as moderator, his legs jittery with restless energy and his hands gesturing broadly as he began by asking each person for their first Michael Jordan memory. Nike wouldn't sink or swim on the strength of this one collaboration. Still, it had been a risk to put the entire project in the hands of a newcomer like Abloh. He had a knack for buzz and a track record for making sure the right audience found his products, but fashion is a fickle business. There are no sure bets.

Abloh also had good reason to worry. If people hated the shoes, if they didn't sell, it would be a reputational disaster for Off-White on a massive scale. And Off-White was his résumé.

Abloh's sneakers were displayed on the surrounding walls like priceless sculptures. Verbiage plastered all around read like chest-thumping bravado, technical blatherings, and existential musings. The room was a graphic designer's nirvana. A Helvetica paradise. Abloh's do-it-yourself philosophy was brought to life.

Each sneaker was distinct, but they all shared a single aesthetic language that was carried through in the details. Despite so much of the work having been done remotely, there was an intimacy to each design, as if you could see the fingerprints of Abloh on the shoe.

The shoes looked like prototypes, as if they were still in the process of being created and as if the wearer had managed to nab something so fresh it was practically unfinished.

The Air Jordan 1, for example, was constructed in its familiar red and white palette, but the black swoosh looked as if it had been cut out by hand from another shoe and roughly basted on the side. The style's original date of introduction was scrawled in black, along with a reference to Nike's headquarters in Beaverton, Oregon. The technology of the shoes—the various elements composing them—was written out like an anatomical diagram. And, of course, red zip ties hung from the eyelets.

As a company, Nike embraced Abloh's creative habits and obsessions. It allowed him to excel at what he was exceptionally good at doing, which was taking a preexisting object and exploiting its design elements. Nike provided him with a group of successful and beloved sneakers that he could alter by his preferred 3 percent, and that was more than enough to make them seem transformed yet still clearly, undeniably Nike. The sneaker giant gave Abloh space to consider sneakers as a statement about culture. It provided a stage for a discussion about the meaning of these shoes and the meaning of Michael Jordan. Nike was the beneficiary of Abloh's confident and engaging aesthetic sensibility. And in return, it took that sensibility and placed it within the context of a brand that had deep roots in sports, popular culture, and the social zeitgeist.

Nike blasted Abloh's talent, ambition, and savvy at full volume. In doing so, his distance from Kanye West expanded. And Abloh got something for which he'd been striving: an opportunity to define himself and his aesthetic within fashion and outside West's orbit. He was building something for himself. He was flexing his singular ambitions. His moment-seizing dalliance with Been Trill, his independence day at Pyrex Vision, and his launch of Off-White were jet fuel. Nike was the billion-dollar blastoff.

"I wouldn't want to give Nike the credit for Virgil's hard work; but I think Nike was the first big sort of accreditation that he needed," Janjer said.

Nike connected to popular culture in a way that was unlike anything within the realm of high fashion. It had dedicated media—Complex, Highsnobiety, Hypebeast—that covered it, along with other sneaker makers, with the kind of unrelenting focus and attention that *The Washington Post* reserved for politics and *The Wall Street Journal* applied to the stock market. The brand understood how to situate itself in the thick of the cultural conversation—whether it was at street level or in ateliers, in art galleries, or at an arena concert. Fraser Cooke and Sami Janjer had long worked to connect Nike to worlds outside sports through collaborations with Riccardo Tisci, Chitose Abe, Martine Rose, and others. That know-how made it the most valuable brand in the world—far ahead of Adidas, as well as luxury labels such as Chanel, Hermès, Gucci, and Dior. Louis Vuitton ranked a distant sixth in the world.

After all the workshops and panel discussions had ratcheted up anticipation, Nike released the first five styles—the group dubbed "revealing"—during fashion weeks in New York, London, Milan, and Paris, with the rest going out to retailers globally soon after. In choosing those cities, the established fashion capitals of the world, Nike made its message clear: sneakers weren't just fashionable; they were fashion at the highest level.

ABLOH'S SNEAKERS SWIFTLY sold out. Nike's quarterly revenue rose by 5 percent compared to the previous year. "Nike is a very loud place," Cooke said. "If you do a product that hits, everyone sees it."

In addition to providing evidence of the shifting nature of luxury fashion, sneakers highlighted demographic shifts and social upheaval that had become more apparent in the country. Sneaker culture had issues of race woven throughout it, from the athletes who promoted the brands to the kids who made the brands cool and the violence that rose up around it. And Nike was at the center of that tension. Its prominence and influence ebbed and flowed, but in the years surrounding Abloh's collaboration and the launch of The Ten, the conversation about racial justice, diversity, and equity increased in both volume and vigor.

The ground had begun to shift as early as 2013 with the creation of the hashtag Black Lives Matter in response to the acquittal of the self-appointed neighborhood watchman who shot and killed seventeen-year-old Trayvon Martin in Florida. In 2014, Eric Garner, Michael Brown, and Tamir Rice were killed by police officers.

The year The Ten debuted, Alton Sterling and Philando Castile were killed by law enforcement. Police violence had become central to the public conversation about systemic racism. And Nike was pulled into that conversation by one of its collaborators.

The San Francisco 49ers football player Colin Kaepernick had an endorsement deal with Nike, and in 2016 Kaepernick began protesting as the National Anthem was performed before games. The playing of the anthem—a long-standing tradition—helped to equate the National Football League with American patriotism. Baseball thought of itself as America's warm-hearted pastime, but football built a reputation as America's swaggering ego, its machismo, and its toughness. Kaepernick's decision to remain seated and then later to "take a knee" during the singing of "The Star-Spangled Banner" aimed to draw attention to police brutality, racism, and social inequality. While many found his actions righteous and brave, others felt nothing but outrage. They accused him of disrespecting the flag, the nation's veterans, and the country itself. During the 2016 presidential campaign, candidate Donald J. Trump gleefully criticized Kaepernick's actions on multiple occasions, at one point even suggesting that the quarterback "find a country that works better for him."

When Kaepernick left the 49ers at the end of the season, no team signed him. Nike was left with a football player who not only wasn't playing football but had become a lead figure in a growing culture war over what it meant to be Black in America. As Kaepernick's visibility grew politically, he essentially became invisible in the Nike ecosystem.

After significant internal debate, Nike finally decided to embrace Kaepernick, as well as his activism.

Nike didn't have to worry about Abloh. He might have been, as Nike initially thought of him, Kanye West's sidekick, but he was not one to use his words like weapons. He didn't fling grenades into the middle of a conversation. He purposefully didn't move through the fashion industry like a race warrior with a bullhorn. "I'm the opposite of a rebel type," Abloh said. He spent much of his time in the digital realm, which made him a global creature. He worked online more than he did from his home in Chicago or in the Off-White offices in Milan. He didn't use social media as a place to document complaints, vent frustrations, or take a virtual knee. He didn't use it as a platform for the public flaying of anyone who didn't see things his way or who refused to see him with the same sense of possibility with which he saw himself. He didn't berate those who underestimated him. He dug deep into his skill set to prove that those who dismissed him were poorer for having done so.

"He was never confrontational," Janjer said. "He never wanted to be the *angry Black man* in the corporate environment.

"We always talked about that. I'm a Black guy. It's so easy for us to look angry," Janjer continued. "We have to look composed; you have to be a chess player. And he was. He was really, really good.

"I think a lot of people who struggle in a predominately White or predominately male or whatever, they would at least acknowledge or complain or identify a level of prejudice," Janjer said. "He just never did. He just worked double time to figure things out." Abloh didn't want to explode corporate culture; he wanted to make it cool.

Janjer was sensitive to what it meant to move through the business world, the fashion industry, the breadth of society, as a Black man. He recognized in Abloh a desire to be measured against a neutral standard. But there really was no such thing—at least not in the fashion business as it had long existed. The standard for creativity had its roots in western Europe, the monarchies, and the aristocratic court. Everything else was viewed in juxtaposition to that—how acceptable it was, how subversive it was, how disorienting it was, how informal it was, how Black it was.

As Abloh stepped deeper into the White corporate culture of fashion, the hurdle was not whether his work was good enough. The days in which fashion had adhered to certain objective rules of quality were long past. Both fine silk and humble nylon had been welcomed into the realm of deeply admired and desired fashion. Haute couture still demanded hand-stitching, but machine-made garments were held in equally high esteem, a comparison celebrated in a 2016 exhibition, *Manus x Machina: Fashion in an Age of Technology,* at the Metropolitan Museum of Art. Price no longer reflected craftsmanship, materials, or even rarity. A T-shirt with the right markings could be a point of pride just as powerful as a bespoke suit.

In the past, fashion's legacy gatekeepers had kept many talented people out, but they had also sifted through the sands to find singular gems. "Now you have a free-for-all. Now, whoever shouts loudly gets the attention," said Teri Agins, author of *The End of Fashion*. The twenty-first-century influencers who sat front row at fashion shows, who had enormous social media followings, weren't gatekeepers; they were bullhorns.

While there were still design houses content to exist outside the mass imagination, content to simply be purveyors of well-made clothes, the big luxury brands had mostly been unable to resist the allure of being something more. Most fashion, particularly men's fashion, trafficked in popular culture, not just attire. And that put it in the thrall of consumers who were young, male, . . . and Black. If connoisseurship still existed to any significant degree anywhere in fashion, it was in the world of sneakers.

"We are more confident in the idea that sneakers are now an emerging alternative asset class that can be bought and sold for both collection, price appreciation and investment," read an alert from TD Securities. Estimates have the sneaker resale market reaching $30 billion by 2030. Indeed, a full collection of The Ten, auctioned by Sotheby's in 2022, sold for $35,280.

Fashion was still a club, only the membership demands had changed. Originally, that club was established for the benefit of those in the upper classes of society. It was a place that could be elitist and intimidating to anyone of modest means and without connections who was trying to penetrate its walls. "It was high society," said Agins, who began writing about the fashion business for *The Wall Street Journal* in 1989. "I was one of the few Black people there. I wanted to look like I fit in. People were not friendly. They were snobby."

Now the rules for membership were shifting. Instead of insider status being determined by one's knowledge of darts and embroidery, it was predicated on intimacy with certain streetwear labels sold through a network of independent boutiques and e-commerce sites rather than grand department stores with elevator operators and doormen. The ability to buy a particularly desirable T-shirt or pair of sneakers wasn't determined by how much money one had—although an enormous bank account certainly helped. Access was based on knowing the right shopkeeper who might put a certain item aside for special customers—not unlike the saleswomen in the old couture houses who required an introduction from an established customer before they'd accept someone new. The modern fashion system still commanded a commitment of time. Rare was the person standing around being fit into muslin; instead, folks were hovering online with itchy fingers trying to snag a limited-edition sneaker at the exact moment of its release.

Fashion editors still held sway in highlighting the next big thing, but that job was shared with those who'd garnered followers on social media. A new kind of socialite drew the affections of designers. These men and women weren't decked out in white tie and ballgowns and heading to opening night at the opera, but make no mistake, they created ripples in another kind of social system in which bouncers still guarded doorways.

Velvet ropes still cordoned off VIP rooms. Bottle service was not available to all. Not everyone was friends with a rapper. Not every Black man had cultivated an online cheering section or had the temperament to be a chess player.

Nike may have needed some convincing that Abloh was more than a rapper's assistant. Many of the fashion industry's editors and critics dismissed Abloh's talent as a designer because he didn't abide by the key tenets of what it meant to create fashion. But the success of The Ten was undeniable. Sneakers had become part of every designer's collection. They weren't intended for a court or a field. They were for the red carpet. They fetched top dollar at auction and they connected with young male consumers in a manner unlike any other fashion object.

The enthusiasm that surrounded Abloh couldn't be ignored. He was exceptionally talented at the things that mattered in a fashion industry transforming itself to be relevant to a new customer base. Those consumers valued the prestige of legacy designer brands. The hip-hop community loved nothing more than reeling off the names of each designer label that hung in their closet: Gucci, Prada, Louis. Fashion meant showing up and showing out.

Working with the big corporations wasn't capitulation. The boardroom was a locus of cool. Aligning with old European fashion houses wasn't selling out; it was winning. Fashion was built on story-telling, stories that felt intimate and personal. Abloh understood that fashion was fundamentally about marketing and communications; he was transparent about it.

In the past, so many institutions within the fashion industry had tried to contain the impact of Black culture and Black people on the clothes they marketed. The most egregious example may well have been the stigmatizing of trends that bubbled up from the hip-hop community as something other than a new variation on designer sportswear. It was not "urban" fashion. It wasn't less-than anything else.

Fashion finally stopped building walls to keep its traditions from being tainted by disruptive outsiders. It relented once hip-hop's dominance in popular culture became indisputable. It relented once hip-hop itself became a little less Black—once it was leavened with streetwear. It relented when confronted by those with the right attitude, which Kanye West did not have.

By the time Abloh collaborated on The Ten, the balance of power in the fashion equation had shifted. Consumers held significant sway. Social media connected and amplified the voices of outliers and activists—as well as fans. Community replaced internships and apprenticeships and design degrees as the most valued asset. How big was your posse? Which tribe did you represent? How many followers did you have? Menswear was a cauldron of creativity increasingly led by a group of designers who'd all been privy to the same sources of inspiration. And siding with Blackness—at least a certain kind of Blackness—was, for a time, proving to be a corporate win.

Abloh embodied all those alliances. He thrived at cultural intersections. Within his community, he was Andy Warhol, Karl Lagerfeld, and the favorite teacher who promised to give his students the shortcuts to success.

"There's been no one, from at least my experience, that I've worked with that has been able to be a communicator, an art director, a fashion designer, and a marketeer all in one," Janjer said.

Louis Vuitton wanted to turn Abloh's friends into their customers.

A Win for the Culture?

IN JANUARY 2018, Louis Vuitton announced that Kim Jones was leaving his post as its menswear designer. Jones had been at the label for seven years. He introduced a credible streetwear sensibility into the brand. He helped to transform the way luxury houses in general looked at their relationship with a generation of label obsessives who cared little for the brand's self-lauded history catering to gray-haired White men, aristocrats, and jet-setters.

Many of fashion's small, family-owned companies that once manufactured distinctive products of admirable quality had been consumed by conglomerates. The brand names were now the product. Labels were a banner under which niche communities gathered, especially in menswear. Instead of wearing the gear of their favorite sports team or the jersey of a beloved player, men lined up behind designer labels. Were you team Givenchy? Or team Gucci? Or Dior? Pick your $3,000 varsity jacket or $700 tee. The necessity and desire for design expertise weren't lost but were under stress. They were being squashed into oblivion.

The changing nature of fashion called for a reassessment of what it meant to be a legacy brand. Increasingly, Louis Vuitton leaned into the idea that it was a purveyor of culture, not simply clothes. During Marc Jacobs's tenure, the women's collection was unveiled on a runway inside a glass box on the site of a former Citroën factory. Later, the show shifted to a temporary tent in the outdoor courtyard of the Louvre Museum. Then the Fondation Louis Vuitton opened in the fall of 2014 in a Frank Gehry–designed building that resembled a glass schooner run aground in Paris's Bois de Boulogne. It housed a permanent collection of contemporary art. To mark its opening, the Louis Vuitton women's collections moved there during Paris Fashion Week. The show itself took place in a subterranean hall devoid of any famous artwork. Still, it was art adjacent. In March 2017, the women's collection moved back to central Paris and into the Richelieu wing of the Louvre. Models sauntered amid the seventeenth- and eighteenth-century sculptures. Louis Vuitton moved from Marc Jacobs's collaborations with artists, to opening its own art foundation, to having its products displayed amid some of the most revered examples of Western art.

When Jones arrived in 2011, the company was flying high. Louis Vuitton had long been the fuel that fired up the fashion and leather goods division of LVMH, and Bernard Arnault crowed about how lucrative the previous year had been. Sales were up; customers lusted after their labels; and Louis Vuitton was a golden child.

During Jones's tenure, Louis Vuitton blossomed as an emblem of luxury, art . . . and streetwear. Jones gave Arnault even more to boast about. The wild success of the 2017 Supreme collaboration received special notice in that year's annual report. That venture reportedly reaped 100 million euros in revenue. But it hadn't just been a commercial success. It connected Louis Vuitton to something more elusive than money: the mood of the moment. In 2011, LVMH revenue was just under 9 billion euros. When Jones departed in 2018, it was well over 18 billion.

As one might expect, LVMH didn't let Jones go far. He left Louis Vuitton and moved to Dior Homme. As soon as Jones's departure was announced, the fashion industry began to speculate on who might fill his shoes at Louis Vuitton.

WHILE SNEAKERHEADS and fashion fans were gobbling up The Ten, the fruits of Abloh's 2017 project with Nike, he continued to focus on building Off-White. He was egoless in his willingness to meet the fashion industry where it was. As Abloh considered his next best steps, there was something old-fashioned, traditional, and nonconfrontational about his mindset.

"I'm not offended by the security guard who, ironically we're the same ethnicity, but he thinks I don't belong there," Abloh said. "That's too low level to get distracted from the larger goal."

Abloh had much in common with the trailblazers of earlier generations. While he didn't preach about the favored status of a talented tenth and its capacity to uplift an entire race, he was, in different respects, both a credit to his race and a race man.

"I think Virgil had a majority mentality. He didn't think small," said Ibrahim Kamara, who worked with Abloh at Off-White and later at Louis Vuitton. The two met when Abloh extended a hand to him over Instagram. Like Abloh, Kamara was a son of immigrants. He came to England as a teenager after growing up in Sierra Leone and The Gambia. Kamara never unlearned the powerful feeling of coming of age in an environment where most everyone—doctors, lawyers, cobblers, waiters—looked like him.

"There was no place [Abloh] thought he couldn't go because he was a Black. I think he just assumed the world was his. And I think building that mindset from a very young age, I think can really set you free," Kamara said. "You know when you have been treated unfairly; you know when you deserve something; you know you should get something because you're good at it."

As the son of Ghanaian immigrants, Abloh moved through his life with the privileges such knowledge and distinction brought.

Abloh exhibited the fresh sense of possibility and heavy responsibility that comes from being the child of parents who traveled to this country chasing the American Dream for themselves and their offspring. The sacrifices of an earlier generation were recent and loomed large. Family history—the successes and the failures and the indefatigable desires—were not blurry memories or casualties of slavery's erasure. Such clarity can be powerfully motivating. The knowledge of his own history was a solid foundation upon which he could build.

Abloh spoke often about having seen the dirt roads of Ghana. He'd seen its poverty, which only made his potential shine brighter. The expectation of success was both a burden and an impetus.

In the hierarchy of America's caste system, Abloh had a bit of distance from the bottom rungs. He wasn't at the top of the ladder looking out over an expansive vista of all life's possibilities, but at least he had a view.

Abloh continued to define Off-White and his role there as something more than merely a fashion brand and the designer who led it. He recast the industry's idea of a designer, shifting it from the image of a tortured creative soul striving to perfect his craft, or a lifestyle guru telling customers how to dress, eat, and shelter, into a kind of cultural impresario—someone who spotted rising trends, who excited a community, who sold a feeling of belonging with a simple logo, and who made the purchase of a varsity jacket feel like a sociopolitical gesture on par with integrating a lunch counter.

His Off-White carried the weight of possibility and transformation. It was a repository for a new way of thinking about how luxury and Blackness converged. Abloh would sometimes say that Off-White wasn't *his* brand—although it very much was—but rather *our* brand. Such positioning was his self-written permission slip to absorb whatever might have been in the air and inject it into a collection. *We're all in this together.*

Abloh demonstrated his talent on terms set by the White establishment; he also helped to transform the terms by which future talent may well be judged. He came to fashion as an outsider, but he checked many—although not all—the boxes deemed necessary for success in the industry. He did this as he loudly professed his disdain for boxes.

To further his ambition, Abloh had hired a public relations team to help him launch Off-White: Karla Otto. Established in 1982, Karla Otto, named after its German-born founder, was part of fashion's old guard. The international firm worked with designers Jean Paul Gaultier and Jil Sander and had even worked with Kanye West on his first runway show in Paris. Otto herself did her part to set West up for success. She assembled key fashion editors in an environment in which they could focus solely on the clothing and not West's fame. The crowd of screaming fans was held at bay as guests entered the Lycée Henri IV and filed into a bare white room with a carved ceiling. They took their places on the two rows of benches that lined either side of the runway. She stood by his side backstage as he fielded questions from editors. When he began to flail, she didn't halt the interviews or otherwise intervene. That was how fashion worked—even for a celebrity.

In selecting Otto's agency, Abloh took a note from Sean "Diddy" Combs. When Combs launched his Sean John collection in 1998, he did so with the assistance of Paul Wilmot Communications, another of the industry's legacy agencies. Even before the unveiling on the main floor of the Bloomingdale's flagship in New York City, the public relations firm had advised Combs on how to engage with the fashion industry, on what he needed to do to be invited inside instead of having to break down the door. And following that advice, Combs dutifully attended other designers' shows. He wooed editors. He took their questions.

At Karla Otto, Abloh was respected for his flexibility, earnestness, and willingness to be amenable to fashion's quirks and traditions.

He wanted to meet the editors of legacy media such as *Elle* and *Vogue* and asked publicist Kevin McIntosh to set up introductions. "Who are the people I need to know?" Abloh asked. "Let me meet them so I can see how the game is played."

Off-White was different from Been Trill and Pyrex Vision. It wasn't an amusing distraction. It wasn't an "art project." Abloh envisioned Off-White as fundamental to his legacy. He was especially eager for an introduction to American *Vogue*'s longtime editor in chief Anna Wintour.

Social media was Abloh's way of circumventing traditional fashion media. But in truth, he loved *Vogue* and wanted the magazine to take note of his accomplishments. "I was doing my thing. I was like looking for a feature," he said. "I was reading things. I was like, 'Man, I think I'm doing better. I'm in Paris. Can I get one of those [stories]?' I used to obsess, when I was young, looking at those magazines and being like, 'This is design. I want that fancy photo in front of like a dog, with maps and all that.'"

Wintour declined, on multiple occasions, to attend an Off-White show. Her reticence was not particularly unusual. Wintour didn't make a habit of going to runway shows of upstart designers—not unless they were being nurtured by *Vogue*. And becoming one of *Vogue*'s babies was, well, a matter of talent, lineage, commercial clout, likability, and the luck of the gods.

Like so many young designers before him, Abloh ferried his collection to the *Vogue* offices to allow its editors to assess his line. As much as folks complained about Wintour's more than thirty-year tenure as editor of *Vogue*, as much as they dismissed the magazine as past its prime, a meeting with Wintour remained one of fashion's stations of the cross, a valuable one.

Vogue finally took real notice of Abloh in 2015, and he was introduced to its readers in the September issue with a story that had him interviewed by phone from various airports as he circled the globe working: Chicago's O'Hare, New York's LaGuardia, Seoul's Incheon. The story focused mostly on his multitasking, on his hopping around the world to deejay, assist Kanye West, and, yes, work on Off-White.

"The first show of his that I seem to recall attending was Fall 2017, which featured so many leaves on the runway it looked like Central Park in November," Wintour said. "[Model] Bella Hadid walked that show, and some years later, she was in conversation with Virgil at our annual Forces of Fashion event. That was his second appearance; his first was with his good friend, Heron Preston, who Virgil had become somewhat of a mentor to. That was something he did a lot; help others, take an interest, show them the way forward.

"Later that year, Virgil and I met in Paris at *Vogue*'s offices on Place du Palais-Bourbon, and we discussed his Princess of Wales–inspired collection," Wintour said. And as was her way, she also introduced Abloh to a group of immigrant soccer players in Paris. He worked with Nike to design jerseys for the Melting Passes team. "Virgil of course had to invite them to his show, taking so many selfies with them.

"I was delighted to go to that show, meet Virgil, and talk—which we ended up doing a lot over the years that followed," Wintour said. She admired his pay-it-forward mentality and the community and excitement he brought to fashion.

About one thing Abloh remained clear: he wanted a big job at one of fashion's big houses. He believed they needed what he could offer: a luxury language understood by young consumers. He'd mused about his chances of being hired at Givenchy when Tisci departed in 2017. But that was just wishful thinking and dreaming. The role went to Clare Waight Keller, who became the first woman to lead the house.

But Abloh was making an impression among fashion executives.

In March of that same year, Abloh had a clandestine meeting with Donatella Versace—who took over the creative direction of the house after her brother was murdered. Abloh and Versace huddled in the South of France to discuss his possibly designing Versus, the brand's youthful diffusion line. Versace looked approvingly and longingly at Abloh's relationships within the music industry, his devoted cadre of fans, and his ability to connect with people across borders—both racial and geographic. Versace wanted to be cool. Or at least cooler.

"Virgil was a true gentleman. He was incredibly kind and courteous when we met, and I loved his energy," Versace said. Like so many others, she was charmed by him and marveled at his capacity to do so much. To be in constant motion. "I don't know where he found the time to do everything he did and deejay as well. I asked him when he slept, and he said that life was for living—not sleeping."

Abloh was intrigued by Donatella's overtures and presented a brief on his vision for Versus. "He had such simple ideas, but they were so strong," Versace said. "I would have loved the chance of working with him more closely."

Ultimately, Abloh decided Versus wasn't the right fit for him. He backed away before an offer was on the table. Another suitor was more attractive.

IN SHORT ORDER after Kim Jones's departure from Louis Vuitton, fashion's rumor mill began to speculate about Abloh succeeding him.

He seemed like a long shot for such a massive job, but Jones agitated for his friend to be his replacement. And on his Instagram, the departing designer posted a photograph of a pair of Off-White x Nike Air Jordan 1 sneakers that Abloh personalized for Jones. "Thanks Virgil," Jones wrote. "Big love."

Abloh's initial response to inquiries about a future at Louis Vuitton was that he had "no clue" about the rumors.

In addition to Jones, Abloh had other supporters within the luxury conglomerate. When Bernard Arnault's son Alexandre became co-chief executive of Rimowa in 2016, he cast about in search of collaborations that could thrust the 120-year-old German luggage maker into the public consciousness. Specifically, he wanted to grab the attention of millennials, who were driving 85 percent of luxury growth. The younger Arnault already had brokered relationships with the Los Angeles–based streetwear brands AntiSocialSocialClub and Supreme. He turned his attention to Off-White and in 2017 promoted a Rimowa collaboration with Abloh's label on social media. In describing the see-through suitcases he'd designed, Abloh argued they represented the "3.0 of personalization." He said, "You become a performance art piece just by using the thing. It's like putting your items on display and rethinking the premise of a product."

A transparent suitcase is also a siren song to thieves. Or a way to obsessively brag. *Fold that Supreme hoodie neatly and make sure the logo is facing outward for all of TSA to see!* Abloh argued that it was an artistic exercise.

Abloh also had Michael Burke in his corner. Burke, who'd facilitated Abloh's unorthodox internship at Fendi, had become CEO of Louis Vuitton, and he remained a fan. He'd continued to talk with Abloh about his career trajectory and about possible projects they might work on together. When menswear designers within the LVMH group began to move around, leaving an opening at Louis Vuitton, Burke had Abloh in mind as Jones's successor.

"We spent time thinking about that and talking about what that would mean and where he would take Vuitton," Burke said. "Where would he want to go with it? And what were my needs and what were my constraints?"

Soon enough, Abloh was sketching his vision for Louis Vuitton menswear. He balanced these aspirations with his daily commitments. Back home in Chicago, he worked to finish a presentation of designs for Louis Vuitton while he was in the midst of an interview with a writer from the *Chicago Tribune*. Abloh was engrossed on his laptop and clearly not paying attention to the writer sitting across from him who was trying desperately to engage him in conversation. Finally, exasperated and baffled, the reporter asked, "What are you doing?" Unable to reveal the truth, Abloh attributed his distraction to his needing to finish up a design for T-shirts in honor of a friend's birthday.

"It really truly was the first iteration of him starting his LVMH conversation," recalled publicist Kevin McIntosh.

The fashion rumors about Abloh were true. He was in talks with a major design house. He quietly sent off sample garments from his collection so executives at Louis Vuitton could see real-world examples of his point of view and the quality of his Italian manufacturing. They needed to see if he had grown into something more than a T-shirt maker. A month later, as the talks with the French firm continued, Abloh participated in *Vogue* magazine's first Forces of Fashion conference held at Milk Studios, a multipurpose space that hosted runway shows, parties, and presentations. Abloh sat with his friend Heron Preston and *Vogue* editor Chioma Nnadi for a conversation about "cool." Just before that talk, in the shared green room, Abloh huddled in a back corner taking a phone call— for once the conversation was not happening via text messages over WhatsApp—about his professional future. When he took the stage, he offered his definition of luxury, which might well have been his view of what Louis Vuitton could mean to the streetwear generation: "My internal tool for digesting the word 'luxury' is to determine whether or not something is coveted. If you covet it, it's luxurious to you." For Abloh, luxury wasn't defined by quality, rarity, or longevity. Luxury was simply something you desperately wanted but didn't necessarily need.

Louis Vuitton was the right European brand for Abloh. Maybe it was the *only* one that could have accommodated him. It was one of fashion's oldest brands, and it had held the imagination of the hip-hop community for decades. It signified a particular kind of success: financial. It was equated with cash that was so freshly earned it was still wet from the printing. The LV logo announced one's ability to buy extremely expensive products that even the most fashion obtuse would recognize. Louis Vuitton didn't measure one's level of sophistication; it highlighted one's bank account.

As the world's largest luxury brand, Louis Vuitton was a force of influence. It was sturdy. It already was a rip-roaring success; it wasn't a brand trying to right itself. Menswear accounted for only 5 to 15 percent of its sales; it was a relatively low-risk division but one with plenty of room to grow.

The company could bear up under the stress of an unconventional talent. It didn't have a history as a couture house. Sure, it had company DNA, but it wasn't mythical. It didn't have the quiet social currency of Hermès, the glamorous hedonistic history of Gucci, the romance of Givenchy, or the idealized haute couture legacies of Dior and Chanel. Louis Vuitton products weren't enshrined in a fashion system with the kind of reverence reserved for Dior's New Look, Chanel's bouclé jackets, or Yves Saint Laurent's *le smoking*. Louis Vuitton made suitcases and handbags, the most familiar of which was probably the Speedy, which did not have the name recognition or aspirational patina of an Hermès Birkin or a Kelly bag. Its designers were talented men, but they were not larger than life. Each one brought a different sensibility to the house. Each had tugged the brand a little bit farther from its French roots, which were never that deeply planted.

"Vuitton had a kind of maturity to it so that it could really embrace disruption in a big way. The foundation was strong enough—as a leather goods company—that they could bring amazing people on and let them loose," said James Greenfield, the former director of Givenchy's men's division. Louis Vuitton "being a leather goods company, its foundation is in something a little bit more neutral, a little bit more lifestyle."

Finally, it was time for Abloh to meet with Bernard Arnault. It seems that every designer has an apocryphal story about the way they were vetted for an LVMH job. Ozwald Boateng recalled being taken onto the balcony outside of Yves Carcelle's immense office to discuss Givenchy. John Galliano told the story of a James Bond–like armored limousine picking him up and ferrying him to LVMH headquarters. But a single tradition stands. A possible new hire of any magnitude met with Arnault over a lunch prepared by his chef and served in his private dining room in his Paris office at 30 Avenue Montaigne.

Arnault was a tall, slender man with gray hair, a high forehead, and a slow, considered manner of speech whether in English or French. He has been described as patrician, but he was not especially charismatic. Any hint of outsize charm may have been due to the fact that he was one of the richest men in the world; and depending on the state of the stock market, he had sometimes been the richest. Immense wealth is its own kind of magnetism.

Arnault was both a cunning businessman with a killer instinct and a connoisseur of expensive wines and vintage champagne, precious jewelry, and, of course, designer frocks. Arnault could have a passionate conversation about the beauty of cashmere socks even as he plotted a hostile takeover of the company that produced them.

When he moved through a fashion crowd gathered for one of his brand's shows, he was surrounded by security as he headed to his seat of honor in the front row. He looked a bit like a human shark patrolling the waters, so there was a tendency for people to both stare and recoil.

As a young man, Arnault studied civil engineering at one of France's most prestigious universities, École Polytechnique, and graduated in 1971. He went on to work as an engineer at Ferret-Savinel, his family's construction company. He entered the fashion industry in 1984 by purchasing the bankrupt Boussac textile business. He was drawn to it because of a single jewel tucked amid the debris: Dior. The brand would later hold a distinct position within the LVMH fashion and leather goods group—and in the heart of Arnault. "Dior is the most magic name in fashion in the world," Arnault once said. But Louis Vuitton was always—and continued to be—the most lucrative one.

The entrance to 30 Avenue Montaigne was watched over by security guards. Before a visitor reached for the door, a watchman stepped from the shadows to inquire about the business that had someone even considering entering the building. These were precautions that one might think more suitable to the Élysée Palace, but these were the offices of Arnault, someone who arguably had as much clout as France's democratically elected president.

Arnault's office was situated in some of Paris's most rarefied retail geography. The quietly elegant streets boasted storefronts for Dior, Chanel, and Valentino, as well as the five-star Plaza Athénée hotel. Arnault referred to his roster of fashion houses as "star brands" and equated their most exquisite efforts with art.

The fashion brands in the LVMH portfolio were among the most distinguished and valuable in the marketplace. The LVMH creative directors were duly compensated for their creativity, with seven-figure baseline salaries along with additional income tied to sales, plus perks such as clothing allowances and chauffeurs. But to be clear, Arnault was neither a dilettante nor an extravagant patron. He was a tactician whom the business community dubbed "the wolf in cashmere."

Arnault worked mightily to keep his taxes low and his profit margins wide. His business interests spanned the globe, and he readily pushed politics and social pressures aside in service to his bottom line.

On the surface, Arnault and Abloh could not have been more different. Separated by more than a generation, Arnault played classical piano while Abloh was an aficionado of hip-hop and electronic dance music. Arnault, a White billionaire with vigilant security, had the ear of presidents both at home and abroad. Abloh, a Black entrepreneur with a penchant for connecting with anyone who popped up in his social media feed, had rappers, streetwear designers, and neighborhood do-gooders among his contacts.

Arnault was judicious with his words. Abloh's words calmly flowed like a river over smooth rocks. Arnault once stood alongside an American president who referred to African nations as "shithole countries." Abloh was a Black man whose roots reached back to Ghana.

And yet, they shared a background in engineering, which required both precise and creative thinking. They each understood fashion as a commercial pursuit while also presenting themselves as deeply connected to art. Abloh had his *practice*; Arnault had his *Fondation*.

The two men sat down for lunch, along with Arnault's daughter Delphine, a statuesque woman with her father's high forehead and a face framed by shoulder-length blond hair. Delphine worked alongside Burke at Louis Vuitton; she also sat on the board of LVMH and shepherded the LVMH Prize for which Abloh had been a finalist. And, of course, Michael Burke was there as well.

The luncheon with Arnault was something between a test and a formality. By the time a job applicant was invited to break bread with the billionaire, a relationship of some sort was practically assured. "It's very rare by that time that something would not go forward, but it can happen," Burke said. "What it would mean is that, well, maybe at this time and at this house, the stars are not aligned. But if Bernard sits down and has lunch with somebody, there will be a relationship that will emanate out of that lunch."

Burke encouraged Abloh to be himself, to not anticipate what he thought Arnault might want. Lunch began with Abloh explaining his vision for Louis Vuitton. In true form, once he began to talk, his opening sentence led into another sentence, which turned into a paragraph, which built into a monologue.

"At that time, everybody had the word *street* on their minds. It's all about street, street, street, street, street, street. And so, he basically explained what *street* meant to him," Burke said. "For him, *street* was very, very complex: basically, it's what we wear in the streets and that includes everything."

As Abloh talked, he scribbled on a sheet of paper. He started in the upper-left corner and kept writing and drawing as he spoke. Arnault mostly listened. Occasionally, the titan posed a question about the role of accessories in relation to ready-to-wear. He asked how shoes fit into Abloh's vision of Louis Vuitton. They talked about architecture too because fashion was retail and luxury retail remained very much a robust brick-and-mortar business. They discussed the things crucial to the success of a business that often go unmentioned—the human factors. Was he ready to take on something so enormous? And as Abloh answered Arnault's questions, he continued to scribble. By the end of the luncheon, Abloh had written his entire game plan for Louis Vuitton on a single sheet of paper, not simply ideas about collaborations or products but the essence of what the collection would be: Who is the Vuitton man as done by

Virgil? The piece of paper was a road map, a preview of what was to come. But that conversation over lunch never anticipated how much the world would change. It couldn't have.

Abloh slid the paper across the table and over to Bernard Arnault, and the two men shook hands.

ON MARCH 26, 2018, Louis Vuitton announced Abloh's appointment as artistic director for the menswear division. In his celebratory remarks, Burke noted that Abloh's creativity and unorthodox background made him not only part of the fashion conversation but part of the pop cultural dialogue as well.

The industry had drastically changed from the days when Paris was the center of creativity and style was defined by strict codes of attire such as cocktail dresses, house dresses, dinner dresses, luncheon suits, and business suits. Business casual upended established corporate dress codes. Urban centers such as Tokyo, Beijing, New York, and Los Angeles captured the imagination of designers, leading them to turn away from Europe for inspiration and to look more globally. Celebrities replaced the models. Influencers were the new social swans. Everyone was a jet-setter, even if they were flying economy. And fashion was slowly knocking down the walls separating streetwear from everything else. As Abloh said, as Kim Jones said, as Jerry Lorenzo said, it was all just clothes.

All those changes made room for Abloh.

"He was disruptive as an outsider coming in, and there was a degree of irony and disruption in the work," Peter Saville said. "The challenge is maintaining that and not being consumed by the system, particularly in fashion, but in popular culture in general."

Fashion loved a person with sharp edges, but it also had a way of smoothing over those rough spots. The very act of celebrating an iconoclast in the pages of American *Vogue,* for instance, involved a makeover, whether the iconoclast was Lady Gaga, Billie Eilish, or Oprah Winfrey. They were all transformed into someone more glamorous, more palatable, and sometimes much thinner, because that was what it meant to be in fashion.

Abloh was elated with his new position; he was also overwhelmed and humbled.

"I wasn't ready for that cultural upswell of shock," he said. "I wasn't ready because I was just thinking, 'I got a new job,' like a normal person. It would be like you got hired at your company and all of a sudden you get emails and texts from people you went to high school with saying things like, 'Wow!'"

"The interview process was like eight months. And you could imagine my close friends having to hear me crying, screaming, moaning, being like, 'What if they don't hire me because of this? What if? What if they had an interview with somebody else and they were like, man, you can't do that?'" he recalled. "That's what I was having to fight through—that it might not happen.

"That magic epiphany of what you thought was impossible, *is* possible, is better than any fashion collection or any shoe that I've released, period."

It was what he'd worked toward in his professional life. With Off-White as his résumé, Louis Vuitton was the job to which he aspired. The seventeen-year-old kid who'd saved up to buy a $75 Louis Vuitton key pouch, one of the least expensive items the company produced in the early 1990s, was now in a position to dictate the next obsession of a teenager living in the stillness of the American Midwest or the cacophony of Beijing. Abloh wanted to create covetable basics.

His fans, the millions of them on social media, were initially confused. On his Instagram, to announce his new position, Abloh had simply posted a picture of a Louis Vuitton trunk with an enormous gold logo. But soon enough the meaning became clear to them. And they were thrilled.

"Past, present, future."

"A star was born."

"Kill everything King!"

"Literally my idol. This man done changed the game entirely."

"Black excellence fr."

"This makes me so hype."

"So proud."

"Virgil is going to WRECK LV!! Can't wait!!"

"Louis Vuitton is seriously about to be a masterpiece."

"Congrats on your work brother . . . you win for all of us!!"

His fans voiced little concern that he might be overwhelmed by the fashion system—consumed by it—or that taking on the grueling work of producing Louis Vuitton menswear, as well as overseeing Off-White, while also collaborating left and right, and racking up airline miles with deejaying gigs and saying "Yes" to a multitude of speaking engagements might be too much. They didn't worry that he'd be spread thin, or that so much multitasking would lead him down a path toward mediocrity. Abloh certainly wasn't selling out. That was something that an older generation said about an indie band that grew in popularity or signed a major label record deal. A younger generation that championed social justice and conscious consumerism didn't let Arnault's business-first philosophy diminish their cheering.

They marveled at Abloh's accomplishments, his ability to do it all. "You're so inspiring it's insane," one fan wrote. "Thank you." Another messaged: "I'm excited to see what you bring to the table of @louisvuitton! This opportunity was earned, not given . . . nothing but the utmost respect from me."

The enthusiasm tilted into ecstatic hyperbole with one social media fan comparing Abloh's arrival at Louis Vuitton to Barack

Obama winning the presidency. Abloh's position was a long way from leader of the free world, but his rise rang with a similar sense of a community seeing one of their own overcome centuries of prejudice and stereotypes. The cultural elites had signed off on a hero of the rank and file.

"He was going to bring his tribe. He was going to bring his language. It wasn't going to be what you think a classical design studio is going to be like," Edward Buchanan recalled thinking when he heard Abloh's news. "They gave him the opportunity and they paid him very well to come in there and bring his world."

Abloh didn't have Savile Row training. He didn't have a degree from Parsons or any other fashion design school. His only apprenticeship was a brief stint as a $500 a month Fendi intern. Ozwald Boateng and Edward Buchanan had tilled the soil in the industry. At Louis Vuitton, Marc Jacobs embraced contemporary culture; Kim Jones delivered street style. Louis Vuitton had been a multitude of things. And now it was a behemoth that was moving unfailingly toward the future but with enough historical ballast to keep it from tipping.

To paraphrase his father, Abloh had come from a long way. He'd moved beyond the silk-screened T-shirts of his beginnings, but the language of community was the same.

HIS FIRST RUNWAY presentation was in four months. And because it was Louis Vuitton, it would be an event the entire fashion industry would be watching. Abloh had to work quickly, but he had the resources of a billion-dollar brand to create an extravaganza that would leave struggling independent designers in awe. It was also a test. Not everyone was convinced Abloh was the man for the job. His design experience was essentially limited to the label he had launched five years earlier—one that was persistently described as streetwear no matter how ill-fitting the term had increasingly become.

"They want to call me a streetwear guy," he said, referring to fashion editors and retailers. "I'm cutting a pattern and they're still looking at the graphic on it or they don't want to buy it if it doesn't have words on it or something like that."

Abloh moved into the Louis Vuitton headquarters on rue du Pont Neuf, into a building with a classically elegant stone exterior and an interior that evoked the glass-and-chrome sterility of the modern business tower. His office retained the signatures of his predecessors, none of which he rushed to change. A Marc Jacobs–era bag from his collaboration with Richard Prince hung from a hook. The floor was ablaze in red carpeting celebrating the Louis Vuitton partnership with Supreme that Kim Jones had orchestrated. Miles Davis played in the background.

Abloh's most immediate decorating touch was to install turntables and several speakers the size of washing machines in front of windows overlooking the busy street below, from which he broadcast a show on Apple Music called *Televised Radio*. He maintained a steady stream of social media posts, updating his fans on the status of his debut.

The twenty-five-member design team that awaited him concentrated on realizing Abloh's vision, which had begun, even at Louis Vuitton, with a T-shirt. But in this case, Abloh was focused on the details of it, not just a logo or graphic. He knew he was under the industry's microscope. He was obsessed with making his T-shirt epitomize luxury in a modern, inclusive way.

"What's the perfect weight? Why are fashion T-shirts usually so tiny?" he said. "I just want to find the size medium that a lot of people could wear, and to not be oversized. People live by the size label in their garments. That affects their whole mental state. Their self-image is related to fit.

"Are we just here leading trend[s] of color and garment, or can I launch a trend thinking about responsibility towards body image, to have an effect on people and society at hand?

"For me, there's a subtlety in focusing on the right shape of [a] T-shirt and pant," he said. "I recognize that it's boring, but the idea is to catch people off-guard and reward them in some valuable way. I'm trying to make something luxurious approachable."

Ultimately, the most distinctive item from that first collection was one that began with an early question to the design team: Why did the leather goods house make clothes at all since that was not part of its history? One might well ask a similar question of brands such as Gucci, Prada, or Hermès, whose histories are in shoes and bags and saddles. But it's hard to dress a model from only the feet down or to tell a cohesive story about style without the help of a few frocks.

Abloh's query was less a complaint about Louis Vuitton's ready-to-wear ambitions and more a challenge for connecting the clothes more obviously to the brand's early lineage. He decided to focus on fusing accessories and garments into hybrid apparel, something he dubbed "accessomorphosis." It was an Abloh-esque way of describing tactical gear, fisherman vests, and utility belts. Jackets came with built-in bags; coats had cutouts to accommodate fanny packs—or, in fashion's new parlance, belt bags.

Accessomorphosis birthed the harness. The aesthetic flourish slipped over the top half of the torso. It merged suspenders with a shoulder holster.

"It can be worn over the outer layer, or worn as a mid-layer, almost like a holster would be for a gun," Abloh said. "It's a utility thing, and you can fashion it up."

The newly minted creative director teased the design on Instagram and then wore a bedazzled custom version to the May 2018 Met Gala—the celebrity traffic jam that functions as a fundraiser for the museum's costume institute. Abloh's harness had been hand-beaded by the Louis Vuitton men's atelier in shades of bronze and ivory to resemble an ecclesiastical raiment in celebration of the spring exhibition *Heavenly Bodies: Fashion and the Catholic Imagination.*

Abloh claimed to have designed his entire debut collection in three hours. He exuded confidence in the face of mounting pressure. "The grade will come back what it is," he said. "But I'm like, I read the book, and I did the work."

As the June runway show drew closer, a stream of messengers delivered what seemed like an entire greenhouse of floral arrangements, fashion's preferred method of communicating good wishes. Assorted influencers—representing millions of fashion followers—wandered through the studios. Model Naomi Campbell bounded through wearing sneakers and leggings and was trailed by an entourage.

Every fashion show setting is a balance between logistics and personal aesthetics. For Abloh's debut on June 21, 2018, he chose a location in the center of Paris. He didn't select some hipster hideaway, a contemporary music venue, or a sports arena. They all would have reflected his interests and his path to Louis Vuitton. Instead, his runway wound through the courtyard of the Palais-Royal in the city's first arrondissement. The seventeenth-century complex took its name from its history as a former palace, but now its gardens were open to the public and its arcade was filled with posh boutiques. The Palais-Royal, which sat not far from the Louvre, served as a backdrop to many fashion shows, including that of Isabel Marant, who regularly unveiled her womenswear collections there. Abloh selected a rainbow-colored runway, and the show was loosely based around *The Wizard of Oz*—the enduring fairytale of a group of misfits in search of a talent that they each eventually learned they'd had all along. All they'd lacked was confidence in their own abilities.

In the moments of anticipation before the show, when the rainbow runway was still immaculate and one could appreciate its borders of lush green trees, when there was a promising glow over the idyllic gardens, Abloh walked the runway alongside his mother Eunice. He was looking down at his phone. She was looking off into the distance. The two of them were alone as she accompanied him to Oz—the boy from the Midwest who'd already proven he had smarts, heart, and courage.

Throughout his rise he had never lost his connection to his roots and the family that grounded him. He had supported his old high school soccer team with jerseys from his partnership with Nike. He helped raise thousands of dollars to feed the less fortunate in Chicago. The lower level of Eunice and Nee's home in Rockford had become an ode to their son's accomplishments. It was filled with photographs from his shows, one of the area rugs he designed in collaboration with IKEA, pictures of ebullient neighborhood kids after receiving Off-White sneakers from the designer himself.

Some one thousand seated guests were invited to that first show, along with his family, including his wife Shannon, whose steadfastness at home in Chicago with their two children allowed Abloh to circumnavigate the globe. The audience was filled with famous faces, those who had helped Abloh along the way as well as those for whom fashion was a lucrative source of self-promotion and for whom Abloh's world was the latest advertising platform. The lineup included Kanye West and his wife Kim Kardashian West, as well as Rihanna, A$AP Rocky, Rita Ora, Travis Scott, Alexander Skarsgård, and assorted pop stars and influencers who represented millions of curious fans on social media. But the most important members of the audience might well have been the hundreds of Parisian fashion school students who were there. Standing behind the rows of seated guests, the students wore T-shirts to match the colorful runway and formed a human rainbow. The words "Not Home" were emblazoned across their shirts in a reference to Dorothy Gale, who in the aftermath of a storm realized with a mix of apprehension and delight that she was no longer in Kansas.

The students were an integral part of the stage set. They allowed Abloh to merge opulence with earnestness. They underscored how his fan base had always seen themselves in him. The students embodied his stated desire to open the fashion system to those still building their credentials. They reflected his sense of himself as an outsider.

It was unusual to have so many civilians in attendance at one of fashion's most anticipated events, although like most things in fashion, it wasn't unprecedented. And for a show that told a story about diversity and harmony, an open-armed approach to who was invited only made sense. For Abloh, debuting his collection before an audience filled with students added to the sense of joy and uplift that was at the heart of it.

The day of Abloh's show, which was scheduled to begin at 2:30 in the afternoon, it was blazingly hot, the kind of searing heat that made perfectly good mobile phones send up high temperature alerts before going haywire. Guests were sweating profusely. The assembled photographers were especially overheated, but mostly about all the celebrities in attendance. It was impossible to see everyone who was there from a single vantage point. The runway was 650 feet long; a guest could lay eyes only on those famous faces in their immediate vicinity. But there was plenty of time to stroll around and take in the view. Rare was the fashion show that began promptly.

For fashion insiders, Abloh's debut was the show of the season. It didn't matter if it was a rousing success or an abject disaster, either way guests had witnessed fashion history. Still, there was an awful lot of goodwill in the audience, which was not always the case. There had been more schadenfreude than anything else in the air that night in Paris when Kanye West showed his first collection.

But here Abloh's awe-shucks midwestern charm served him well. "In thirty-two years of modeling," said Naomi Campbell, "I'd never felt that feeling of unified love from every single person there."

Abloh explained himself on Instagram in advance of the show to the only critics who ultimately mattered: his would-be customers. "The biggest goal for a first collection in any scenario is to start so that people can understand the new vocabulary," he wrote. To make sure that everyone was speaking the same language, each guest received a dictionary of Abloh-isms. In this manual, F was for "fandom: two-way worship between a designer and his clientele." D was for "Dorothy: A farm girl from the Midwest transported to Oz, a fairy tale land where she experiences things beyond her imagination. As an outsider, she soon discovers she was taken to Oz for a reason."

The dictionary was a lot to take in, and for those who weren't interested in reading the entire volume, it at least served as an efficient fan to beat back the summer heat, which seemed even hotter for those guests who found themselves positioned along the bright-yellow portion of Abloh's rainbow. It was a bit like being seated on the sun itself.

The fifty-six-look collection, called Color Theory, was said to include models from every continent except Antarctica, which was the kind of statement that sounded like quite an accomplishment until one paused to note there were only seven continents and it was not that much of a stretch out of fifty-six looks to have at least one model from North America, South America, Europe, Asia, Africa, and Australia. Still, the models were an impressively diverse group that also included musicians Kid Cudi, Playboi Carti, Dev Hynes, and Theophilus London. The models wore clothes that showcased Abloh's desire for a size medium that really reflected a median body type rather than a lithe Hedi Slimane schoolboy.

The modern jazz band BadBadNotGood played a live soundtrack. But one also heard West's song "I Thought About Killing You," echoing from the speakers. The show opened simply, with a dark-skinned Black man in loose-fitting, but not oversize, white trousers, a white shirt, and a matching double-breasted blazer. His sneakers were white, and so was the bag he carried, from which a white chain dangled. The contrast between the model's dark skin and the white attire was beautiful and served as an aesthetic reminder of the glory of differences.

The first dozen looks were studies in white as the collection slowly moved into shades of off-white, ivory, and then camel before it burst into a full kaleidoscope of yellow and fuchsia.

Color Theory was a nod to diversity and to finding one's dreams at the end of a rainbow. It reflected Abloh's beginnings silk-screening T-shirts.

The collection began where menswear once was rooted, in tailored silhouettes, but it moved quickly to where menswear now thrived with pullovers, T-shirts, and nicely cut hoodies. On Abloh's runway, the traditions of menswear hadn't been abolished. They coexisted with the more informal present. It wasn't an either/or proposition.

In many respects, the clothes were simple and familiar. They did not upend the fashion orthodoxy. But Abloh's distinctive voice was present in the poppy graphics, the abstract prints, the generously sized T-shirts and the many vests and harnesses and utility bags. Many of the garments had an ephemeral quality because they were so light and translucent. That added to the optimistic mood of the show. The bold colors spoke of joy and youthfulness. Abloh luxuriated in hope, a far more powerful gesture than wallowing in pearls, fur, or exotic leathers. He also paid homage to *The Wizard of Oz* with an intarsia sweater with Dorothy, the Scarecrow, the Tin Man, and the Cowardly Lion silhouetted in black.

"Virgil's cosmology, if you will, was kind of flexible enough to accommodate all manner of criticism and just kind of turn it into part of the point," said writer Matthew Schneier, who had followed Abloh's work and attended his Louis Vuitton debut. "There was something very Teflon about him in that way."

Not everyone was fully committed to Abloh's verbiage, but he managed to reframe any criticism as part of an artistic debate. For those who found his work derivative, Abloh defended it as postmodern. If some found it lacked design finesse, that was okay because Abloh avoided calling himself a designer. When it seemed unsophisticated, well, that was because it was meant to speak to the seventeen-year-old mindset. Overpriced? Value is about desire, not labor and material. To support him was to celebrate disruption and open-mindedness. To criticize him was to defend the status quo, to be a snob. Abloh declined to call himself a designer, so what exactly was he? Wildly creative? Or an incredibly creative bullshitter?

For many observers, it seemed as though Abloh had made an unimaginable leap akin to a street corner busker's suddenly performing at Carnegie Hall—or, as Michael Burke put it, that Abloh, a basketball fan, had awakened one morning to find that he'd become Michael Jordan. The journey had been swift. But it had come in discrete steps, from the graduate school T-shirts, to the Been Trill promotional merchandise, to the Pyrex Vision audacity, to the Off-White gamesmanship, to the Nike collaboration seen around the world. Step by step, Abloh had tested his theories and his philosophy. Bit by bit, the fashion ground had softened and become more amenable to the seeds he was planting. In hindsight, the spring 2019 menswear show was a fait accompli. It hadn't gone off without a hitch. But it happened, and that was a marvel.

"The tempo was slow. The guys didn't know how to walk," Burke said, as he offered his assessment of the day. "There were some things that were ill-fitting. . . . I mean, there were all sorts of things. It was not a perfect show, but it was a perfect *first* show."

The finale featured the usual promenade of models down the runway so that the audience could get one last look at the collection. As the last model passed, Abloh emerged from backstage to take his bows. Dressed in loose-fitting purple cargo pants and a black Louis Vuitton T-shirt, he walked down the runway with his hands clasped in front of him in a gesture of gratitude. When he spotted his friend Kanye West, Abloh pointed to him with affection. West stood and the two men wrapped each other in a tearful embrace. It was more than a quick gesture of friendship; it was more emotional than the masculine ritual of affection that had two guys clasping hands and drawing each other in for a chest bump. Abloh and West held on to each other—two men who'd been intertwined for a decade, each of them standing at the doorway to the fashion industry, West pounding on it with bravado and demanding entry, Abloh quietly knocking, unwilling to be shooed away.

"Kanye was the guy, when it was completely unpopular, that said, 'I am not going to be typecast into a box.' He willed it for us. That dream is just as much his as mine—in my dream, it was him down the runway," Abloh said. "It actually wasn't me on the runway, it was the community. That show was us."

A thousand cameras clicked as the Louis Vuitton Don ceded his title. Abloh had achieved what West could not. As West later said, "Nobody owes me anything, but I'm still going to feel the way I feel." Abloh's accomplishment brought feelings of pride, envy, joy. He'd scored a win for everyone.

That hug, not the clothes on the runway, was the image of the day. It circulated around the world.

"Your first takeaway was the circumstances—not that this was someone with a powerful idea about what clothing is or should be or how we should dress," Schneier recalled. "But that's also a very high standard to hold someone. I think most fashion shows don't tell us that."

The collection didn't have the bombshell impact of Tom Ford's earliest shows at Gucci in the mid-1990s, when he abruptly shifted menswear into a hypersexual, mod phase. Abloh didn't force a rethinking of silhouettes, as did Thom Browne with his cropped trousers and shrunken blazers. He wasn't Hedi Slimane or Raf Simons, lionizing skinny, disaffected youth and causing a generation of fashion-obsessed men to aspire to the physique of a twelve-year-old. Few designers ever achieve that level of impact.

But Abloh offered a credible fashion proposition. With his mix of tailored jackets, sweatshirts, pleated trousers, sneakers, and duffel bags with chain-link handles, he added to the ongoing aesthetic conversation about the role of streetwear in the fashion industry and the relevance of luxury to a generation raised on hip-hop, skateboarding, and self-branding. His mix of models was wildly diverse. His audience was filled with insiders and outsiders. Abloh had said something from his new perch. And that was significant.

His Louis Vuitton registered within popular culture. The actor Timothée Chalamet wore one of Abloh's harnesses to the Golden Globe Awards in January 2019. It had been customized with jet beads, and Chalamet—or rather his stylist—paired it with a black shirt and trousers. The curious bedazzled accoutrement caused a media stir because of its presumed reference to a particular kind of aggressive sex. The baby-faced Chalamet, for his part, insisted he thought the accessory was a bib. Shortly after the Chalamet outing, actor Michael B. Jordan chose a floral iteration of the harness for his appearance at the SAG Awards. The harness didn't particularly flatter either actor. They looked as though they were about to be hoisted into the air as part of an aerial act. But the thing became a sartorial talking point, which meant it cast a bright spotlight on Louis Vuitton menswear. Thus Abloh had done his job.

Helming a design house of the size and reputation of Louis Vuitton meant that what Abloh did and said and showed on the runway resonated more widely than ever before. It was amplified and dissected. That was made jarringly clear with his sophomore collection in January.

Abloh looked to the music of his youth for inspiration. He turned to Michael Jackson and the African American parable *The Wiz*. Abloh sent guests white rhinestone gloves as invitations, and the show's location—a darkened tent in the Jardins des Tuileries—nodded to the sidewalk tableau from Jackson's "Billie Jean" video. The collection included bedazzled tops, as well as a T-shirt printed with an image of Jackson's loafer-clad feet in the midst of one of his signature dance moves.

It was a woefully timed point of reference. Eight days after the collection was unveiled, five thousand miles away at the Sundance Film Festival, the four-hour documentary *Leaving Neverland* screened. In it, two young men told a story of grooming and sexual abuse by Jackson, whom they met when they were children and Jackson was a global celebrity. Abloh's Louis Vuitton collection met with a backlash and multiple news cycles were dedicated to its troubling associations. The media asked Abloh to explain his celebration of Jackson against the backdrop of the documentary and in light of the significant legal and reputational baggage Jackson had long been carrying regarding inappropriate relationships with children. Abloh professed ignorance about the film and noted that his admiring gaze was focused on Jackson as a humanitarian and fashion influencer—both of which were arguably the least of Jackson's accomplishments. Abloh seemed unprepared for the uproar, dismayed that so many people noticed and cared about what he put on the runway. His famous temperament—unflappable, nonconfrontational, forgiving—had allowed him to siphon the tantalizing mythology of Jackson from the entertainer's disturbing dark side. Louis Vuitton issued an apology and announced that it would not produce the few designs that directly referenced Jackson.

The contretemps died down. Louis Vuitton was unscathed. And Abloh's renown only grew.

HIS STATURE WAS helped along by a propitiously timed exhibition in his honor. In the summer of 2016, a little more than a year after Abloh was a finalist for the LVMH Prize, Michael Darling, the chief curator at the Museum of Contemporary Art Chicago, had emailed him. This was long before Abloh forged his relationship with Nike and before there were even rumors about a job at Louis Vuitton. Abloh had just moved from background player to founder of Off-White.

Abloh and Darling had never met, but the curator was intrigued by the Chicago-based designer who'd made a name for himself in the Paris fashion world. Darling, who is White, was also interested in ways to bring a more diverse audience into the museum, which had been established in 1967 and, like most fine art institutes, had a history of predominantly attracting the White elite. Darling's determination to expand the reach of the museum was, in part, affirmed by the community response to its David Bowie exhibition, which closed in January 2015. *David Bowie Is* examined the artist's career through his handwritten lyrics, costumes, album covers, and other memorabilia. That exhibition brought in two hundred thousand visitors during its four-month run and set a record as the most attended show in the museum's history. Darling wondered if Abloh, with his connections to popular culture, high-end fashion, and the city itself, might open the museum's doors even further.

"I always like to celebrate the creatives that we have here," Darling said. "You know, it's Chicago. It's not New York or L.A. where they're everywhere. For somebody to launch an international career from Chicago, especially in the world of fashion, is like totally unique."

Darling invited Abloh to meet him at the museum, and Abloh obliged. "He thought I was inviting him to deejay an event at the museum. And I said, 'No, we should do an exhibition.' He said, 'I've been doing all this work waiting for somebody to ask me to do that—to invite me to do something like this.'"

Abloh didn't exactly have an archive, not in the traditional sense. His was not a catalogued, carefully preserved collection of papers and products. It was akin to a hoarder's stash, the treasure trove of a pack rat. Abloh kept everything. Not in the meticulous manner that a museum requires, but his legacy, as brief as it was in the summer of 2016, was intact.

While it's audacious that Abloh felt himself ready for a career retrospective at only thirty-five years old, it's not surprising that he had the wherewithal to keep a record of his work. Owning one's history is something to which younger designers had been more attuned than were their elders. They'd seen the lavish fashion exhibitions mounted by the Victoria and Albert Museum in London and the Metropolitan Museum of Art in New York. They understood that while fashion might not be art, it was a reflection of the culture. It was part of the language of modern life. Fashion was anthropology.

In the past, society ladies who purchased some of the most representative work of designers might simply give their castoffs to a younger relative or an assistant. They might alter a couture garment to extend its life. Dresses were in museums because of their provenance—because of who wore them and where they were worn—not simply because they existed. Some of the most revered designers in the world, such as Oscar de la Renta, did not aggressively collect their own work. When Alexander McQueen died in 2010, his colleagues had to work feverishly to preserve his archive, but despite their efforts it remained incomplete. Financial woes early in his career had him giving away runway pieces to his models in lieu of their regular fees. And he sometimes ripped apart sample garments from the previous year's collection to produce the next one.

Sometimes as their reputation soared and their finances stabilized, designers tried to buy back some of their most distinguished work through vintage shops and auction houses—only to be outbid by private collectors who'd recognized the value in old clothes.

But Abloh kept things; he kept unrealized ideas, doodles, hard drives, architectural models. They weren't organized; but they were there. There was, however, a much higher hurdle to an exhibition than cataloging the objects: most people at the museum had no idea who Abloh was. They'd never heard of Off-White or any of the projects that led up to it. Darling had to write a proposal that not only explained how an exhibition dedicated to Abloh would look but who Abloh was and why he mattered. Why was his work, rather than that of more experienced and enduring designers, worthy of a considered evaluation? The answer was that Darling saw Abloh as a gateway to the future.

The marketing team was first to grasp the possibilities, which was only fitting. Abloh understood how to sell himself and his ideas. They saw how deeply Abloh was embedded in social media. They knew he was in constant communication with his customer base and with his fans. The story to be told about Abloh was not one that focused on fashion in the way that it might be examined at the Met, where the garment was central. Abloh's impact wasn't on the way a garment looked. It was on the way he made it possible for certain young people to engage with fashion. He influenced the culture's thinking about the hierarchy of the industry, which had always put French haute couture at the top of the pyramid and items such as sneakers and T-shirts at the bottom. Fashion had placed the highest value on the obsessions of its wealthy White clients. Abloh put the spotlight on the interests of Black youth and then set those obsessions on a foundation of intellectualism. He encouraged his fans to make their own merchandise, to put his signature markings on their own garments. He referred to Off-White as a communal effort, not his own rigorously copywritten business.

Abloh was full of contradictions. And he readily admitted that. He spoke often of feeling like an outsider who didn't have the right contacts or credentials to enter fashion's interior spaces; and yet, from the beginning of his fashion career, he was celebrity adjacent, which is like having a skeleton key to the industry. It didn't get him to the highest of heights, but it unlocked a side door. He bemoaned how even ten years ago, he hadn't known of "any young Black artists making work that couldn't comfortably be put in a box and labeled 'Black art.'"

But that was a sentiment that spoke to Abloh's historical lapses, his occasional nearsightedness. In his enthusiasm to make a point, he reframed history in a way that burnished his already remarkable accomplishments. What exactly is Black art, after all? That question was provocatively mulled in 2001's influential *Freestyle* exhibition at the Studio Museum in Harlem. Curated by Thelma Golden, *Freestyle* was a survey of artists—average age thirty-two—that she described as "post-multicultural, post-identity, post-conceptual and post-Black."

Abloh was far from the first Black creative person to balk at being placed inside a Black box, nor was he the first to convincingly work outside those confines. Veteran artists such as Sam Gilliam and Alma Thomas quickly come to mind.

Maybe Abloh was speaking a truth. Maybe it was confident gibberish. Much of what the culture views as important is perceived as such because certain straight White men have soberly proclaimed it so. With calm, measured tones, Abloh declared sneakers and T-shirts significant—not just as pieces of commerce but as part of an artful practice. And fashion believed him.

It took nearly three years of conversations and planning before the

MCA exhibition was ready to open in June of 2019—just a year after Abloh's Louis Vuitton debut. His improvisational nature challenged the museum to keep an open mind and to question whether the traditional way of doing things was the only way or even the best way.

"He didn't care about museum procedures. This big black billboard that he made for the exhibition, he put it right in the middle of the show. He wanted to tag it with graffiti, and the timing was such that he couldn't do it before it was brought into the museum. So it had to be done in the galleries, which meant that we had to shut down all the installations and put plastic wrap on everything," Darling said. "On the one hand, I was needing to hold the line for the museum, but on the other hand, it was sort of like, 'Yeah, Virgil. This is great!'"

Everything was a work in progress or an opportunity to be subversive, whether it was covering a billboard in the middle of the museum with graffiti or filling a suitcase from Rimowa, one of Abloh's collaborators, with plastic toys and squirt guns purchased from a nearby Walgreens.

Darling, who sometimes felt as though he was chasing after a runaway train, struggled to conceive how Abloh's ever-growing list of partners and artistic projects would fit into a cohesive exhibition—one that didn't simply look like a gallery filled with merchandise. As it turned out, Abloh himself solved that problem. The pivotal section of the show was an exploration of what Darling described as "the Black gaze." To a large degree, Abloh's race provided the substructure for the exhibition. Race wasn't a box into which Abloh was shuttered; but it was the base upon which the show's intellectual heft was built. It was Abloh's persistent subverting of expectations, his ignoring the negative and determinedly existing in the in-between spaces that shored up the exhibition.

"That was the way to really bring out the political aspect of the work, the racism he'd experienced in the industry, the critiques of white supremacy and things that he was building into his clothes that were just below the surface. You could ignore them if you wanted to; but they were there," Darling said. "That was a whole gallery unto itself.

"Once we had that, I felt like, 'Okay, I think this is really working.' We can get the chronology that I wanted as the historian, curator. We could get the breadth that he wanted to portray of his practice," Darling continued. "And then we also could get this important social critique that's in the work."

Central to the mission of that gallery was the bright yellow neon sign Abloh had commissioned as the backdrop to his Fall 2016 women's Off-White show, which was his first formal runway presentation of the line. The throbbing art piece cribbed a line of dialogue from a scene in the film *Pretty Woman* in which Julia Roberts's character, a scantily clad hooker with a girl-next-door demeanor, enters a high-end clothing boutique to burnish her image, delight in fashion, and prepare for her dream date. She is rebuffed by snobbish saleswomen who serve as gatekeepers to the premises and her aspirations. "You're obviously in the wrong place," they scold her. And in some ways, that was precisely how Abloh felt many in the fashion industry had responded to him: the curious and condescending looks he received as a tourist attending his first fashion week in Paris, the dismissal of Pyrex Vision as just overpriced screen printing on bargain-bin flannels, the early refusal of Anna Wintour to attend one of his Off-White shows, the hurdles of getting fashion publications to write about him as a designer and not a celebrity-adjacent curiosity, the persistent description of Off-White as streetwear no matter how much creative effort went into it.

The discussion of race in the exhibition was nuanced, in keeping with the way in which Abloh had engaged with it as he made his way through the industry. He saw his mere presence as a provocation—one that he didn't have to heighten with political rhetoric, angry rants, or self-conscious swagger.

"I'm throwing a Molotov cocktail at the temple, but in a non-antagonistic way. I'm not punk; I'm not trying to overthrow the temple. The Molotov cocktail is just being there after starting the race from the furthest position," Abloh said. "When people heard that I became the head of menswear at Louis Vuitton, they were like '*Damn!*' Well, where does that shocked reaction come from? I mean, I design clothes just like the next guy. The shock is that you can count on one hand the number of Black people in positions of power in this industry.

"Race is the elephant in the room. But I've never let race be a limiting factor. I have contemporaries, those who came before me. Granted, they came at a different time, so it's not really comparable but . . . Take Kanye, for example. In his brain, he has this anger. He can't go to a meeting without putting it at the forefront. He wants to confront people's prejudice. All across the board, but in fashion specifically. That's just his personality. My personality is different. I've accepted these things. I don't hold a grudge. Part of the reason as to why I think I'm here is that I've accepted the reality and then been able to put it aside to get on with my work."

Abloh was the right kind of Black man. He understood that. That was his intention. This is not to suggest that he didn't have an internal fire that allowed him to be a trailblazer or that he was a long-suffering Saint Sebastian pierced by a thousand arrows. He noticed when the Black security guards at Louis Vuitton eyed him with suspicion. He knew that it would be difficult for his clothes to be seen as something other than streetwear for the same reason that the work of all those Black designers who preceded him was described as urban. He recognized that the greatest upheaval—the ultimate revolutionary act—would come from his fitting in to the fashion industry, rather than standing out. He maneuvered over and around the land mines, propelled by his majority mentality.

As the museum worked to mount the exhibition, Abloh's fame and influence continued to grow. And the museum benefited from Abloh's close relationship with his admirers.

"Instagram was really just starting to become a powerful tool," Darling said. "I don't think the museum knew how to use it effectively, but Virgil already was the king of Instagram. So the museum turned over its marketing campaign to him. He was really driving a lot of the marketing ideas."

When the doors to *Figures of Speech* opened in 2019, with the sponsorship of Louis Vuitton, Conagra, and the Joyce Foundation, among others, there was a sense of amazement and breathlessness from visitors. It was stunning that ten thousand square feet of space had been dedicated to a designer whose career in streetwear, in luxury fashion, in sneaker culture, was not even a decade old. And yet, few designers had surfed such a tidal wave of hype, accessibility, and creative output. Abloh was well on his way to becoming an icon.

The museum commemorated the opening with the usual dinners and galas. Organizers power-washed the parking garage and set up tables and mood lighting. Dev Hynes performed. And for once, Abloh didn't deejay his own party.

He did, however, create merchandise just for the gift shop. There were the expected high-priced items, which included Off-White blazers and dresses with four-figure price tags, but Abloh supplied plenty of inexpensive offerings that were distinct from Louis Vuitton and even his own Off-White label. He created notebooks, keychains, magnets, and trucker hats that were simply attributed to "Virgil Abloh." He also made blue Air Force 1s for the security guards who stood sentinel during the show.

The line to enter the exhibition would sometimes wind around the block, and the museum organized the queue so visitors would be funneled through the exhibition. They wanted to focus attention on Abloh's practice and to prevent folks from simply showing up to shop. Museum staff also spent no small amount of time refuting a stubborn rumor that the MCA was the site of an impending Nike drop—one of those overly hyped deliveries of new collaborative merchandise bearing the sneaker brand's swoosh and Abloh's fingerprints. Denial was futile. There was no drop, but the ever-hopeful and faithful sneakerheads came anyway.

For Darling, the pleasure was in looking out over the galleries and seeing young adults, Black Chicagoans, and preteens dragging their reluctant parents through the exhibition. "There was this hunger to see someone like him recognized in this way and to be adjacent to it that was just really infectious," Darling said. "It felt like people were really wearing all their cool clothes and communicating to each other through their shoe choices or their shirts or hoodies."

The exhibition attracted 180,000 viewers, making it the third-most-visited show in the museum's history. *Figures of Speech* later traveled to the High Museum in Atlanta, the Institute of Contemporary Art Boston, Qatar Museums, and the Brooklyn Museum in New York. There were, of course, exhibition T-shirts. And many of them were printed by Abloh's old friend Jay Green from Custom Kings. The entrepreneur known as Jay Boogie was still working, still inspiring young people with big ideas and few resources. Green didn't begrudge Abloh his fame or fortune. But he was glad that Abloh's definition of community hadn't expanded so much that his early days became little more than a pinpoint in the distance. Abloh commissioned Green to produce shirts for the MCA, as well as the Qatar exhibition—some $700,000 worth in total.

A Once-in-a-Century Storm

ABLOH LED LOUIS VUITTON menswear down a path toward significant treasure. He imbued it with buzz. Circumstances beyond Abloh's control would magnify those accomplishments. Events far outside the realm of fashion would resonate within the industry and make his every step forward seem like a kind of miracle. His achievements within the fashion industry would be seen as another victory in the warriors' march toward equity.

Abloh's debut at Louis Vuitton preceded the cultural provocations, social upheaval, and racial unrest that would ultimately define the 2020s. His first collection appeared during a quiet interlude when fashion was still telling kind stories about itself, about its progress toward diversity, about its ability to move forward toward inclusivity, and about its connection to next-generation consumers. Fashion reveled in its embrace of streetwear, characterizing it as an opening up of the luxury market to younger and more diverse customers.

The calm, however, was short-lived. Abloh had one glorious year of runway shows in Paris before the real struggles began. He would soon be forced to address race more directly than he ever had in his professional life. His standing in the fashion industry would be magnified by the culture's evolving relationship with Black consumers and Black identity. He would be transformed into an icon, and he'd have to address the impossible demands the public makes of them.

As he juggled the workload of designing both Off-White and Louis Vuitton menswear—along with a multitude of side projects—Abloh was diagnosed with cardiac angiosarcoma, a particularly fast-growing form of cancer. He and his wife Shannon kept the news close, although Michael Burke was told. Abloh didn't want to field endless questions about his health; he wanted to keep working. His time would likely be short. For the fashion industry at large, and even among some of his cohort, the only inkling that something was amiss was Abloh's September announcement that he would not be in Paris for the upcoming shows. He told people his doctors had forbidden him to travel. Everyone presumed that the man who was in constant motion simply needed to rest.

By December of that year, a mysterious virus was reported in Wuhan, China, and within four months the world had shut down and Covid-19 was declared a pandemic. The man for whom his phone was his office, who traveled 320 days a year and sometimes made eight international flights in a week, hunkered down with his family. In some ways, the timing was a gift.

Meanwhile, the election of President Trump had untethered American racism from the forces of civility, decorum, and a constitutional democracy that had kept it from floating freely. It was no longer an embarrassment to be a racist; it was simply a political position, a cultural preference, an expression of disdain for tiptoeing around the sensitivities of the overly sensitive. And in response, people felt empowered to raise hell.

The fashion industry wrestled with accusations of racial insensitivity in a way that was different from the past when consumers had expressed their frustration over the lack of Black models or high-profile designers. That had been a matter of omission, the result of which was racism. These were acts of aggression. Their vividness jarred the senses, and young Black men and women, empowered with social media as both a spotlight and a bullhorn, made their anger and frustration known.

It's hard to put a finger on precisely when both insiders and outsiders began to lose patience with the fashion industry's sloppy and dismissive understanding of race, but in December 2018, Chinyere Ezie, a Black staff attorney at the Center for Constitutional Rights, expressed her exasperation and disdain on social media. It was a marker of sorts.

Ezie stepped out of the New York City subway on Prince Street and walked past the Prada store. It was the same place where Abloh had spotted the work of Michael Rock and his design agency 2 x 4. What Ezie saw in the windows stopped her cold. She was returning from a trip to Washington where she'd visited the National Museum of African American History and Culture, and the decorative tchotchkes in the Prada vitrine recalled the racist Golliwog dolls she'd just seen in the museum—the same Golliwogs that Patrick Kelly had reclaimed in his work. With dark-brown coloring, wild hair, and a bright red mouth, Golliwogs were a visual slur used against Black people.

Ezie was stunned. She went into the store, took pictures of the offending objects, and then showed those images to friends and family. Was she wrong to be offended? Was she too sensitive? They assured her she was not. Ezie uploaded those images to social media because "I didn't want to have to grieve in silence," she said. After her complaints were amplified by others, Prada issued an apology, dismantled the display, and pulled the $550 charms from circulation. The company also pledged to donate proceeds from the products' sale to a New York–based organization focused on racial justice, which was what Ezie suggested as part of the company's atonement.

Soon after, Gucci stumbled into an uproar over blackface. News stories had drawn attention to several examples of public officials with a history of wearing blackface—not as uninformed children, but as adults. And then social media discovered a black Gucci turtleneck sweater, designed by Alessandro Michele, with an exaggerated collar. The neckline covered the nose but with a cutout for the mouth that was delineated with bright red lips. It was a Golliwog in sweater form, a Sambo in wool knit. The sweater had been in stores for months. It had been produced in numerous color combinations. But the version that combined black with red set off a chain reaction of confusion, accusations, outrage, and, finally, customers pledging to burn their Gucci belongings in an act of protest.

At the time, Gucci's chief executive Marco Bizzarri believed he'd been nurturing a company that put diversity and inclusivity at the center of its brand philosophy. But Bizzarri also understood the times in which he was doing business. "In the digital era, if someone says this is blackface, it's blackface," he said.

And so the company responded accordingly. The sweater was taken off the market and the company increased its efforts to support a more diverse and inclusive workforce. It already had programs aimed at widening the pipeline of creative talent into the fashion industry. It decided to educate its staff and increase its executive ranks. It brought in an academic named Kimberly Jenkins as its diversity coach. Jenkins had created the Fashion and Race Database, a clearinghouse of history and culture that helped designers get at least a beginner's understanding of the various traditions from which they so liberally borrowed. Antoine Phillips was also hired. A young Black public relations professional who'd worked for Giorgio Armani and Coach, Phillips focused on Gucci's Changemakers project, which aimed to connect the company to an increasingly diverse marketplace of ideas and desires.

In 2020, it seemed that every day someone felt emboldened to point to a racial offense within the fashion industry. These weren't brazen new offenses. These were nagging irritations and systemic harassments that had long been present. But now people were willing to speak up because it seemed like some sort of ameliorative action might be taken. They didn't feel so alone in bringing these things to light. Reporting their concerns no longer felt like a lost cause. And in a whack-a-mole manner, the industry responded.

At the magazine publishing house Condé Nast, which owned *Vogue, Teen Vogue, Bon Appétit*, and *Glamour*, the staff was ready to confront and litigate decades of microaggressions and macro- ones too. Adam Rapoport, who'd been the editor in chief of *Bon Appétit* for a decade, resigned hours after a photograph of him and his wife resurfaced on social media showing Rapoport, who is White, wearing a baseball cap, a white tank top, and a metallic medallion hanging around his neck. His wife, who had initially made the image public, referred to Rapoport as "papi" and included the hashtag "Boricua." The image was decried as brownface and served as a flashpoint in what had been a long-standing frustration by *Bon Appétit* staff over its tone-deaf coverage of diverse cuisines and its treatment of non-White staff. He was replaced by Dawn Davis, a veteran book editor and Black woman.

Internal critics revolted against longtime *Vogue* editor Anna Wintour and the magazine's practice of using predominantly White photographers, stylists, and editors. Readers recalled the April 2008 cover featuring basketball player LeBron James and model Giselle Bundchën and its seeming reference to an old movie poster for *King Kong*. The challenges of being a person of color within a fashion company that historically elevated and glorified White women— and men—rose to the surface. And amid that anger, Wintour was forced to apologize for her failures and to make changes, saying that she would be accountable—although she never clarified exactly what that meant—if signs of improvement were not evident within one year's time.

Black men and women in fashion were emboldened by events

unfolding around them that made addressing systemic racism more urgent than ever. On March 13, 2020, a Black woman named Breonna Taylor was shot in her own home after police officers stormed in armed with a no-knock warrant, massive firepower, and a belief in their own omnipotence. They had identified and invaded the wrong house. On May 25, 2020, George Floyd pleaded in vain for mercy, for grace, and for his life. Floyd was arrested for allegedly trying to make a purchase in a convenience store with a counterfeit twenty-dollar bill.

In response to these deaths, crowds flooded into the streets all over the world. They chanted George Floyd's name, and they fought to make sure Breonna Taylor's name would not be forgotten. At a time when a pandemic made human contact possibly deadly, protesters donned surgical masks, grabbed bottles of hand sanitizer, and banded together, believing that what they were doing as a group was more important than their individual risk.

The value of Black lives seemed negligible when they were in the hands of the police. But the lived experiences of Black people were also being devalued or simply ignored by a White majority. The death of George Floyd sparked a conversation about the nature of racism and prejudice at a time when fashion's growth was becoming dependent on an increasingly diverse and activist consumer base. The influence of baby boomer shoppers—as well as the sliver of folks known as Generation X—had given way to the whims of millennials. And that cohort was being pushed aside for a rising Gen Z. By 2019, Gen Z represented some 40 percent of global consumers and about $150 billion in annual spending power in the United States alone. But more importantly, nine out of ten Gen Z consumers believed that companies had a responsibility to publicly address social issues. The emphasis on social justice represented a shift in how shoppers related to companies. Companies were no longer simply organs of capitalism; they were a representation of a consumer's values.

Race mattered. Companies were forced to make a statement about Floyd's death, about police violence, and about the need to amplify Black voices. Institutions went on a hiring spree for diversity and equity specialists. Companies pledged their financial support to Black-owned businesses and ventures. Instagram accounts of major corporations filled up with black squares in solidarity with the Black Lives Matter movement and pronouncements about with whom they "stood." They funded organizations dedicated to racial justice or diversity or some other warmhearted, fuzzy, feel-good goal.

One of the few clearly defined actions that came out of the many black squares and statements of solidarity began as a response to the impotence of that very symbolism. The Fifteen Percent Pledge, essentially founded on Instagram in 2020, was born out of Aurora James's desire for more tangible and measurable actions. The idea was simple. Black people make up close to 15 percent of the population; businesses should pledge to fill 15 percent of their shelf space with products from Black-owned companies, to spend 15 percent of their dollars with Black-owned firms. Macy's, Sephora, and West Elm were among the earliest companies to take the pledge. To be clear, the pledge was not an order to buy. Mostly, it was a public commitment to do something that had a dollar value attached to it.

These statements and actions all unfolded when Abloh was sitting atop the Louis Vuitton mountain. His success was recognized and lauded in a way that no other Black designer's success had been before. His accomplishments were hailed not just as a professional victory but as a win for the culture. Race was no longer something that one had to overcome. Race had become something to own.

This was not a moment that celebrated the nonconfrontational and the well-behaved. Abloh learned that quickly. As some of those involved in the protests turned to looting, Abloh decried those actions, commenting on an Instagram post by business owner and sneaker designer Sean Wotherspoon who'd recorded a video of damage to his shop.

"This disgusts me. . . . We're part of a culture together. Is this what you want?? When you walk past [Wotherspoon] in the future please have the dignity to not look him in the eye, hang your head in shame."

Abloh wasn't quite reaching back to an era of respectability politics, but he was making an abbreviated case for nuance, for working within a system rather than destroying it. That's what he'd done.

"The race conversation was always sort of an unspoken conversation that happened with his actions: who he chose to work with or how he articulated something or what cultural nuances he was pulling from. At the end of the day, whatever is culturally relevant to him, in one way or another, should be somewhat culturally relevant for Black folks because he's a Black man," Janjer said. "There's a lot of instances of shared experiences.

"Even if he had an agenda, he would do it in this 'Virgil way' rather than to be like, 'This whole team needs to be Black or this thing isn't happening,'" Janjer added. "He would find his way to do it and still get a similar output if not the same."

"There was a situation where a gallery director was really keen on having him involved in doing something, but she didn't regard him as a full-on 'artist' to be in the exhibition space. They were keen on doing something with him in the gift shop. It was a merch thing," Janjer explained. "Maybe it wasn't about race. But in that scenario, a lot of people would be like, 'Well, but why not? You're asking for all this, but you're not seeing me as worthy of an exhibit. You're happy to have *my* world queue up outside of *your* gallery, but for the wrong position.' But here's the Virgil way: He would just put them on ice and go and do something with someone else. He would do it in a bigger way on his own. And then lo and behold, the gallery owner would be like, 'Why didn't you do that with me?'

"For every 'no,' he would go like double time," Janjer said. "For every resistance that he received, he would find a way of proving that person or that institute or that group wrong." Indeed, instead of a small show in that single gallery, Abloh was the subject of a museum exhibition that traveled around the world.

After Abloh criticized the looting, for the first time Black folks on social media rose up en masse against him. A generation of digital warriors understood that they could force change by sending a few sentences of outrage into the universe. As they understood his comments, Abloh was prioritizing belongings over lives. He was elevating capitalism over social justice. He was siding with the system over those who had been sidelined by it.

The fury blindsided him. He was fashion's inside man, the guy who'd cracked the code and promised to share the secret with everyone else. He was changing the definition of luxury. He wasn't making luxury more accessible. That was never the point. He was transforming the dream and who was reflected in the fantasy. Succeeding at capitalism had always been part of what it meant to win.

Critics took special offense at his publicizing a fifty-dollar donation he'd made to a bail fund for protesters arrested while campaigning for racial justice. He'd highlighted that modest donation to encourage others to do the same. But he was ridiculed for the paltry sum and dismissed as a dilettante. Abloh, who'd always been rewarded for his amiable temperament, who managed a delicate balancing act between intrepid creator and earnest marketer, between postmodern artist and unrepentant copycat, between disrupter and company man, was in the crosshairs. The populace was fed up with being accommodating. The angry and exasperated masses pounced on anyone who suggested, even obliquely, that perhaps they should take a breath and go slowly. Observers weren't willing to shrug off the status quo or silently fume about disparities. They had no patience for anyone who suggested they should.

Black folks on social media turned on Abloh. Where once they'd given one of his so-so collections an A for his effort, they now lashed out in revisionist reviews. If they'd been willing to look the other way when Abloh made minor tweaks to someone else's work and called it his own, they were less willing to do so now. They called him a thief.

Abloh explained his looting remarks in a series of lengthy online statements. He wrote about his fears as a dark-skinned Black man whose success and fame couldn't shield him from a police officer who was quicker to rely on bullets than words.

"Let me start with a few central facts," he wrote in June 2020. "I am a Black man. A dark Black man. Like dark-dark. On an average trip to the grocery store in Chicago, I fear I will die. The risk of literal death is the normal walk of life for us. I almost live as if I'm walking on my tiptoes. When I apply for a job, I fear I won't get it. It's my nature to be extra polite, but I'm extra polite because before I open my mouth 9 times outta 10 I see people judge."

He continued: "Any interaction with the police could be fatal to me. A split-second interaction I could have with them, Off-White™ sneakers mean nothing . . . or that I'm head designer of this . . . or I showed art work at such and such place doesn't apply in the heat of an exchange. 'SIRRR! Come here!!' sends chills down my spine . . . 39 years of my life could be reduced in a 1 second radio call to the police: 'A tall black man was . . .'"

Abloh acknowledged that when considering the hierarchy of privilege, he had more personal agency than Black women or queer women or transgender people or those who didn't have two striving, caring middle-class parents with the hardworking ethos of immigrants as well as a deep sense of personal history and culture that could be traced back to Ghana. So in many ways he was lucky. Abloh also explained that his fifty-dollar donation was part of a tag team of donations organized by a group of his friends and that he'd contributed $20,500 to bail relief and other causes but that he hadn't wanted to publicize that because it seemed crass. Instead, he wanted to emphasize the fifty-dollar donation to underscore that even modest gifts are important to the cause. And as for his tsk-tsking the looters, he stepped back from that too, noting that no building was more important than human lives and that "if looting eases pain and furthers the overall mission, it is within good standing with me."

Abloh's was a breathless unloading of frustration and commiseration along with backpedaling, from a man who'd spent his professional life making sure that feathers remained unruffled, whether he was at the helm of Louis Vuitton's menswear or collaborating with Nike.

"When he got criticized for what looked like a $50 donation, I'll never forget it because he said, 'I thought I was just talking to my friends up until today.' And I think what he meant by that is he saw his social media as a way of talking amongst his peers. But what he hadn't realized in the time frame of those few years, there were now six million strangers following him, you know, and seeking his guidance," Janjer said. "He was like, 'I feel like I'm on a playground on a campus where Nike, IKEA, Louis Vuitton are all looking at me being stoned in the middle.' He just felt like he was alone at that moment. I was like, 'use it to your advantage. Use it to show us your Blackness more than ever.'

"I think that moment really helped him go, you know, 'I have to overdrive this because me being sort of cute about it just doesn't work, not when even my own people think I'm not there,'" Janjer said. "I think that's when he realized his social media isn't a group of friends anymore and it's obviously a good platform, but it could also be a really sort of nasty place."

The life and murder of George Floyd—the would-be rapper and poet, security guard, struggling addict, dreamer, and former convict—amplified the ways in which racism was embedded within the systems that governed our communities. His life and death illustrated how racism complicated even the simplest aspirations. His story revealed the depths of our denial about the role race played in our culture.

In the months following Floyd's murder, Abloh's social media was more overt in addressing race. Less subtle. Not as coy. What he'd already been doing became clearer. He noted that he'd leveraged his relationship with Nike to organize a Black-led creative team to work on projects with Off-White. He encouraged followers to vote, announced that he'd joined a coalition of Black fashion designers, and highlighted a project to promote Black-owned businesses.

In 2020, he met Aleta Clark, who often went by the nickname "Englewood Barbie," when she posted a note on social media asking for help with her charity. A Black woman with long, wavy hair and bright eyes, Clark was dedicated to feeding Chicago's unhoused residents. Abloh messaged her and asked what he could do. Stunned by the offer, she suggested helping her distribute meals. He told her to think bigger. What would she do with an influx of money? Abloh held a sneaker auction and raised more than $180,000 for Clark's mission.

His collections for Louis Vuitton delved deeper and deeper into Black identity. The spring 2020 collection was to have been held in front of Notre-Dame, but a fire at the cathedral meant the location had to be shifted to the cobblestone streets of place Dauphine on the western end of the Île de la Cité. He sent his guests kite-making kits as invitations and used wildflowers as a metaphor for diversity.

He followed that with shows in Shanghai and Tokyo during the pandemic and during the height of the Black Lives Matter protests. He worked with a team of Black collaborators, including Ibrahim Kamara, found inspiration in Africa and the Caribbean, and added biographical notes about his parents Eunice and Nee Abloh and their journey from Ghana to Illinois.

His fall 2021 show was his most accomplished. Presented as a film and inspired by the 1953 James Baldwin essay "Stranger in the Village," it celebrated Black cultural heritage with a mix of long, flowing coats, African fabrics, wide-brimmed hats, do-rags, and sharp suits richly styled by Kamara, who had become an influential editor and a permanent member of Abloh's creative circle. The accompanying film, *Peculiar Contrast, Perfect Light,* set against snowy mountains and a sterile office interior, was a merging of poetry, dance, fashion, and storytelling. Abloh surrounded himself with artists including poet Saul Williams, performer Kai-Isaiah Jamal, and Yasiin Bey, who didn't shy away from discussing politics, gender, and race in their work. In the film's soundtrack, a voice proclaimed: "I think as Black people, and as trans people, as marginalized people, the world is here for our taking—for it takes so much from us."

With his collections, Abloh had begun to consider what it meant to be Black within the creative breadth of the fashion industry. His first collection had been an almost facile celebration of accomplishment; this was the beginning of an examination of what success costs, what it's worth, and how it endures. It was a recognition of the challenges of living in the gray area—the off-white area.

But now there was no live audience for the presentation. There were no rows of editors and celebrities and students all holding their telephones aloft to capture the best image of the dancers who moved to the choreography of Josh Johnson. The show existed outside the realm of fashion. It was connected to the broader world in a way that none of his other presentations had been.

This one answered the question that so many in fashion struggled with during that period of upheaval and uncertainty. Fashion could be relevant as a way of expressing identity. It told a story of history and possibility. Abloh hadn't reinvented tailoring or haberdashery, but he'd at last made clear the questions he'd been getting at for so many years. Who owned luxury? Who owned this idea

267

of desirability, value, and longevity? Whoever owned history also owned the future.

Even as a young man, Abloh seemed conscious of the legacy he would leave. He wanted to pass on wisdom he'd accumulated practically in real time. He was a twenty-something who wanted to mentor his own peers. He was a thirty-something who was already impatient for a museum to examine his life's work.

While West was thinking about solving hunger and brokering world peace, Abloh, too, was considering his place in making social change, albeit on a smaller scale, a more human scale. He focused on his desire to mentor. Abloh was thankful to people like Jay Boogie, Michael Rock, and West who'd taken him seriously and given him helpful bits of wisdom and encouraged him to be fearless.

For many people, mentoring isn't something that occurs to them until much later in their career; it's often seen as a retirement project. But Abloh cast himself as a mentor even when he himself still had much to learn. Perhaps, in thinking about the seventeen-year-old Abloh, he knew that there were things even his peers might have taught him.

As early as 2008, Abloh had talked about not wanting to be hemmed into a box, about wanting to follow his passions. Shawn Agyeman, who was then a young fan and blogger, asked Abloh if he thought his and West's fashion pursuits would expand into something "big like Louis Vuitton." Abloh responded that he was terrible at planning. He was simply going from task to task; and if he took care of each task, he felt confident his trajectory would be skyward. His larger goal was to "be a mentor to kids who want to get into this line of work. To give talks to kids in schools," Abloh told Agyeman. "Give kids the basics in how to design a T shirt, how to take measurements to send to a factory. Take away the mystique."

Even though Abloh was then still in his twenties, he already had a sense of what it meant to be a public figure and to symbolize something larger than his own accomplishments. He saw fans swirling around West and waiting in lines at nightclubs. Abloh had also been a fan, standing around outside fashion shows. He saw kids swooning over streetwear brands like Supreme and over limited-edition sneakers. Abloh had swooned too. In some ways, he still was.

"The life of a designer is you're only as good as your last design," Abloh said. "What defines you is how you behave in the low moments, not when you've done something super fresh."

In the aftermath of George Floyd's death, when Abloh had a cancer diagnosis hanging over his head, he turned his full attention to that seventeen-year-old he once was, to mentoring. He began working with the Fashion Scholarship Fund—an organization founded in 1937 as the Young Menswear Association, an informal group focused on developing the next generation of (White) professionals. Over the years, it evolved into its current iteration: helping college students looking to enter the fashion field, not only as designers but also as merchants and executives.

Through his connections, Abloh raised more than $1 million, accepted a position on the FSF board of directors, focused his attention on Black students, and established a scholarship in his name. "Instead of starting something on his own, he could kind of leverage our existence and our structure and our reach and the relationships that we have on campus with educators and really quickly set up this Post-Modern Scholarship Fund with this targeted population of students," said Peter Arnold, FSF executive director.

The Virgil Abloh Post-Modern Scholarship Fund was born.

He was just in time. After the surge in allyships and racial awakenings and reckonings, the country entered a state of backlash that included book banning, historical revisionism, and shrill accusations about a tyranny of "woke-ism." The term meant many things depending on who was using it but for many conservatives, who derided the term, invoking "woke-ism" quickly became a way of conflating political correctness, liberalism, radical social change, and even basic civility.

Fearmongers described a woke mob stampeding across the plains trying to overturn the culture in the name of diversity and inclusivity. There was no mob, and *woke* was a term drained of any real meaning. But the culture was, in fact, being disrupted.

Abloh was part of the change. He was leading, sometimes clumsily and awkwardly, sometimes with bold confidence and strokes of breathtaking audacity. He worked hard to avoid being hemmed in by walls that could separate him from the cultural milieu within which he'd grown up. He referred to himself as a kid even though he was very much an adult. He operated with the cut-and-paste mentality of the digital age. He borrowed willy-nilly, and he was sued—or told to cease and desist—by everyone from the United Nations to the Norwegian sportswear company Helly Hansen.

Being a leader in the age of digital bullhorns, community watchdogs, and impatience with fallibility was daunting. But Abloh pressed onward—sometimes benefiting from sheer luck, but always with a sense of urgency.

Abloh had only managed to present one Louis Vuitton collection before his world started to turn upside down. That collection was months in the making, and the show was ten minutes of grandeur. But it all had really begun with the seventeen-year-old Abloh: the dutiful son of immigrants who didn't take his middle-class advantage for granted. The pragmatic optimist. The sneaker aficionado. The smart, even-tempered guy who didn't bring rage—no matter how righteous it might be—to the bargaining table, or to lunch with Bernard Arnault. Abloh's success was a lot to take in. It only made his death more startling.

Abloh unveiled his final collection in June 2021. The highlight was a film he'd made, *Amen Break,* which looked at the way in which origins and provenance for Black men and women became a matter of blurred lines and cultural erasure. Abloh broached the question of who created what and how it was passed along in an era of sampling and within the context of his own malleable design philosophy. He turned again to Johnson for choreography and to Kamara for styling. The clothes came in searing colors—lime, cobalt blue, fuchsia—and referenced the mental strength of samurai and the intellectual gamesmanship of chess.

ABLOH DIED FIVE MONTHS later on November 28.

"It wasn't like we knew that he was going to pass," Shannon Abloh said. "Even though we knew the challenge of what he was fighting, it went a lot faster than we thought it was going to.

"So we never had the 'this is the legacy that I want you to work toward' discussion. But because I was with him for so long, I knew every inch of him. I knew every inch of his brain."

Louis Vuitton's Michael Burke spoke to Abloh in the hours before his death and listened as he lamented not being able to continue on, to see his projects through. "Virgil's passing remains inconceivable to me," Burke said. "He was born the same year as my oldest child, and I considered him like a son."

That final Spring 2022 collection quickly became an homage to what was and what could have been. A live show, with a few changes, traveled to Miami only three days after Abloh died. Instead of simply planting a flag during Art Basel Miami Beach, as was originally planned, it served as a memorial. It was what his family wanted.

The presentation took place at Miami Marine Stadium in Biscayne Bay. The audience, some fifteen hundred strong, was ferried to the location by boat. Once there, they were greeted by a three-story-tall statue of Abloh dressed in jeans, a sweater, and an LV belt buckle at his waist. The statue wore sunglasses and looked skyward in a gesture of hope. It was an outsize gesture in acknowledgment of the briefest career.

Karl Lagerfeld shaped the fortunes of Chanel for three decades. Gianni Versace rewrote the definition of glamour and unleashed the era of supermodels. Neither was commemorated with a statue the size of a small apartment building. But in the midst of a storm involving race, power, and identity, no flourish was too big for Abloh's family, colleagues, famous friends, and famous people—Kanye West, Pharrell Williams, A$AP Rocky, Bernard Arnault—who assembled to honor his work. They wanted to appreciate the stubborn dreamer who'd planted himself in a fashion environment that had become more amenable to change—and flourished.

"When we talk about fashion, we often think about the idea of 'garments,' but it was so much more than garments to Virgil," said designer Aurora James. "It was really about culture, about identity, about the youth. He also made a lot of people feel seen; for him, it was always 'us' and 'we,' never 'I,' and that's really important. I've also never seen anyone be able to output so much incredible work. It was mind-blowing. I'm honored to be here."

While some guests arrived dressed in mourning black, many more came wearing Abloh's designs for Louis Vuitton—and his optimistic embrace of every moment of every day was reflected in his jubilant use of color. He'd dictated the details of this memorial and celebration. "The deeply moving show we are about to see was born out of an idea Virgil first discussed with me three years ago," Burke said. "It was based around the traditional coming-of-age narrative—of course, being Virgil, he spun and recontextualized the concept for the 21st century, and in doing so, he was expressing his own unique talents and vision.

"This idea of coming-of-age was important to Virgil because inspiring and empowering younger generations defined who he was. He used the platform he had to break boundaries and to open doors, to shed light on his creative passions—art, design, music and, of course, fashion—so that everybody could see inside, not only to dream of being part of that world, but to also find ways to make that dream a reality," he continued. "Virgil showed them the way."

Abloh hadn't succeeded in fashion by instilling fear or exerting force. He'd gotten ahead due to faith in his own abilities, a multitude of fortuitous connections and the capacity of an entrenched establishment to give way to a Black man who was the flagbearer of a community's bold new ideas.

As the sun set, Abloh's optimism was reflected in the bright-red hot-air balloon anchored nearby and in the paper plane sculpture that served as a set piece for the runway. The models, some of them with tears in their eyes, weaved through a forest of birch trees.

For that final collection, Abloh collaborated with Nike. His two beloved brands had come together for a new version of the Air Force sneaker. His seventeen-year-old self would have been delighted.

When the show ended, fireworks exploded over the bay. Many in the audience hugged and wept. A drone wrote a message to the crowd and to anyone who happened to be looking up at the night sky: "Virgil was here."

There was a postshow gathering. But there was no celebratory champagne. And more important than any varsity jacket, sneaker, or T-shirt was the message delivered to outsiders and dreamers in Abloh's own quiet voice broadcast over the sound system.

"Life is so short that you can't waste even a day subscribing to what someone thinks you can do, versus knowing what you can do."

Epilogue

ABLOH'S DEATH WAS met with a great outpouring of grief, not simply from those who knew him, but also from those who admired what he'd accomplished and believed that his success cleared a path on which others could travel.

Abloh summited a particular peak in the fashion world—one that made his advancement easy to understand. Everyone knew Louis Vuitton. The sheer size of the company meant that most consumers had, at some point, stumbled across its LV-branded handbags in a fancy department store, in an airport duty-free shop, or in one of its more than 460 boutiques across the globe. The brand wasn't selling subtlety. Louis Vuitton made its presence felt with both volume and bravado. People who had little interest in or familiarity with fashion knew Abloh had made something of himself within an industry that seemed closed off, opaque, and extremely White.

In the aftermath of his death, Abloh's stature only grew. Like actors and musicians who died young, who died when it seemed that their talent had yet to fully blossom, they became legends. They were forever youthful and full of promise; their flaws dimmed in the glowing light of admiration and loss.

In his home state, a few weeks after his death, State Rep. Kambium Buckner (D) introduced House Resolution 0569 memorializing Abloh. In true legislative style, it was a litany of "whereas this" and "whereas that." It ended the list of his accomplishments with a simple acknowledgment: "Be it resolved, by the House of Representatives of the one hundred second General Assembly of the state of Illinois, that we mourn the passing of Virgil Abloh and extend our sincere condolences to his family, friends, and all who knew and loved him; and be it further resolved, that a suitable copy of this resolution be presented to the family of Virgil Abloh as an expression of our deepest sympathy."

The resolution was adopted on January 5, 2022. That same year, the Illinois House also resolved to mark what would have been the hundredth birthday of Harold Washington, who'd made history as well. He was the first African American elected mayor of Chicago, serving from 1983 to 1987. Abloh was in fine company.

The Fashion Scholarship Fund suddenly found itself not simply the organizing body for Abloh's mentoring program but a repository for much of his legacy. He established the mentoring program in 2020, in the aftermath of George Floyd's death, and dubbed the recipients of his awards "Post-Modern" scholars. From the beginning, with the program launching during a pandemic, the logistics had been a challenge. It was hard to establish a supportive mentoring relationship virtually. The 2022 scholars faced a different kind of challenge. Abloh wasn't just holding the door to fashion open for them; they were asked to embody what he represented. They weren't simply beneficiaries of his largesse; they represented his legacy.

They were honored in mid-April, on a clear, cool evening in New York at the Glass House on Twelfth Avenue. Guests assembled to praise Abloh and to behold the next generation of fashion designers, merchants, and entrepreneurs. The event evoked memories of the LVMH Prize that had figured so prominently in Abloh's rise. The large, open loft space, dotted with ottomans and settees and an open bar, was mostly given over to installations highlighting the work of the students. Of 123 students, 23 had been designated Post-

Modern scholars. All the students had tackled case studies in design, marketing, fashion, or beauty. They stood in front of their presentations—a kind of PowerPoint meets mural—and did their best to answer questions, make industry small talk, and simply be charming. The students came from fashion industry stalwarts such as Savannah College of Art and Design and Parsons, as well as Florida A&M University—one of several historically Black colleges and universities represented. It was the most diverse student cohort to date, said Peter Arnold, executive director of the FSF.

Abloh was present in pictures, words, and spirit. That evening, his wife, Shannon, dressed in black pajama-style trousers and a matching shirt piped in white, with her blond hair hanging straight, accepted an award on her husband's behalf. She'd always avoided the spotlight that shone so brightly on her husband. She noted that throughout his career, his focus wasn't "simply about opening the doors but laying the groundwork to ensure that these doors remain open permanently for others to walk through."

And that night, Naecia Dixon walked through those doors as the $25,000 grand prize winner. Dixon had grown up in Jamaica and studied at Savannah College of Art and Design. In her remarks that evening, she recalled seeing *Figures of Speech,* Abloh's museum exhibition that traveled to the High Museum in Atlanta.

"I'd never seen so many Black people in an art museum," she said. "Everyone was so inspired and captivated by an artist they had never met. Yet somehow it felt as though they had."

She finally had the chance to meet Abloh, at least virtually over a video call for the scholarship finalists, and she'd felt a kinship when he supported her ideas about creating a fashion line that was sustainable.

"Supporting the Virgil Abloh Post-Modern Scholarship develops a future reality where Black creatives are finally allowed to exist in the spaces they've been dreaming of," she said. "Systems are designed.

So we, as designers and as creatives, we can choose to design something better."

What had begun as a scrappy scholarship now had considerable financial weight. In early February 2022, Sotheby's auctioned two hundred pairs of limited-edition Air Force 1 sneakers to benefit Abloh's scholarship. Abloh had introduced the Air Force 1s on the Louis Vuitton runway in his Spring 2022 collection. He'd remade the basketball shoe with its familiar swoosh using leather printed with signature Louis Vuitton logos and patterns and then embellished them with his beloved irony: "air." For the auction, each pair of trainers was packaged with its own bright orange, monogrammed carrying case.

"A cultural symbol in its own right, today the Nike Air Force 1 serves as an *objet d'art* emblematic of self-generated subcultural provenance," Sotheby's proclaimed in the catalog. Sneakers had come a long way. They were now an *objet d'art*.

Sotheby's estimated the sale would raise $3 million for Abloh's scholarship. But once the bidding began, it was clear the auction was on pace to raise far more. By the time the virtual gavel came down, the sneaker sale had made $25.3 million, with a single pair selling for $352,800. Suddenly, the modest scholarship fund that had been the source of such pride for Abloh had overtaken the program under which it was housed.

Students applied to be Post-Modern scholars because they could envision themselves walking through the doors that Abloh opened. He wasn't the first to stand at the top of the fashion pyramid, but he was the first to whom they could relate.

"While Virgil was alive, I was very critical of his design. I always said that. I always thought, which I still do, that the impact of his *presence* was far more valuable than his actual talents," said designer Willy Chavarria, whose work is often inspired by his Mexican

American roots. "When he passed, I think it just hit so hard. It broke my heart. And I realized how important this man was.

"I look to him now as inspiration," added Chavarria. "I want to do what he did. I want to have the same sort of positive impact on humanity that he did through design."

AS IN SO MANY FIELDS, the fashion industry's agitation after the death of George Floyd led to increased attention to racial disparities and the need to take corrective action. Certainly, the fashion industry had a great deal of work to do. Progress that already had been made received new attention. Benchmarks were greeted with broad acclaim, and every success story registered louder than ever. And on social media, people demanded more diversity, more visibility, and more power.

A new generation of Blacks in the fashion industry rose alongside Abloh. Others were lifted in the fallout after George Floyd's death. They arrived via less traveled paths as well as on more traditional routes. How they came to their roles was less important than the fact that they arrived.

In 2018, Edward Enninful, a son of Ghanaian immigrants to England, took over *British Vogue* and transformed an overwhelmingly White publication into a template for diversity and inclusivity. Enninful demonstrated how everyone could participate in the glamour of fashion without its magic dissipating.

That same year Lindsay Peoples was appointed editor in chief of *Teen Vogue,* where she had once been an intern. Peoples had risen to prominence as a writer at *The Cut* for her examination of what it was like to be a Black person working in fashion, a treatise that read like a combination of investigative reporting, confessional, and notes from a communal therapy session. She furthered *Teen Vogue*'s mission as an outlet for the political, social, and sartorial desires of young people of color—something that had started under her predecessors.

Shiona Turini came into her own with her costume work on the 2019 film *Queen & Slim,* a retelling of the young lovers-on-the-run myth as a pulse-pounding examination of Blackness, doomed relationships, and policing. She later styled Beyoncé on her "Renaissance" tour in a dizzying array of bedazzled designer bodysuits and onesies.

In 2021, Pierre A. M'Pelé, who garnered fame on social media as "Pam Boy" with his assessments of runway collections, became head of editorial content at *GQ France.* Black American designers such as Sergio Hudson and Christopher John Rogers had their signature collections celebrated simply for their artistry and creativity; their work was in no danger of being labeled streetwear or urban. It would not be othered. They were Black designers who simply made stylish clothes. British designer Grace Wales Bonner garnered praise for her tailoring and at the same time celebrated the Black diaspora. She found inspiration in African nobility, bringing nuance and breadth to fashion's too-often clichéd representation of the African continent.

As fashion's landscape changed, designer Ozwald Boateng, who had resisted referencing race in his work, began to pull from his African roots and allowed them to inform his work. In 2019, he presented a gala fashion show in Harlem at the historic Apollo Theater. He called the collection "AI," for *authentic identity,* and the show marked the one-hundredth anniversary of the Harlem Renaissance. He did this because the kinds of conversations happening in fashion and in the broader culture had changed. Patrick Robinson, a Black man from California, had a run at the helm at Paco Rabanne. Martin Cooper, born in South Carolina, rose to chief creative officer of Belstaff. Olivier Rousteing won the top job at Balmain. And Abloh debuted at Louis Vuitton.

The success of Abloh's first show, with its Black models, its front row full of Black celebrities, and its hordes of Black youth watching virtually, marked a moment of Black greatness. In some respects, Abloh freed Boateng to be more fully himself. For decades, Boateng had worked within the constraints of the fashion system. He had pushed up against its confines and even delighted in the establishment rules. At last, he was adding his own unique rules to the mix.

And by 2022, five Italy-based luxury brands claimed creative directors who were men of color. British designer Maximilian Davis, whose family roots extended to Trinidad and Jamaica, was appointed to the Florentine luxury leather goods house Ferragamo with a mandate to make it cool.

Ibrahim Kamara, who'd worked closely with Abloh as a stylist, stepped up as the creative director of Off-White after Abloh's death. Benjamin A. Huseby and Serhat Işik took the design reins at Trussardi. And veteran designer Lawrence Steele was appointed creative director of Aspesi.

"That wouldn't have happened ten years ago," Edward Buchanan said. "Are we happy that it happened today? Yes. Are they deserving and talented individuals? Yes. Was a part of the decision-making related to what happened [with Abloh and George Floyd]? Yes. I think that the pool of talent and what they look like had to open up. I think people had to be conscious in making sure that when they were looking at CVs they were not only those of White creatives. I think people had to do that or they'd be called out."

None of these advancements came without individual struggles. Professionals had their judgment and stature doubted even when they were veterans in their field. One editor was called the n-word during one of their earliest experiences on a fashion shoot. One had a more senior Black professional question their decision to wear their hair in braids or to display a quote from the rapper Kendrick Lamar at their desk: "Every nigga is a star."

The industry watched designer Kerby Jean-Raymond rise like Icarus. He was applauded for his deeply researched, socially conscious runway shows in service to his brand Pyer Moss. Jean-Raymond turned the spotlight on police violence, Black cowboys, and the power of Black leisure. In 2021, he became the first Black American designer invited to join Paris's haute couture schedule with his own label. Jean-Raymond set his couture show at Villa Lewaro in Irvington, New York. The expansive estate belonged to Madam C. J. Walker, the hair product entrepreneur who became one of the first self-made African American millionaires. Jean-Raymond revealed a high-minded collection inspired by unsung Black inventors. It reflected his enduring philosophy of reclaiming and elevating the contributions of Black people to American culture.

But the clothes themselves? They had little finesse. It was a disheartening collection by a designer whose attention had drifted from perfecting the craftsmanship of his clothes to other endeavors such as philanthropy, politics, and personal bravado. His business financially unraveled and ostensibly shut down.

Fashion has moved forward, but not in a straight line. Many of the same frustrations that stymied previous generations have stubbornly refused to fall. Many of the old pressures have simply mutated into another kind of stress.

The Council of Fashion Designers of America, the industry's premiere trade group in New York, struggled in its mission to help Black designers. Should the CFDA focus solely on Black men and women in the early stages of their career, or should it include those who are midcareer and have ostensibly suffered the most from systemic racism? Should the CFDA focus solely on issues of diversity within the fashion industry, or should it consider the broader social context in which it exists? Should it earmark programs for Black designers, or should it also consider financial circumstances or gender? Should anyone be able to apply, or should there be a vetting process? And if so, who would pass judgment, the same gatekeepers who had historically barred the entryway? The council expanded its membership with an eye toward diversity, but it was in upheaval over the right answers to the difficult question of inclusivity.

After the Sotheby's auction, the Post-Modern Scholarship Fund was no longer as reliant on the largesse of corporations, although it still needed them to provide mentorships. And the Fashion Scholarship Fund was not immune from the vicissitudes of corporate gift giving. While it was fashionable for corporations to use discretionary dollars to benefit young Black students and entrepreneurs in the immediate aftermath of George Floyd's death—and Abloh's, too—that sense of duty quickly faded, particularly as companies hit financial struggles.

"I think that there was a lot of, I won't say lip service, but a lot of noise," Arnold said. "For the first year or two, virtually everybody said they wanted to do something, and they started to spend money to do something. I've seen a total drop-off, and there are organizations in my ecosystem that are really suffering because the folks who started to fund them said, 'We're not doing it anymore.'"

In fashion, consultants who'd been hired to help corporations navigate race moved on. Boards remained stubbornly homogeneous. And Kering, despite hiring regional diversity and inclusivity officers, ended 2023 with all White men serving as creative leads for its six fashion brands. Indeed, an industry expert estimated that 70 percent of the design directors or heads of design at major fashion houses were White men.

But Antoine Phillips was a beacon. A California native who'd started his fashion career in retail, Phillips was a strategic thinker who looked beyond the expected and the familiar. Tall, slim, and brown-skinned, he was charming and good-humored, a listener as much as an assertive actor. He knew that sometimes his mere presence was as revolutionary as anything he might say.

As he rose through the ranks of fashion communications, Phillips found mentors and champions along the way, such as the late George Kolasa at Giorgio Armani. Phillips was doing yeoman's work in reaching out to diverse communities and bringing them in to the luxury fashion conversation.

He brought luxury brands onto the campuses of historically Black colleges and universities. At Coach, he helped recruit actor Michael B. Jordan as a brand ambassador. At Gucci, he encouraged the company to engage with Black consumers, artists, and students in ways that were authentic to the brand as well as each distinct community Gucci was trying to reach.

In 2023, he made a career move that he thought would be an especially prestigious feather in his cap. He left Gucci to become a vice president in communications at Chanel. The French firm remained a private company but released limited financial data, mostly to crow about its revenue, which in 2022 was $17.2 billion. Chanel continued to support an haute couture atelier and through its investment in artisanal trades such as embroidery and lacemaking had kept those specialty crafts alive. The typical Chanel customer bought its fragrances and cosmetics and perhaps splurged on one of its $10,000 quilted handbags—the price of which continually ticked up and up. But Chanel also sold couture, a world of $100,000 garments, and that placed it in an exceptional category within fashion.

Phillips arrived in Paris on February 28, eager to experience his first Chanel ready-to-wear show. He stepped off the plane carrying a large Chanel tote bag and wearing a Chanel cashmere coat; he was also wearing a baseball cap. The retail cost of his traveling ensemble totaled several times the average mortgage payment of an American. Phillips felt good. He felt accomplished. He collected his luggage and exited the baggage claim area. He scanned the waiting crowd. He was searching for his name, which was on a sign, held by his driver. But before he could make his way toward his future, he was confronted by echoes of the past.

A group of French police officers stopped him and interrogated him: Who are you? Why are you here? What is your title?

The scene recalled those moments almost thirty years earlier when Edward Buchanan stepped off a plane in Venice eager to helm the new ready-to-wear division at Bottega Veneta, only to be treated with suspicion, disdain, and disrespect. Buchanan was alone when Italian police officers searched him for drugs. But Phillips was not.

More than twenty-three thousand French citizens, angered after the killing of George Floyd in 2020, protested in the streets of Paris, Lyon, Bordeaux, and Nice. They demanded racial justice, in America, in France, everywhere. They marched with signs expressing solidarity with the Black Lives Matter movement. They'd also been enraged when racist commentary that police officers made in private social media groups became public. They were tired of overpolicing in immigrant neighborhoods. They'd had enough.

As Phillips stood his ground in front of French authorities, two Black men—African men—waited nearby listening to the exchange. They didn't say anything to the officers; they didn't move. But they kept their eyes on the police and their ears trained on Phillips's words—just in case he needed help.

In the airport that day, Phillips had allies. That was a reassuring thing. But it was disheartening to know that even in 2023, allies were still required, perhaps more than ever. How many barriers could a Black man break on his own before he needed a rest?

Phillips departed Chanel a few months later. It was, he said, one of his most difficult moments. He'd been thrilled to add the company to his résumé, but never felt the staff made space for him on the long-standing team he was joining. He was there but not there.

He was the invisible man. Diversity was easy; inclusivity required clarity and conviction.

In resigning, Phillips felt the weight not only of his own disappointment but also that of other Black men and women in fashion who saw his career trajectory as indicative of what theirs could be. Like so many trailblazers, Phillips felt as though he'd let people down. He was also frustrated with Chanel.

"It's my hope that you all will consider the totality of someone's identity, not just their CV, contacts and relationships when attempting to shift or adapt team dynamics," Phillips wrote to his colleagues at Chanel when he left. "Equity and inclusion truly require the work of everyone involved to create meaningful change, and I do fear that not doing that work will simply lead to repeating the cycle I just experienced."

There were no quick routes to equity and inclusivity. Yet no one believed in shortcuts more than Abloh. He talked about cheat codes and all the ways in which he believed one could game the system to get ahead. But he did not consider that he was unique in temperament, talent, and background—and that he moved through fashion at a particular time when fashion wanted the same things that he did. Abloh shaped himself into a twenty-first-century celebrity. He wasn't famous because he was on television or on the covers of magazines. His fame was built on social media, word of mouth, the winds of cultural change. All those things in combination made his journey swift and steep.

"Virgil was good at seeking out what was going to drive him forward. He was not so much a fantastic designer but somebody who wanted to sell stuff and be known. He wanted to be a star," said Chavarria, who worked on Kanye West's Yeezy line. "He knew the importance of celebrity, and he knew how to navigate fame and social media."

A shortcut is, by definition, a way of getting to the finish line without having to do all the work. It's a way of skipping ahead. In some cases, it's simply cheating.

A 2021 lawsuit filed by April Walker was a stinging, public rebuke of shortcuts. Walker, who is Black and Mexican, is the founder of Walker Wear. She was one of the few women of color in the forefront of establishing streetwear as a fashion category. Friends on social media alerted Walker to Abloh's varsity jackets emblazoned with a close facsimile of her WW logo. She voiced her displeasure in an essay on *Medium*.

"As we walked into Women's History Month, I noticed in an Instagram ad that Off-White introduced a WW Letterman jacket that felt too close for comfort in the design. It was a classic design that we've been using for years," Walker wrote. "As a founder and legend in this space, I'm flattered that some creatives have been inspired, but the best way to pay homage is to do just that, without duplicity and forgetting to give credit where credit is due. The problem that exists here is a lack of integrity, lack of respect for culture and a lack of appreciation for women. The irony is that without me and others that have created this streetwear lane, Virgil wouldn't be here today."

Walker eventually settled her lawsuit, and it's something that she won't discuss. But in making her accusations public, she made sure her wins, for which she'd taken the long way around, weren't erased amid the Abloh adulation.

Some might argue that at their best, shortcuts were a way of avoiding unnecessary busywork. Or that choosing a more direct route was simply smarter than taking a longer, more time-consuming path. Yet there was something to be said for all the experience one gained through years of labor or the sense of grounding and perspective achieved by following a trail with more forgiving, energy-reserving switchbacks. Sometimes taking the long way was the only way everyone learned what was necessary to effect enduring change.

Abloh preached a gospel of urgency and impatience to a

generation weaned on text messages so hurriedly written there was no time for punctuation. In Abloh's view, shortcuts were a form of wisdom that was being withheld from those standing outside the fashion system who didn't have the benefit of insider information.

But shortcuts were also a disavowal of expertise. They reflected a belief that certain knowledge and experiences were superfluous to success. Fashion wasn't alone in devaluing experience or treating the slow, sometimes painful process of learning as a kind of hindrance rather than help. Similar evolutions were underway in politics, science, and education. The rise of the individual and one's personal truth were increasingly seen, not as additions to formal expertise, but as alternatives to it and, in some cases, better alternatives.

In fashion, Abloh's dedication to shortcuts was another way of saying that schooling, interning, and apprenticing were a waste of time. That was a balm to those who hadn't chosen a traditional route or for whom that was never an option. But what of those students taking on debt to attend design school? Where did that leave young designers paying dues in someone else's workroom?

"I'm not the consumer of Vuitton and I never have been," Buchanan said, "but I can look at the optics. I understand the decisions that were made. And from a business perspective, I understand how that can be very lucrative. But I would like to think that in the future of design and creativity and the creative process, there are going to be more designers that are being offered these types of positions. I would hope."

In the optimistic vision of Abloh, he was opening doors for unlikely designers: the kid silk-screening T-shirts at his neighborhood print shop, the deejay with an impeccable eye for trends, the computer geek with a creative streak, or the architecture student who couldn't get enough of fashion. He made people believe in the unlikely. But finding that one bit of gold takes patience, hard work, and tremendous luck. It can be easier to make do with pyrite.

"I think the reality is the industry thinks that there's a load of Virgils around," Janjer said. "And there isn't."

FIFTEEN MONTHS AFTER Abloh's death, Louis Vuitton named Pharrell Williams its new creative director of menswear. In the formal announcement, the company highlighted Williams's musical successes but also underscored his lobbying efforts to make Juneteenth a state holiday in Virginia and then a federal one. The company's new CEO, Pietro Beccari, noted that Williams's "creative vision beyond fashion will undoubtedly lead Louis Vuitton towards a new and very exciting chapter."

The choice of Williams underscored the impact that hip-hop, sneakers, and streetwear had had on the men's luxury business. Williams was an accomplished music producer and performer. He partnered with Nigo on the brand Billionaire Boys Club, among other fashion projects. Williams dabbled in sneaker collaborations. He checked all the boxes.

"When I look at Pharrell, I think, 'Wow, it would be great if that went to a trained designer.' But then I can look at it from the perspective of that large machine of a company. They're checking off boxes in that house," Buchanan said. "They want to have that consumer, those kids that are interested in [streetwear culture]. But they're only going to get that if they hire the person who actually has that magic wand to bring that consumer in."

A Black man from Virginia Beach, Virginia, Williams had much in common with Abloh. But he was also resoundingly different. Williams was a global celebrity when he entered the fashion arena.

He was not someone who'd made his way in from the shadows. Williams hadn't entered the fashion industry through design schools and internships, but his route was not especially unusual either. He was part of a lineage of celebrities who had launched their own fashion lines, who had signed up as brand ambassadors for luxury labels, and who had put their names on micro-collections that were meant to inject excitement into a brand that was drifting into the doldrums.

Williams also marked a turning point. He was the first celebrity to be appointed to a top position at a European luxury house. In 2019, Rihanna came close. LVMH announced its investment in Fenty, a new fashion label with Rihanna. The conglomerate hadn't attempted to build a high-end brand from the ground up since it launched Christian Lacroix in 1987 and, after years of losses, finally sold it in defeat in 2005. Rihanna's style was widely admired. She had previous experience developing her own fashion line and had started a successful beauty brand that distinguished itself with its vast range of foundation shades. She had millions of fans around the world.

But in 2021, the Fenty fashion house ceased production. Even Rihanna couldn't move high-priced merchandise during a pandemic. Still, LVMH did not hire Rihanna as creative director of Dior or Givenchy or Céline.

In selecting Williams, Louis Vuitton put an exclamation point on its positioning as a pop culture brand. Williams could bring heat and attention to the luxury house. He wasn't someone merely aware of rising trends in music; he sparked them. He was a creative director who was also a voracious consumer, someone who conversed in the language of high-wattage, look-at-me success. Williams was his own brand ambassador, red-carpet model, and social media influencer. He was a public-facing representative of the zeitgeist.

Louis Vuitton retained its atelier of skilled designers and craftspeople who could translate Williams's ideas into sketches then patterns and finally samples. But Louis Vuitton had also made plain its lack of faith in fashion's ability to excite the culture on its own terms. Abloh stretched the relationship between fashion and the broader culture. Williams snapped it.

A pure fashion designer, that is someone who'd built their fame and fortune through frocks and footwear, was no longer trusted to dazzle consumers. In the past, fashion catapulted Tom Ford into the lyrics of a Jay-Z song and into filmmaking. Fashion established Karl Lagerfeld as an icon renowned far beyond the borders of runways and ateliers. But Louis Vuitton wasn't willing to make the bet that such leaps still were possible.

Williams brought diversity to the top ranks of creative directors, but he also signified that the very definition of the job no longer had anything to do with technical fashion expertise. Men such as Marc Jacobs and Kim Jones brought streetwear into the luxury arena, but they'd ushered it in with their design credentials and their atelier experience. Over the years, the creative director's responsibilities grew. They were as much a merchant and advertising director as a designer. But now, the creative director was something much closer to a deejay, someone who manipulated the desires and moods of consumers, who sampled and mixed music but didn't write the lyrics or assemble the notes.

The choice of Williams didn't amplify the hope and possibility that Abloh signified for aspiring fashion designers. It underscored a sense of loss—of technical expertise and formal training, or even the little guy winning. The elevation of Williams was a shortcut, but not for the aspiring designer or even the struggling MC. It was a shortcut for Louis Vuitton.

Williams debuted on the runway during the week of Paris menswear shows in June 2023. He was part of the new guard. The traditionalists were few. At Dior, Kim Jones bridged the divide between tradition and heresy. Nigo, one of the godfathers of streetwear, was the creative director at Kenzo. Matthew Williams had long ago moved past Been Trill. He not only had his own brand but also was designing for Givenchy. Mike Amiri, who presented his collection outdoors in a garden party, was known for distressing his $1,000 jeans and cashmere sweaters as if blasted with a shotgun. A few months after his show, Amiri posted a note on his social media reminding his followers: "The kids that are screen printing tees in a garage, distressing jeans, upcycling vintage, and hand painting shirts are the ones that will take over the luxury retail streets in the next 5 years."

Jerry Lorenzo opted out of the menswear show cycle. Two months earlier, he mounted his first runway presentation for Fear of God at the Hollywood Bowl in Los Angeles. It was an impressive combination of luxury, sportswear, and allusions to the African American journey from enslavement to empowerment. The heartache of the past was embedded in Lorenzo's clothes—along with the promise of the future. And they were beautiful.

Pharrell Williams's show was a spectacle of music, merchandise, celebrity, and money. In advance of it, Williams stoked the anticipation by revealing his inaugural advertising campaign, which starred Rihanna. In a billboard that loomed over the Seine, she stood in the foreground of an elegant cityscape. Her pregnant belly was bursting from a Louis Vuitton leather shirt, and her arms were weighed down by Louis Vuitton bags in bright candy colors of red, yellow, and green. She clutched a to-go coffee cup in one hand. Her hair hung in waves down her back, and she stared off into the distance as if she was marching toward her limousine after a busy morning of shopping. It was an image that spoke of money. Spending money. Bragging about money. Money as a defining element of fame.

The advertisement didn't depict Rihanna the performer, so it didn't highlight the talent that brought her so much success and money. It didn't illuminate her personal style, the way in which she took clothes and transformed them into a statement about her identity. The picture was a commentary on abundance. Rihanna hadn't made a studied choice of the perfect bag. She'd walked off with all of them.

It was a startling contrast to the advertising campaign that marked Abloh's arrival at Louis Vuitton. Abloh's starred a Black toddler seated against a white backdrop and draped in one of the adult-size "Wizard of Oz" sweaters from the collection. The crewneck was a swirl of cheerful colors along with silhouettes of the band of serendipitous friends. The photograph highlighted the smooth, inky black of the child's face. It was a snapshot of possibility and change. The image spoke to the glory of talent and ambition in its infancy when both seem limitless. The sweater was lovely. But it was the toddler who tantalized the viewer.

The Pont Neuf, the oldest of the bridges across the Seine, served as Williams's runway. Guests didn't just walk along the docks and onto the bridge to find their seat. Their arrival was far more elaborate. They were told to assemble about a mile away on the Quai Valéry-Giscard-d'Estaing, where they boarded boats under the two-story Rihanna.

The day had been warm and humid with the clouds periodically unleashing just enough rain to ruin a well-chosen ensemble, but by 8:40 p.m., when the first of the boats departed, the air had cleared, and it was turning into a glorious night. With its Louis Vuitton flag flapping in the breeze, the open-top boat moved briskly along the Seine toward Notre-Dame, passing under the Pont des Arts with its weathered wooden planks. Tourists and residents sat along the banks of the river watching the parade of fashion editors, influencers, and other guests who were decked out in Louis Vuitton finery, as they arrived at the Pont Neuf, which had been painted like a golden checkerboard to mimic Louis Vuitton's signature Damier pattern.

As guests stood on the bridge looking toward the Right Bank, they could see several LVMH institutions. The five-star Cheval Blanc hotel had a prime position on the river. Nearby, polka dots adorned the Louis Vuitton headquarters in celebration of a collaboration with Japanese artist Yayoi Kusama. Folks could also see La Samaritaine department store, which LVMH had finally finished renovating. In some ways, the gilding of the bridge was just a formality; this was already another of LVMH's well-heeled little corners of Paris.

As always, there was plenty of time to gawk and kibitz before the show began. Williams lined up an impressive array of celebrities for his debut. Basketball star LeBron James came to pay his respects, and so did Zendaya. Musician and actor Lenny Kravitz strode in and greeted rows of editors from competing news organizations like a skilled diplomat. Beyoncé arrived wearing marigold-yellow Louis Vuitton lounging pajamas that were almost the same golden hue as her hair. Accompanied by husband Jay-Z, in a dark three-piece Louis Vuitton suit with a reimagined Damier print, the two had seats of honor at the center of the runway next to Bernard Arnault.

Rihanna arrived with her pregnant belly and A$AP Rocky after the show began. She showcased her tummy with a strategically unbuttoned Louis Vuitton denim jumpsuit along with a matching bra. The two looked like they'd been dipped in a vat of indigo dye and etched with various Louis Vuitton logos. They tucked themselves into a corner at the top of the runway from which they cheered Williams on.

He'd reinvented the tourism mantra of his home state—Virginia is for Lovers—as LVers. Working with the Louis Vuitton design team, he spliced the Damier checkerboard pattern with a camouflage print and called it "damoflage." He embroidered figures from the paintings of African American artist Henry Taylor onto tailored pieces. The collection included furs and leather coats, crocodile varsity jackets and glittery Moon Boots. Many of the models walking the runway were Williams's doppelgangers, preternaturally youthful Black men dressed in short pants, cropped jackets, and bedazzled sunglasses. Some of the most extravagant garments were encrusted with pearls, which had become a favored flourish within menswear. Models carried multiple bags based on the back-alley knockoffs hawked by street hustlers, the same ones in the Rihanna advertisement. Some of the models even drove golf carts bearing steamer trunks. Williams's first collection was an eye-popping expression of money, arriviste splendor, and street savvy.

As one might expect, the musical soundtrack was stellar and reflected the evolution of the brand from its traditionalist past to its embrace of hip-hop and its expansive sense of itself as a company that transcends fashion. The show opened with "Peace Be Still," a classical melody featuring the Chinese pianist Lang Lang. Next came the sharp rap of "Chains & Whips" by Clipse, the hip-hop duo originating in Virginia Beach and produced by Williams.

> Uncle said, "nigga, you must be sick
> All you talk about is just gettin' rich"
> Choke my neck, nigga, and ice my bitch
> Beat the system with chains and whips.

Clipse's early lyrics undergirded Pyrex Vision, Abloh's first solo foray into fashion. The duo, composed of brothers Gene "No Malice" and Terrence "Pusha T" Thornton, had been silent for a decade. They returned to the spotlight with a new tune for Williams's debut and to walk his runway.

The signature song of the evening, "Joy (Unspeakable)," was

performed by the Voices of Fire gospel choir, which had been the subject of a reality series that starred Williams and his uncle, who had founded a nondenominational church in Norfolk, Virginia.

The choir members, dressed in white robes with a white Damier print, filled the top of the runway and chanted the single word *joy* for nearly one minute. They swayed and danced as they sang a song of praise while the models walked out for one final promenade and Williams took his bows. It was hard not to be moved by the choir's soulful voices and passion. It was a bit like being in church, Black church. If the song signified anything, it was that this evening, this success, was a blessing for which Black people were particularly thankful. *Giving praise to God. The Lord works in mysterious ways. Amen.*

Williams wore a damoflage suit and matching baseball cap along with his diamond adorned sunglasses—no matter that the sun had set long ago. And unlike most designers at their debut, who emerged from backstage looking shell-shocked and like they'd just slipped off a work smock and a bracelet of pincushions, Williams was trailed by security. He walked halfway down the runway. He doffed his hat to Arnault, and the politically agnostic billionaire who'd made it all possible reciprocated with a thumbs-up. Beccari smiled broadly and applauded vigorously. Williams moved a few more steps down the runway, took a knee in gratitude, and then stood and walked over to embrace his wife and children, whose own attire matched his. They were a damoflage family.

As Williams returned to the top of the runway, he was met by the design team, a predominantly White group of young men and women who'd served as the translators of Williams's vision of dandies, diversity, and French *savoir faire*. In a dramatic gesture of respect for their skill, Williams bowed before them.

By the time Williams disappeared backstage, the runway was already transforming into an open-air concert hall. Waiters bearing cocktails and hors d'oeuvres moved through the crowd. Reggae began to boom over the sound system. But that was just a place-holder until Jay-Z slipped out of his suit coat and into a Louis Vuitton motorcycle jacket. He took the stage and gave the crowd a version of "Niggas in Paris," one of the hits from *Watch the Throne*, the album he'd recorded with Kanye West, the album Abloh had art-directed, the album for which Riccardo Tisci had created the cover art, the album Williams had helped produce. The song was a soliloquy on success, along with a roll call of bragging rights brands that included Louis Vuitton and, of course, Jordan brand sneakers.

A single musical gesture contained virtually all the landmarks on fashion's long road to transformation.

Then Williams stepped out and joined Jay-Z in "I Just Wanna Love U (Give It 2 Me)"—a song that opened with a simple pro-nouncement: "I'm a hustler, baby." Williams's falsetto pinged across the crowd and drifted into the night to serenade Paris. Some design-ers don't even take a bow. Others walk out and give a tentative wave. Abloh had been known to deejay an after-party. Williams was his own Grammy-winning entertainment.

In between songs, Williams expressed his gratitude to Jay-Z for attending the show, noting that the rapper could have been any-where in the world but "he chose to be here." Jay-Z returned the admiration, expressing his pride in Williams's accomplishment and adding that it was "a win for the culture."

But whose culture? That of the freshly minted millionaire and billionaire Black moguls who sit at the top or the strivers at the bot-tom? Williams equated gross consumerism as something more than a by-product of success. He—and Jay-Z—declared it a civil rights victory.

To see the merchandise at close range the next day at the Louis

Vuitton showroom was to be bowled over by just how extravagant it really was. The materials included leather, crocodile, and fur. Indeed, one crocodile jacket was so precious that it had a dedicated handler who twirled it around for visitors, all of whom were prohibited from touching it.

Over the next few days, Williams made a victory lap, attending the presentations of his LVMH colleagues—Nigo and Kim Jones. He did so carrying one of the items from his own collection: one of those Speedy bags, glitzed up with diamonds and bearing a $1 million price tag.

Williams's debut collection recalled another trend that had bubbled up from hip-hop and into the world of high-end designer fashion. Within the fashion press, the look was referred to as ghetto fabulous. Surely, if anyone used such a moniker in the twenty-first century they would be banished to purgatory for their reliance on stereotypes and racially charged tropes. But in its day, which was the early to mid-1990s, ghetto fabulous was viewed as a glorious urban riff on luxury fashion. It was a rebuke to those luxury brands that shunned Black consumers and ran away from hip-hop's overtures. The aesthetic relied on flash and swagger. It co-opted designer logos.

Ghetto fabulous was a belief in more always being better. The designer Coco Chanel was credited with saying, "Elegance is refusal." That was interpreted by many as meaning everything from a refusal of calories to a shunning of excessive flourishes, accessories, and showmanship. It was a belief that shades of beige were intrinsically more elegant than searing fuchsia or yellow. That a single perfect diamond was more sophisticated than a watch bedazzled by Jacob Arabo—who became known as Jacob the Jeweler—with hundreds of diamonds. Ghetto fabulous tested the boundaries of good taste by simply questioning who had the power to set boundaries in the first place.

Williams now had that power. Indeed, luxury fashion had come running to him.

LOUIS VUITTON HELPED climbers and dreamers show their worth through their possessions. With the help of Abloh, those same possessions were imbued with political and social relevance. Abloh was a marvel because he was the first Black man from the world of hip-hop who'd been tasked with setting up fashion's new rules and boundaries on a global scale. He meant something to sneakerheads, Black creatives, and awkward outsiders. But his voice was amplified far beyond the niche communities that had been so influential in its maturation.

He made a lot of folks feel like they were inside fashion's hallowed walls standing alongside him. Abloh made people feel like they belonged, no matter how unlikely their success might have seemed to themselves or anyone else.

When Louis Vuitton hired Williams, it invited him to become a fashion insider, and what he created was ostentatiously fabulous, but it wasn't ghetto because it wasn't niche.

It celebrated hip-hop, Black men, and the empires they built. That was beautiful whether one liked the clothes or not.

Williams added grand flourishes to the conversation that Abloh began. But did he move it forward or broaden its scope?

Fashion is not merely about the clothes one wears. It's essential to our understanding of who and what are prized. Abloh made it clear that Black men dreamed of seemingly impossible achievements in roped-off places. He brought along a diverse community of colleagues and supporters upon whose shoulders he stood. He led with a genteel spirit. He dealt with racism with a nimbleness, and sometimes the naiveté, of someone unburdened by America's history of slavery.

Abloh succeeded. His unlikely victory made it seem as though anything was possible. And indeed, it was. Abloh took the baton from those who came before him and he ran with it. He covered a mighty distance in a terribly short time.

Pharrell Williams took up the baton. He raised it high, and with gratitude, he took a bow.

ACKNOWLEDGMENTS

This book is ultimately a story about optimism. It's about believing in small changes and awe-inspiring prospects.

Abloh was an optimist. He was also tenacious and talented. But so many of those who shared their memories of him, began by noting that he was nice. At first, I thought this was just a bit of throat-clearing before they got to the heart of things. But I learned that while there was much to say about Abloh, his kindness was not an aside. It was central to his achievements and his enduring impact. That's something we should all remember as we try to scramble up the ladder of success.

Eunice and Nee Abloh extended both kindness and grace when they allowed me into their home and shared memories of their beloved son. You are remarkable. And I am forever grateful.

I am indebted to the optimism and kindness of editor Kevin Doughten. His encouragement, enthusiasm, and wisdom midwived this book into the world. Every conversation left me energized and determined—and a bit more clear-eyed. He is a masterful editor. I'm not sure how I got so lucky.

Thank you to Christopher Brand for a wonderfully elegant and thoughtful cover design—and with a little bit of sparkle too. And to the entire team at Crown, including Elisabeth Magnus, Terry Deal, Dan Novack, Aubrey Khan, Andrea Lau, and Jessica Scott—I'm grateful for the editing, the lawyering, the designing, the corralling, and the hand-holding. Dyana Messina, Chantelle Walker, Mary Moates, and Josie McRoberts had such wonderful ways of ushering this book out into the world.

As always, I am so thankful for my agent, David Kuhn at Aevitas Creative Management. He and Nate Muscato nurtured a seed of an idea and helped it grow into a book. Thank you and thank you, again.

I offer my sincerest appreciation to the members of the fashion, design, and art worlds, and beyond, who spoke to me on-the-record and off-the-record, who helped me consider Abloh's work in a multitude of contexts and who kindly helped me connect so many dots and let me pester them again and again. Thank you: Shawn Agyeman, Peter Arnold, Ingrid Asoni, Ozwald Boateng, Anthony Brooks, Edward Buchanan, Michael Burke, Meaghan Cohen, Susan Conger-Austin, Fraser Cooke, Franck Couetil, Michael Darling, Cecile Durieux, Frank Flury, Jonas Gustavsson, Laron Howard, Walker Inge, Sami Janjer, Kim Jones, Jerry Lorenzo, Stella McCartney, Bonnie Morrison, Dao Nguyen, Amy Ott, Jay Paavonpera, Lindsay Peoples, Nancy Pearlstein, Antoine Phillips, Heron Preston, Daniel Rasmussen, Michael Rock, Debra Thom, Tommy Ton, Katie Weisman, Kristine Westerby, Matthew Williams, and Julie Zerbo.

The work of two books informed my research. Yuniya Kawamura's *Sneakers: Fashion, Genders, and Subculture* (Bloomsbury Academic, 2016) and *His Name Is George Floyd: One Man's Life and the Struggle for Racial Justice* by Robert Samuels and Toluse Olarunnipa (Viking, 2022). I thank them for their thoughtful, enlightening, and rigorous research.

My colleagues from the world of journalism were generous with their contacts, their support, and their guidance. And no institution is more supportive of its writers' extracurricular endeavors than *The Washington Post*. Thank you: Keith Alexander, Sally Buzbee, Bronwyn Cosgrave, Ann Gerhart, Blake Gopnik, Lisa Green, Booth

Moore, Long Nguyen, Steven Pearlstein, Liz Seymour, Lauren Sherman, Rachel Tashjian, Krissah Thompson, Emil Wilbekin, and Teresa Wiltz.

Hugs to my friends and family for the cheerleading and the cocktails—and for knowing when not to ask, "How's the book going?" And, of course, to my parents, for whom I have endless love and gratitude.

NOTES

PROLOGUE

ix **More than 3.5 million people:** Farida B. Ahmad, Jodi A. Cisewski, and Robert N. Anderson, "Provisional Mortality Data—United States, 2021," Centers for Disease Control and Prevention, April 29, 2022, https://www.cdc.gov/mmwr/ volumes/71/wr/mm7117e1.htm#:~:text=NVSS%20routinely%20releases %20provisional%20mortality,occurred%20in%20the%20United%20States.

x **"That's the problem":** Malcolm Gladwell, "Black Unlike Me," *The Washington Post*, July 11, 1995.

xi **"god in the flesh":** Antoine Sargent, "In Search of Virgil Abloh," *GQ*, February 15, 2022, https://www.gq.com/story/in-search-of-virgil-abloh.

xi **The mourners wept and they sang:** Michael Darling, interview with author, April 2023.

xi **"He did what he *knew*":** "Celebrities attend Virgil Abloh's memorial service in Chicago. Rihanna, Kim Kardashian, Kanye West," YouTube, https://www .youtube.com/watch?v=klHNFVcFmws.

INTRODUCTION

2 **"The term *streetwear*":** Kim Jones, interview with author, March 2023.

3 **He saw himself as a leader:** Shawn Agyeman, tape recording of Virgil Abloh in 2008.

5 **Abloh had numerous lawyers:** Ezra Marcus, "The Off-White Papers: Inside Virgil Abloh's Trademark Ballet," *The New York Times*, April 21, 2021.

5 **He filed to trademark a series:** Marcus, "Off-White Papers."

6 **"He wouldn't network":** Jones, interview with author, March 2023.

10 **The country lived through a summer:** Robin Givhan, "The Verdict: His Life Mattered," *The Washington Post*, April 20, 2021.

10 **Some die within months:** Melinda Wenner Moyer, "What Is Cardiac Angiosarcoma?," *The New York Times*, November 29, 2021.

CHAPTER ONE

15 **"When I was starting":** Aria Hughes, "Virgil Abloh Thinks Streetwear Can Be a Trap," *Women's Wear Daily*, November 6, 2018, https://wwd.com/ feature/virgil-abloh-thinks-streetwear-can-be-a-trap-1202897025/.

16   The city's modern-day population: U.S. Census 2023, "City and Town Population Totals: 2020–2023," population estimate (as of July 1), 2023, https://www.census.gov/data/tables/time-series/demo/popest/2020s-total -cities-and-towns.html.

17   The first wave of Black residents: Chris Jaffe, "The Race Line in Rockford to 1930," *Journal of the Illinois State Historical Society* 103, no. 1 (Spring 2010): 7–42.

18   Rockford even had its own: V. Dion Haynes, "Racial Tensions Still Dog Rockford," *Chicago Tribune,* September 1, 1991.

18   Eventually, Black residents: U.S. Census 2024, "QuickFacts: Rockford City, Illinois," https://www.census.gov/quickfacts/fact/table/rockfordcityillinois/ PST045224.

19   "The west side was not considered": Deryk Hayes, interview with author, April 2023.

20   Eunice Abloh was a tall, brown-skinned woman: Eunice Abloh, interview with author, March 2023.

22   When Nee considered: Nee Abloh, interview with author, March 2023.

23   "A lot of the Africans": Shawn Agyeman, interview with author, April 2023.

23   "Being an African in Africa": Agyeman, interview with author, April 2023.

24   By the time Abloh entered: Elizabeth Austin, "A River Knifes Through It," *Chicago Tribune,* September 27, 1998.

24   "I remember it being a big issue": Hayes, interview with author, April 2023.

24   "I was amazed something like this": Joseph Kirby, interview with author, June 2023.

25   De facto segregation: Austin, "A River Knifes Through It."

25   So a group of parents: Austin, "A River Knifes Through It."

25   When a federal judge finally issued: Linda P. Campbell and Joseph A. Kirby, "School Bias Is Rife in Rockford," *Chicago Tribune*, November 4, 1993.

25   By 1994, as Abloh was preparing: Ron Grossman et al., "In North, Desegregation Still Unfinished Business," *Chicago Tribune,* May 17, 1994.

26   "Virgil was an African American": Hayes, interview with author, April 2023.

27   The school was founded in 1960: Amy Ott, president of Boylan Catholic High School, interview with author, March 2023.

27   "We never have a problem": Ott, interview with author, March 2023.

27   Abloh might not have been Catholic: Interview with Nee and Eunice Abloh, December 2024.

28   "He was a part of the whole process": Eric Eiss, interview with author, March 2023.

28   He was an introvert: Eunice Abloh, interview with author, March 2023.

30   It also designated billions: Glenn Kessler, "Joe Biden's Defense of the 1994 Crime Bill's Role in Mass Incarceration," *The Washington Post*, March 16, 2019.

30   "Rap is now a worldwide phenomenon": Chuck D, *Fight the Power: Rap, Race, and Reality* (New York: Delacorte Press, 1997), 256.

31 **"Black male elegance"**: Robin Givhan, "Basic Black," *The Washington Post*, March 1, 1999.

32 **"Everyone likes the pretty boys"**: Treach, interview with author, February 1996.

32 **"I'm not fashion"**: Robin Givhan, "Ralph Lauren's Corporate Look," *The Washington Post*, October 2, 1997.

33 **He was a Jewish kid**: "Ralph Lauren" (bio), company website, accessed December 22, 2024, https://corporate.ralphlauren.com/leadership-ralph -lauren-full-bio.html.

33 **"I earned the money"**: Givhan, "Ralph Lauren's Corporate Look."

35 **"One aspect of fashion"**: Long Nguyen, contribution to *My Beutyfull Lyfe: Davide Sorrenti, 1995–1997*, ed. Francesca Sorrenti (London: IDEA, 2021).

35 **In large measure, 1997 also marked the implosion**: Amy Spindler, "A Death Tarnishes Fashion's 'Heroin Look,' " *The New York Times*, May 20, 1997.

36 **"But the glorification of heroin"**: Christopher S. Wren, "Clinton Calls Fashion Ads' 'Heroin Chic' Deplorable," *The New York Times*, May 22, 1997.

37 **"What drew me to his work"**: Katherine Bernard, "Kanye West's Creative Director Virgil Abloh on His Obsession with the Work of Raf Simons," *Vogue*, June 2, 2014, https://www.vogue.com/article/kanye-wests-creative -director-virgil-abloh-on-raf-simons.

38 **"Gucci, especially under Tom Ford"**: Robin Givhan, "Gucci's Moment," *The Washington Post*, November 15, 2021.

39 **"white washing"**: Robin Givhan, "The White Stuff," *The Washington Post*, June 5, 1996.

39 **"an homage to different Black women"**: Robin Givhan, "Black Chic," *The Washington Post*, December 1, 1997.

40 **"The mid-1990s were a period"**: Nguyen, contribution to *My Beutyfull Lyfe*.

41 **Diana was one of the few**: Tariro Mzezewa, "For the African Women Who Love Diana," *The New York Times*, November 24, 2020.

42 **the year to which Abloh so often referred**: Virgil Abloh, as told to Véronique Hyland, " 'I'm Just Trying to Dress Like the 17-Year-Old Version of Myself,' " *The Cut*, February 16, 2016.

CHAPTER TWO

45 **"When you're a first"**: Edward Enninful, interview with author, February 2024.

47 **Kelly died in 1990**: Thelma Golden, "Patrick Kelly: A Retrospective," exhibition note, Brooklyn Museum, 2004, https://www.brooklynmuseum .org/exhibitions/patrick_kelly.

48 **"I could have really taken you"**: Woody Hochswender, "Realism Takes Henderson to Top," *The New York Times*, November 28, 1989.

48 **"Gordon was amazing for me"**: Edward Buchanan, interview with author, March 2023.

48   **"Laura created, in the seventies":** Buchanan, interview with author, March 2023.

49   **When he arrived in Italy:** Jennifer Parmelee, "Beautiful Florence Faces an Ugly Problem: Violence Against Immigrants," *The Washington Post*, April 5, 1990.

50   **"They start checking my bags":** Buchanan, interview with author, March 2023.

50   **"There was no formal 'Okay, we're done'":** Buchanan, interview with author, March 2023.

52   **"The pictures were there on Style.com":** Style.com launched in 2000 and was the online home for *Vogue* and W magazines. It became famous for its extensive catalogue of runway photography. That archive now lives at Vogue .com.

52   **"The majority of the Italian press":** Buchanan, interview with author, March 2023.

53   **"To see someone like me":** Buchanan, interview with author, March 2023.

58   **"My mother used to make clothes":** Ozwald Boateng, interview with author, September 2022.

59   **Nutter made clothing for Mick Jagger:** Lance Richardson, "Everything You Need to Know About Rebel Savile Row Tailor, Tommy Nutter," *Another Man*, May 10, 2018, https://www.anothermanmag.com/style-grooming/ 10328/everything-you-need-to-know-about-rebel-savile-row-tailor-tommy -nutter.

59   **"There is something about being self-taught":** Boateng, interview with author, September 2022.

60   **"I love the tradition of being British":** Robin Givhan, "Unbuttoning Stuffed Shirts," *The Washington Post*, October 22, 1998.

60   **And that has been an archetype:** Monica L. Miller, interview with author, October 2024.

61   **"I didn't want anyone to know":** Boateng, interview with author, September 2022.

62   **"It's a different world now":** Boateng, interview with author, September 2022.

62   **Remnants of the building's original owner:** Susan Tunick, "The City's Exuberant Ceramic Facades," *The New York Times*, December 13, 1992.

63   **In 2002, Boateng moved:** Rebecca Lowthorpe, "Savile Rows," *The Sunday Times*, August 25, 2002.

65   **The idea of working on menswear:** Boateng, interview with author, September 2022.

65   **After a year of courtship:** Boateng, interview with author, September 2022.

65   **"There was a lot of change":** James Greenfield, interview with author, November 2023.

66   **"His models crunched down a catwalk":** Hilary Alexander, "Boateng Conquers Paris: The British Designer with a Penchant for Firsts Has Just Made Fashion History in France," *The Daily Telegraph*, July 6, 2004.

66   **"Boateng's collection displayed more self-belief":** Hadley Freeman, "Hadley

Freeman Thought Men's Fashion Shows Would Be Camp or Dull. She Hadn't Counted on the Influence of David Hockney and Nirvana," *The Guardian*, July 9, 2004, https://www.theguardian.com/lifeandstyle/2004/jul/09/shopping.fashion.

66 **"Givenchy benefited from the enthusiastic reception":** LVMH Moët Hennessy Louis Vuitton annual report, 2004, https://www.annualreports.com/HostedData/AnnualReportArchive/l/OTC_LVMUY_2004.pdf.

66 **"We really embraced it":** Greenfield, interview with author, November 2023.

68 **"I'd never experienced that type of conflict":** Boateng, interview with author, September 2022.

69 **"The last possible thought about it":** Marco Gobbetti, interview with author, November 2024.

69 **"A lot of people say":** "The New Man at Givenchy," *British Vogue*, March 1, 2005, https://www.vogue.co.uk/article/the-new-man-at-givenchy.

69 **"Of twenty-nine outfits":** Cathy Horyn, "Couture Steps Lively for a Corpse," *The New York Times*, July 14, 2005.

70 **Instead, there was number-crunching curiosity:** James Sherwood, "Tailor-Made for the Job," *The Times*, December 15, 2003.

70 **"He has more charm than Hogwarts":** Sherwood, "Tailor-Made."

CHAPTER THREE

73 **"the architectural father":** Lee Bey, "Van der Rohe Building May Get Landmark Status," *Chicago Sun-Times*, October 2, 1996.

75 **The school was just over an hour's drive north:** Nee Abloh, interview with author, March 2023.

76 **"Architecture would be my bridge":** Virgil Abloh, conversation with Michael Rock, unpublished transcript, December 2013.

77 **"women who could buy Balenciaga":** Robin Givhan, "The Wind of Change; Michelle Obama Has Put Chicago's Conservative Chic on World's Stage," *The Washington Post*, January 15, 2009.

77 **When Abloh arrived:** "Chicago Mayor Daley Wins Fifth Term," CNN.com, March 3, 2003.

78 **But by 2005, the city:** Gretchen Ruethling, "Homicide Capital in 2003, Chicago Has a Turnaround," *The New York Times*, January 2, 2005.

80 **"The interesting part about architecture training":** Frank Flury, interview with author, March 2023.

81 **"I wouldn't say he was":** Flury, interview with author, March 2023.

81 **something he never explicitly confided:** Interview with Nee and Eunice Abloh, December 2024.

82 **"I liked the idea of taking a program":** Abloh, conversation with Rock, unpublished transcript, December 2013.

82 **"Virgil always was like, it's a prototype":** Matthew Williams, interview with author, July 2023.

83 **"Virgil dealt with a lot of—":** Williams, interview with author, July 2023.

83   **"as apt to conjure notions"**: Nicolai Ouroussoff, "Tunnel Vision—A Good Kind," *Los Angeles Times*, November 2, 2003.

84   **"You could think about deconstruction"**: Michael Rock, interview with author, March 2023.

84   **"A building could actually *cause*"**: Rock, interview with author, March 2023.

84   **He hadn't honed a singular vision**: Nicolai Ouroussoff, "Why Is Rem Koolhaas the World's Most Controversial Architect?," *Smithsonian Magazine*, September 2012, https://www.smithsonianmag.com/arts-culture/why-is-rem-koolhaas-the-worlds-most-controversial-architect-18254921/.

85   **"It's a way of analyzing something"**: Rock, interview with author, March 2023.

85   **"I think some of the criticism"**: Rock, interview with author, March 2023.

86   **The tabletop model**: Izzy Kornblatt, "In Brooklyn, Virgil Abloh's Architectural Legacy on Display," *Architectural Record*, August 16, 2022.

86   **"like a tree bending"**: Andrew Connor, "Remembering Alumnus Virgil Abloh, a Pioneering Designer Inspired by Architecture," Illinois Institute of Technology website, December 16, 2021, https://www.iit.edu/news/remembering-alumnus-virgil-abloh-pioneering-designer-inspired-architecture.

86   **"He recognized that if you had a visual brand"**: Rock, interview with author, March 2023.

88   **But he was styling himself**: In 2023, Sean Combs denied multiple allegations of sexual assault and rape raised in lawsuits that were filed when New York passed legislation opening a limited window during which people could file civil lawsuits for sexual abuse even if the statute of limitations had passed.

89   **"*Urban*. I was always insulted"**: Robin Givhan, "They Laughed When Diddy Launched a Fashion Line. Then He Changed the Industry," *The Washington Post,* April 21, 2016.

89   **"When I came to L.A."**: Robin Givhan, "Fashion at the Highest Level," *The Washington Post*, April 27, 1998.

89   **"All-Star weekend you have to look nice"**: Givhan, "Fashion at the Highest Level."

90   **In 2003, player Kobe Bryant**: Kevin Draper, "Kobe Bryant and the Sexual Assault Case That Was Dropped but Not Forgotten," *The New York Times,* January 27, 2020.

91   **"We have a minimum standard"**: Draper, "Kobe Bryant."

91   **"They're targeting my generation"**: Zack Graham, "How David Stern's NBA Dress Code Changed Men's Fashion," *Rolling Stone,* November 4, 2016, https://www.rollingstone.com/culture/culture-sports/how-david-sterns-nba-dress-code-changed-mens-fashion-104719/.

92   **By 2005, 75 percent of men**: Robin Givhan, "NBA Players Take Style off Court," *The Washington Post,* June 3, 2013.

95   **"You know how you pull a jolly-rancher"**: Benjamin Edgar, "Edamame . . . If You Don't Know, You Better Ask Somebody," *The Brilliance,* March 6, 2005, https://www.thebrilliance.com/posts?page=110.

95 **"What can I say . . ."**: Virgil Abloh, "Interview! > Virgil Abloh!," *The Brilliance*, n.d., accessed January 4, 2025, https://www.thebrilliance.com/interviews/virgil-abloh-e4273bf4-4108-4305-92e8-358055d1c9c6.

95 **"During the week"**: Virgil Abloh, "Find Space and Sell!," *The Brilliance*, July 21, 2006, https://www.thebrilliance.com/posts?page=60.

97 **"I hate the way they portray us"**: Helena Andrews-Dyer, "Actor Mike Myers Says Kanye West Spoke 'a Truth' During That Infamous Hurricane Katrina Telethon," *The Washington Post*, May 21, 2014.

98 **"I was into fashion that intersected"**: Thom Bettridge, "Group Chat: The Oral History of Virgil Abloh," *GQ*, March 4, 2019.

99 **"Daley Making Dollars"**: Vic Lloyd, interview with author, December 2023.

100 **"If you had an ounce of creativity"**: Jay "Jay Boogie" Green, interview with author, December 2023.

101 **Green quickly hired Abloh**: Green, interview with author, December 2023.

101 **Soon Abloh was invited**: Taiye Selasi, "How to Be Both," in *Virgil Abloh: Figures of Speech* (Chicago: Museum of Contemporary Art Chicago; New York: DelMonico Books, 2019), 133.

102 **West threw himself fully into his passions**: Jim Moore, who has spent in excess of forty years at *GQ* magazine, more than half of that as creative director, interview with author, May 2023.

102 **In the crush of academic work**: Selasi, "How to Be Both," 133.

102 **"All this stuff happened"**: Lloyd, interview with author, December 2023.

103 **"He said he liked our work"**: Mark Peters, interview with author, December 2023.

103 **"I'd never done that before"**: Peters, interview with author, December 2023.

103 **"I'm the only one"**: Peters, interview with author, December 2023.

104 **"Virgil had the best social IQ"**: Dirk Standen, interview with author, May 2023.

106 **In 2009, while DW was percolating**: Vanessa Friedman, "Shannon Abloh Is Ready to Talk," *The New York Times*, November 29, 2022.

107 **"He would do crazy flights"**: Christine Centenera, "Keeping Virgil: Shannon Abloh on Carrying on Her Late Husband's Fashion Legacy," *Vogue Australia*, April 3, 2023.

107 **"I saw Kanye and his posse"**: Brooke Bobb, "Remember When Kanye West Carried a Goyard Briefcase to Paris Fashion Week?," *Vogue*, February 28, 2017.

108 **Abloh carried his laptop**: Debra Thom, interview with author, May 2022.

110 **"Tokyo was, for menswear back then"**: Michael Burke, interview with author, July 2022.

112 **"I'm the only White guy"**: Burke, interview with author, July 2022.

112 **"I was very impressed by the silence"**: Burke, interview with author, July 2022.

113 **"You just can't show up one day"**: Burke, interview with author, July 2022.

114 **"That seems to be a leitmotif"**: Burke, interview with author, July 2022.

115 **"When that happened"**: Burke, interview with author, July 2022.

115 **When he presented his DW collection:** Terry Richardson was later accused of sexual harassment. Vanessa Friedman and Elizabeth Paton, "'Terry Richardson Is Just the Tip of the Iceberg,'" *The New York Times,* October 27, 2017.

116 **"I'm so scared":** Robin Givhan, "Kanye West Paris Fashion Show Spring 2012: DW by Kanye West," *Daily Beast*, October 2, 2011, https://www.thedailybeast.com/kanye-west-paris-fashion-show-spring-2012-dw-by-kanye-west.

117 **"It was kooky":** Rock, interview with author, March 2023.

117 **"They were all sitting around":** Rock, interview with author, March 2023.

118 **"The example I always use":** Rock, interview with author, March 2023.

119 **He felt belittled:** Kanye West, interview with Charlamagne tha God, 2018, https://www.youtube.com/watch?v=zxwfDlhJIpw.

119 **"Hey, come over here":** Abloh, conversation with Rock, unpublished transcript, December 2013.

119 **"When I first met him":** Abloh, conversation with Rock, unpublished transcript, December 2013.

120 **Abloh was the lead researcher:** Abloh, conversation with Rock, unpublished transcript, December 2013.

120 **"I have a kind of add-on function":** Abloh, conversation with Rock, unpublished transcript, December 2013.

120 **"The story is secondary":** Steven Zeitchik, "Kanye's Journey: The Hip-Hop Star Ventures a Bit Further into the Film World with His 30-Minute 'Cruel Summer,'" *Los Angeles Times,* May 25, 2012.

121 **"I realized I have an identity too":** Abloh, conversation with Rock, unpublished transcript, December 2013.

CHAPTER FOUR

124 **"I developed these woven labels":** Heron Preston, interview with author, March 2023.

124 **"I had my little filing cabinet":** Preston, interview with author, March 2023.

125 **"sort of like Studio 54":** Frank Bruni, "A Secret Too Dark to Keep," *The New York Times*, August 31, 2005.

126 **"Nike was really smart":** Preston, interview with author, March 2023.

127 **"They were all bedroom creatives":** Preston, interview with author, March 2023.

128 **"Ever since college I have this knack":** Abloh, conversation with Rock, unpublished transcript, December 2013.

128 **"Don C and I started the shop":** Virgil Abloh, "Interview! > Virgil Abloh!," *The Brilliance*, n.d., accessed January 4, 2025, https://www.thebrilliance.com/interviews/virgil-abloh-e4273bf4-4108-4305-92e8-358055d1c9c6.

132 **"Fashion is so multidimensional":** Matthew Williams, interview with author, July 2023.

133 **"We were traveling around":** Williams, interview with author, July 2023.

135 **"We started throwing parties together"**: Preston, interview with author, March 2023.

135 **"non-headlining bands"**: Melissa Locker, "9 Non-headlining Bands You Must See at Coachella 2013," *Time*, April 11, 2013, https://entertainment .time.com/2013/04/12/9-non-headlining-bands-you-must-see-at-coachella -2013/.

135 **"There was something so interesting"**: Julie Gilhart, interview with author, March 2023.

136 **"Been Trill was an open source idea"**: Matthew Williams, "#BeenTrill# (2012)," *Grailed*, July 26, 2018, https://www.grailed.com/drycleanonly/ matthew-williams-35-1.

136 **"The brand itself is a perfect example"**: Nick Matthies, "Remembering Been Trill," StockX, March 28, 2019, https://stockx.com/news/been-trill-virgil -abloh-matthew-williams-heron-preston/.

137 **"When I would go back to Chicago"**: Jerry Lorenzo, interview with author, April 2023.

138 **"I never intended or desired"**: Lorenzo, interview with author, April 2023.

139 **"I just honestly, narcissistically, felt"**: Lorenzo, interview with author, April 2023.

140 **"I was brought into that conversation"**: Lorenzo, interview with author, April 2023.

140 **"We were just trying"**: Lorenzo, interview with author, April 2023.

141 **"I think our strength is"**: Abloh, conversation with Rock, unpublished transcript, December 2013.

CHAPTER FIVE

144 **"I branded it to death"**: Abloh, conversation with Rock, unpublished transcript, December 2013.

145 **"My first encounters around Virgil"**: Ian Stonebrook, "The Oral History of Virgil Abloh's Pyrex Vision," *Boardroom*, December 13, 2023, https:// boardroom.tv/the-oral-history-of-pyrex-vision/.

146 **"There's no arguing"**: Jian DeLeon, "No One Pyrex Should Have All Those Rugby Flannels," *Complex*, January 4, 2013, https://www.complex.com/ style/a/jiand/no-one-pyrex-should-have-all-those-rugby-flannels.

147 **"If he didn't charge"**: Jian DeLeon, interview with author, March 2023.

148 **"Gucci is now making real versions"**: Virgil Abloh, "$200 for Real Fake Gucci!," *The Brilliance*, June 28, 2006, https://www.thebrilliance.com/ posts/200-for-real-fake-gucci.

149 **"Can you still be the wizard"**: DeLeon, interview with author, March 2023.

149 **"We met at the airport"**: Benjamin Edgar, " 'A Moment' via Virgil Abloh, Louis Vuitton, Blogs, Cold Emails, and . . . the Wapity," *The Brilliance*, June 23, 2018, https://www.thebrilliance.com/posts/a-moment-via-virgil-abloh -louis-vuitton-blogs-cold-emails-and-the-wapity.

151 **"It was very, very cool"**: Jim Moore, interview with author, May 2023.

152   "When [Duchamp] takes a urinal": Blake Gopnik, interview with author, March 2023.

153   "What makes me a little bit nervous": Gopnik, interview with author, March 2023.

154   the company donated $10 million: Jacqueline Trescott, "$13 Million Lauren Gift Will Fund Flag Project," *The Washington Post*, July 13, 1998.

154   "With Pyrex, the first thing I thought": Peter Saville, interview with author, March 2023.

155   Saville, who was born in Manchester: Jon Savage, "Radical Clique," *The World of Interiors*, December 2022, https://www.worldofinteriors.com/story/hacienda-nightclub-manchester-design.

156   "All the things that I was drawn to": Saville, interview with author, March 2023.

157   "Our paths crossed in the lobby": Saville, interview with author, March 2023.

157   "So, I might have been": Saville, interview with author, March 2023.

158   "It was competitiveness": Matthew Williams, interview with author, July 2023.

160   "Don't let anyone put you in any box": Virgil Abloh, interview with author, Fashion Scholarship Fund, July 2020.

161   Abloh partnered with a group: Vikram Alexei Kansara, "The Mystery Mogul Behind Off-White," *The Business of Fashion*, April 25, 2019.

162   "He could talk anyone into backing him": Moore, interview with author, May 2023.

162   "My premise is to create a brand": Matthew Schneier, "Virgil Abloh, Kanye West's Creative Director, Puts Street Wear in the Spotlight with His Off-White Line," *The New York Times*, November 5, 2014.

163   "The one thing that I think the luxury market needs": Joelle Diderich, "Off-White's Virgil Abloh Is Streetwear's New Star," *Women's Wear Daily*, August 17, 2016, https://wwd.com/feature/off-whites-virgil-abloh-is-streetwears-new-star-10507943/.

163   "A 17-year-old can be more advanced": Diderich, "Off-White's Virgil Abloh."

164   Saville was flummoxed and flattered: Saville, interview with author, March 2023.

164   "Instances through which your work is kept alive": Saville, interview with author, March 2023.

165   "Fashion doesn't exist if we don't exist": Noah Johnson, "Raf Simons on Life in New York, Designing Under Trump, and the New Generation of Designers Who Look Up to Him," *GQ Style*, January 27, 2017, https://www.gq.com/story/raf-simons-exclusive-interview.

166   Serdari sometimes told corporate chieftains": Robin Givhan, "The Case for Luxury," *The Washington Post*, November 21, 2017.

166   It was a generational investment: Givhan, "Case for Luxury."

167   "I'm trying to redefine how people see": Jerry Lorenzo, interview with author, April 2023.

168   **founded by hip-hop entrepreneur Sean Combs:** In 2024, Sean Combs was charged in Manhattan federal court with sex trafficking and racketeering. He was also the subject of multiple lawsuits accusing him of sexual assault. He has maintained his innocence.

168   **"I understood what it meant":** Edward Buchanan, interview with author, March 2023.

169   **"When you see a Black man working,":** Buchanan, interview with author, March 2023.

170   **"He wanted to fuck up the idea":** Buchanan, interview with author, March 2023.

170   **"Nothing could ever be really formulated":** Buchanan, interview with author, March 2023.

170   **"I was impressed with how fast":** Kim Jones, interview with author, March 2023.

171   **"We'd sit in a corner":** Jones, interview with author, March 2023.

171   **"He was very open to stuff,":** Jones, interview with author, March 2023.

172   **"Off-White is sort of my résumé":** Diderich, "Off-White's Virgil Abloh."

173   **LVMH wraps all its commerce:** In English, we use *savoir faire* to refer to social sophistication. The French, specifically Bernard Arnault, uses it to refer to a kind of mythical know-how that is passed down through the generations.

173   **Oliver's aesthetic came from "me being a queen":** Robin Givhan, "How Designer Shayne Oliver Won Over Kanye West, A$AP Rocky—and the Fashion World," *The Washington Post*, September 4, 2014.

174   **"It was just all the things":** Julie Gilhart, interview with author, March 2023.

175   **"I had gone and taken a look":** Gilhart, interview with author, March 2023.

176   **"Every no is perfect for me":** Virgil Abloh, "Virgil Abloh Is Saving Luxury with T-Shirts," *The New York Times*, September 28, 2017.

177   **"Is this the god of London?":** Matthew Schneier, "LVMH Celebrates Its Designer Search," *The New York Times*, March 5, 2015.

179   **"When we were going through the applicants":** Gilhart, interview with author, March 2023.

179   **"It wasn't a thing of like, *woe is me*":** Gilhart, interview with author, March 2023.

180   **"But he understood his talent":** Gilhart, interview with author, March 2023.

CHAPTER SIX

183   **By the time Nike noticed Virgil:** "Value of the Sneakers Market Worldwide from 2014 to 2027," *Statista*, February 14, 2023, https://www.statista.com/forecasts/1017918/sneakers-market-value-forecast-worldwide.

184   **It sold more than $100 million worth:** Kurt Badenhaussen, "Michael Jordan Has Made over $1 Billion from Nike—the Biggest Endorsement Bargain in Sports," *Forbes*, May 3, 2020, https://www.forbes.com/sites/kurtbadenhausen/

2020/05/03/michael-jordans-1-billion-nike-endorsement-is-the-biggest
-bargain-in-sports/.

185 **By 1990, the company's annual revenue:** Bill Brubaker, "Athletic Shoes
Beyond Big Business," *The Washington Post*, March 10, 1991.

185 **"We don't consider sneakers to be feminine":** Robin Givhan, "How a Sexist
Sneaker Culture Turned Men into Fashion Addicts," *The Washington Post*,
July 10, 2015.

186 **"Sneaker collecting, done by many men":** Givhan, "How a Sexist Sneaker
Culture."

187 **"They're insecure. They need a little story":** Jim Moore, interview with
author, May 2023.

188 **"Men's fashion is being transformed":** Givhan, "How a Sexist Sneaker
Culture."

188 **Puma renamed that shoe the Clyde:** "The History of the Puma Suede,"
Puma website under "Archive Stories," accessed December 23, 2024, https://
about.puma.com/en/this-is-puma/archive-stories/history-of-suede.

189 **"My Adidas and me close as can be":** Darryl McDaniels, Joseph Simmons,
and Rick Rubin, "My Adidas," Universal Music Publishing Group, Warner
Chappell Music, Inc., 1986.

189 **An industry run by White businessmen:** Brubaker, "Athletic Shoes."

190 **In Detroit, an eighteen-year-old was shot:** Frank Currier, "Killing for
Clothes," *CBS Evening News,* transcript, April 24, 1990.

190 **It wasn't uncommon for some cities:** Rick Telander, "Senseless," *Sports
Illustrated*, May 14, 1990.

191 **And parents mourned the loss:** Brubaker, "Athletic Shoes."

191 **In July 2003, Nike bought:** Peter Verry, "*Air* Reminds People That Nike Inc.
Owns Converse," *Footwear News*, March 29, 2023, https://footwearnews
.com/shoes/outdoor-footwear/does-nike-own-converse-1203439476/.

193 **Adidas sold eight million pairs:** Ellen Emmerentze Jervell, "Retro Sneaker
Styles Give Shoemakers a Boost," *Wall Street Journal*, June 20, 2016.

193 **after a dispute regarding royalty payments:** In a radio interview on Hot 97,
Kanye West explained that Nike had refused to pay him royalties because he
wasn't a professional athlete.

193 **Adidas lured West:** Megan Twohey, "Kanye and Adidas: Money, Misconduct
and the Price of Appeasement," *The New York Times*, October 27, 2023.

193 **And Yeezys soon accounted for 8 percent:** Trefor Moss, "Adidas Profit Falls
83% After Split with Yeezy," *Wall Street Journal*, March 8, 2023.

193 **Adidas expected net sales of Yeezys to grow:** Twohey, "Kanye and Adidas."

194 **In 2016, that honor went to the Adidas Superstar:** Marc Bain, "The Top 10
Sneaker List for 2016 Was Dominated by Retro Adidas," *Quartz*, April 3,
2017, https://qz.com/948439/the-top-10-best-selling-sneakers-in-2016
-adidas-beats-nike.

194 **"I think Nike just felt":** Fraser Cooke, interview with author, March 2023.

195 **"I was looking at these guys":** Cooke, interview with author, March 2023.

196 **"I think that made people warm to him"**: Cooke, interview with author, March 2023.

196 **"It's graphitized stuff"**: Cooke, interview with author, March 2023.

198 **"It was something about the way"**: Cooke, interview with author, March 2023.

198 **"And then, three years later"**: Sami Janjer, interview with author, March 2023.

200 **"In that golden era of the '90s"**: Christina Binkley, "For Kicks," *ARTnews,* Winter 2020.

200 **"I hold sneakers as art"**: Binkley, "For Kicks."

200 **And at one of his earliest studio meetings**: Email interview with Fraser Cooke, January 2025.

201 **His manner of communicating was disruptive**: Email interview with Cooke, January 2025.

201 **"I think one of the reasons"**: Cooke, interview with author, March 2023.

202 **When Abloh thought about the look**: Mark Anthony Green, "Virgil Abloh and Nike Unveil 'The Ten' Sneaker Collection," *GQ Style,* August 21, 2017, https://www.gq.com/gallery/virgil-abloh-nike-sneaker-full-collection-the-ten.

203 **"a really, really hardworking, well-educated engineer"**: Janjer, interview with author, March 2023.

204 **Large seating cubes were scattered**: In 2017, Aleali May became the second woman to collaborate with Nike on her own Jordan Brand sneaker. The first was Vashtie Kola, whose sneaker debuted in 2010.

206 **"I wouldn't want to give Nike the credit"**: Janjer, interview with author, March 2023.

206 **Louis Vuitton ranked a distant sixth**: Brand Finance Brand Directory, "Apparel 50 2017 Rankings," https://brandirectory.com/rankings/apparel/2017/table.

206 **"If you do a product that hits"**: Cooke, interview with author, March 2023.

208 **During the 2016 presidential campaign**: Sean Sullivan, "Trump Slams Colin Kaepernick: 'Maybe He Should Find a Country That Works Better for Him,'" *The Washington Post,* August 29, 2016.

208 **After significant internal debate**: Julie Creswell, Kevin Draper, and Sapna Maheshwari, "Nike Nearly Dropped Colin Kaepernick Before Embracing Him," *The New York Times,* September 26, 2018.

208 **"I'm the opposite of a rebel type"**: "Naomi Campbell Meets Virgil Abloh," video interview, *British Vogue,* June 28, 2018, YouTube, https://www.youtube.com/watch?app=desktop&v=DdRcWYiJecs&t=491s.

209 **"He just never did"**: Janjer, interview with author, March 2023.

210 **"Now you have a free-for-all"**: Teri Agins, interview with author, May 2023.

210 **Estimates have the sneaker resale market**: John Kernan, Oliver Chen, Krista Zuber, and Jared Orr, "Sneakers as an Alternative Asset Class, Part II," https://www.cowen.com/insights/sneakers-as-an-alternative-asset-class-part-ii/.

210   **"I was one of the few Black people there"**: Agins, interview with author, May 2023.

213   **"There's been no one"**: Janjer, interview with author, March 2023.

CHAPTER SEVEN

216   **That venture reportedly reaped**: Joelle Diderich, "Virgil Abloh Writes New Chapter at Louis Vuitton," *Women's Wear Daily*, June 20, 2018, https://wwd.com/fashion-news/designer-luxury/virgil-abloh-debut-louis-vuitton-kanye-west-1202720839/.

217   **"That's too low level to get distracted"**: Virgil Abloh, "Figures of Speech," talk at the High Museum, Atlanta, Georgia, March 1, 2020.

217   **"You know when you have been treated unfairly"**: Ibrahim Kamara, interview with author, November 2024.

220   **"Let me meet them so I can see"**: Kevin McIntosh, interview with author, June 2022.

220   **"I was reading things"**: Virgil Abloh, interview with author, July 2020.

221   **She admired his pay-it-forward mentality**: Anna Wintour, interview with author, November 2024.

222   **"I don't know where he found the time"**: Donatella Versace, statement to author, February 2024.

222   **"I would have loved the chance"**: Versace, statement to author, February 2024.

223   **Abloh's initial response**: Elizabeth Paton and Matthew Schneier, "Kim Jones to Exit Louis Vuitton, Reviving Speculation About What's Next," *The New York Times*, January 17, 2018.

223   **Specifically, he wanted to grab**: Christopher Morency, "Inside Rimowa's Off-White Collaboration with Virgil Abloh and Alexandre Arnault," *The Business of Fashion*, June 5, 2018.

223   **He said, "You become"**: Morency, "Inside Rimowa's Off-White Collaboration."

223   **"Where would he want to go with it?"**: Michael Burke, interview with author, July 2022.

224   **"It really truly was the first iteration"**: McIntosh, interview with author, June 2022.

225   **"My internal tool for digesting the word"**: Brook Bobb, "In 2018, Let's Not Price Cotton Hoodies at $800," *Vogue*, January 12, 2018, https://www.vogue.com/article/virgil-abloh-for-all-streetwear.

225   **Menswear accounted for only 5 to 15 percent**: Kati Chitrakorn, "Louis Vuitton Recreates Pharrell's Debut Show for Retail Launch," *Vogue Business*, January 4, 2024.

226   **Louis Vuitton "being a leather goods company"**: James Greenfield, interview with author, November 2023.

226   **John Galliano told the story**: *High & Low—John Galliano*, directed by Kevin Macdonald, KGB Films and Condé Nast Entertainment, 2024.

227   **"Dior is the most magic name"**: Robin Givhan, "The French Connection:

Bernard Arnault Built a Fashion Empire. But Don't Expect Any Air Kisses," *The Washington Post,* April 28, 2002.

229   **"It's very rare by that time"**: Burke, interview with author, July 2022.

229   **"At that time, everybody"**: Burke, interview with author, July 2022.

230   **"The challenge is maintaining that"**: Peter Saville, interview with author, March 2023.

231   **"That magic epiphany"**: Abloh, interview with author, July 2020.

232   **"Congrats on your work brother"**: Virgil Abloh, Instagram, March 26, 2018.

232   **Another messaged: "I'm excited to see"**: Abloh, Instagram, March 26, 2018.

233   **"They gave him the opportunity"**: Edward Buchanan, interview with author, July 2023.

234   **"They want to call me a streetwear guy"**: Abloh, interview with author, July 2020.

234   **Miles Davis played in the background:** Charlie Porter, "Virgil Abloh—'The World Is Looking for the Second Coming,'" *Financial Times,* June 19, 2018.

234   **Abloh's most immediate decorating touch:** Steff Yotka, "Virgil Abloh Is Launching His Own Beat 1 Radio Show on Apple Music," *Vogue,* June 15, 2018, https://www.ft.com/content/9cdf0158-730e-11e8-b6ad-3823e4384287.

235   **"For me, there's a subtlety"**: Porter, "Virgil Abloh."

235   **"It can be worn over the outer layer"**: Porter, "Virgil Abloh."

236   **"The grade will come back what it is"**: Porter, "Virgil Abloh."

236   **Model Naomi Campbell:** Guy Trebay, "Virgil Abloh Tells Louis Vuitton's Story of Fashion," *The New York Times*, June 22, 2018.

239   **"In thirty-two years of modeling"**: Virgil Abloh, "Naomi Campbell Meets Virgil Abloh," video interview, *British Vogue,* June 28, 2018, YouTube, https://www.youtube.com/watch?app=desktop&v=DdRcWYiJecs&t=491s.

239   **D was for "Dorothy"**: Scarlett Conlon, "V Is for Virgil: Abloh Makes Debut for Louis Vuitton in Paris," *The Guardian,* June 21, 2018, https://www .theguardian.com/fashion/2018/jun/21/virgil-abloh-louis-vuitton-debut-show -paris-menswear-spring-summer-2019.

241   **"There was something very Teflon"**: Matthew Schneier, interview with author, April 2023.

241   **"There were some things that were ill-fitting"**: Burke, interview with author, July 2022.

242   **"It actually wasn't me"**: Abloh, "Naomi Campbell Meets Virgil Abloh."

242   **As West later said:** West, interview with Charlamagne tha God, 2018.

242   **"Your first takeaway"**: Schneier, interview with author, April 2023.

245   **"I always like to celebrate"**: Michael Darling, interview with author, March 2023.

246   **"He thought I was inviting him to deejay"**: Darling, interview with author, March 2023.

248   **He bemoaned how even ten years ago:** "Virgil Abloh: A Hundred Percent, as Told to Anja Aronowsky Cronberg," in *Virgil Abloh: Figures of Speech,* ed. Michael Darling (Chicago: Museum of Contemporary Art Chicago; New York: DelMonico Books, 2019), 149.

248   **Curated by Thelma Golden:** Jerry Saltz, "Post-Black," *Village Voice*, May 15, 2001.

249   **"On the one hand, I was needing to hold the line":** Darling, interview with author, March 2023.

250   **"And then we also could get this":** Darling, interview with author, March 2023.

251   **"Race is the elephant in the room":** "Virgil Abloh: A Hundred Percent," 149–50.

252   **"Instagram was really just starting":** Darling, interview with author, March 2023.

253   **"It felt like people were really wearing":** Darling, interview with author, March 2023.

253   **The exhibition attracted 180,000 viewers:** Felicia Feaster, "The Many Talents of Virgil Abloh on Display at the High," *Atlanta Journal-Constitution,* October 23, 2019.

253   **Abloh commissioned Green:** Jay Green, interview with author, December 2023.

CHAPTER EIGHT

256   **Everyone presumed:** Vanessa Friedman, "Shannon Abloh Is Ready to Talk," *The New York Times,* November 29, 2022.

257   **Ezie uploaded those images:** Chinyere Ezie, interview with author, December 2018.

257   **The company also pledged:** Robin Givhan, "Seriously, Prada, What Were You Thinking? Why the Fashion Industry Keeps Bumbling into Racist Imagery," *The Washington Post*, December 15, 2018.

258   **"In the digital era":** Marco Bizzarri, interview with author, May 2019.

260   **The influence of baby boomer shoppers:** Baby boomers were born between 1946 and 1964. Virgil Abloh was technically part of Generation X, born between 1965 and 1980, but claimed greater synergy with Millennials, who came along between 1981 and 1996. Gen Z spans 1997–2013.

260   **By 2019, Gen Z represented some 40 percent:** The Business of Fashion and McKinsey & Company, *State of Fashion 2019*, annual report, https://www.mckinsey.com/~/media/mckinsey/industries/retail/our%20insights/fashion%20on%20demand/the-state-of-fashion-2019.pdf.

260   **The emphasis on social justice:** The Business of Fashion and McKinsey & Company, *State of Fashion 2019*.

262   **"He would find his way to do it":** Sami Janjer, interview with author, March 2023.

263   **"For every 'no,' he would go like double time":** Janjer, interview with author, March 2023.

265   **"I think that's when he realized":** Janjer, interview with author, March 2023.

266   **Abloh held a sneaker auction:** Nee Abloh, interview with author, March 2023.

268   "Give kids the basics": Shawn Agyeman, tape recording of Virgil Abloh in 2008.

269   "The life of a designer": Agyeman, tapes, 2008.

269   "Instead of starting something on his own": Peter Arnold, interview with author, May 2022.

271   "So we never had": Friedman, "Shannon Abloh Is Ready to Talk."

271   "He was born the same year": Diana Tsui, "Louis Vuitton Show in Miami Becomes a Virgil Abloh Tribute," *The New York Times*, December 1, 2021.

272   "When we talk about fashion": Laurie Brookins, "Critic's Notebook: Louis Vuitton's Virgil Abloh Tribute Sparked Gamut of Emotions for Star-Studded Front Row," *Hollywood Reporter*, December 1, 2021, https://www .hollywoodreporter.com/lifestyle/style/critics-notebook-virgil-abloh-tribute -1235055557/.

273   "Virgil showed them the way": Brookins, "Critic's Notebook."

273   The models, some of them: Samuel Hine, "Inside Virgil Abloh's Emotional Final Show for Louis Vuitton," *GQ*, December 1, 2021, https://www.gq.com/ story/virgil-abloh-final-show-louis-vuitton-miami.

273   But there was no celebratory champagne: Brookins, "Critic's Notebook."

273   "Life is so short": Hine, "Inside Virgil Abloh's Emotional Final Show."

EPILOGUE

276   "Be it resolved, by the House": Illinois General Assembly, full text of HR 0569, December 7, 2021.

277   It was the most diverse student cohort: Peter Arnold, interview with author, May 2022.

277   his focus wasn't "simply about opening the doors": Shannon Abloh, remarks at the Fashion Scholarship Fund gala, April 2022.

277   "I'd never seen so many Black people": Naecia Dixon, remarks at the Fashion Scholarship Fund gala, April 2022.

277   "Supporting the Virgil Abloh Post-Modern Scholarship": Dixon, remarks.

278   "While Virgil was alive, I was very critical": Willy Chavarria, interview with author, September 2022.

281   "That wouldn't have happened ten years ago": Edward Buchanan, interview with author, March 2023.

283   "I think that there was a lot": Arnold, interview with author, November 2023.

283   Indeed, an industry expert estimated: Vanessa Friedman, "Fashion's Groupthink Problem," *The New York Times,* October 11, 2023.

284   released limited financial data: Chanel, "Limited Financial Results for the Year Ended 31 December 2022," https://www.chanel.com/emea/img/prd -emea/sys-master/content/P1/hac/h4d/10202336657438-Press%20release %20(2022%20Results)%20ENG%20-%20FINAL_.pdf.

285   A group of French police officers: Antoine Phillips, interview with author, October 2023.

285   They demanded racial justice: France 24, "Black Lives Matter Movement

Gains Momentum Worldwide with Fresh Weekend of Protests," June 6, 2020, https://www.france24.com/en/20200606-black-lives-matter-movement -gains-momentum-worldwide-with-fresh-weekend-of-protests.

285 **But they kept their eyes on the police:** Phillips, interview with author, October 2023.

286 **"It's my hope that you all will consider":** Phillips, interview with author, October 2023.

286 **"Virgil was good at seeking out":** Chavarria, interview with author, September 2022.

287 **"As we walked into Women's History Month":** April Walker, "Fashion Looters, Originators, and Gender Inequality; A Need for Change," *Medium,* March 6, 2021, https://iamaprilwalker.medium.com/fashion -copycatters-innovators-and-gender-inequality-a-need-for-change -e49e13f41d21.

288 **"I'm not the consumer of Vuitton":** Buchanan, interview with author, March 2023.

289 **"I think the reality is the industry thinks":** Sami Janjer, interview with author, March 2023.

289 **"creative vision beyond fashion":** "Louis Vuitton appoints Pharrell Williams as its new Men's Creative Director," Louis Vuitton, press release, February 14, 2023.

289 **"When I look at Pharrell":** Buchanan, interview with author, March 2023.

295 **"Uncle said, 'nigga, you must be sick'":** Clipse, "Chains & Whips," performed June 20, 2023, at the Louis Vuitton spring 2024 men's collection runway show.